General Principles of Law

Nijhoff Law Specials

VOLUME 110

The titles published in this series are listed at *brill.com/nlsp*

General Principles of Law

Natural Rights, Legal Methods and System Principles

By

Daiga Rezevska

BRILL | NIJHOFF

LEIDEN | BOSTON

Library of Congress Cataloging-in-Publication Data

Names: Rezevska, Daiga, author.
Title: General principles of law : natural rights, legal methods and system principles / by Daiga Rezevska.
Description: Leiden ; Boston : Brill/Nijhoff, 2024. | Series: Nijhoff law specials, 0924–4549 ; volume 110 | Includes bibliographical references and index.
Identifiers: LCCN 2024002345 (print) | LCCN 2024002346 (ebook) | ISBN 9789004690509 (paperback) | ISBN 9789004690516 (ebook)
Subjects: LCSH: Law–Philosophy. | Rule of law–Philosophy. | Civil rights. | Democracy.
Classification: LCC K231 .R49 2024 (print) | LCC K231 (ebook) | DDC 340/.1–dc23/eng/20240129
LC record available at https://lccn.loc.gov/2024002345
LC ebook record available at https://lccn.loc.gov/2024002346

Typeface for the Latin, Greek, and Cyrillic scripts: “Brill”. See and download: brill.com/brill-typeface.

ISSN 0924-4549
ISBN 978-90-04-69050-9 (paperback)
ISBN 978-90-04-69051-6 (e-book)
DOI 10.1163/9789004690516

This book is printed on acid-free paper and produced in a sustainable manner.

Contents

Foreword VII
Ineta Ziemele

1 **Introduction** 1
1 Conclusions 14

2 **Understanding and Types of General Principles of Law** 15
1 Definition 15
2 The Origin of General Principles of Law and Basic Groups of Meaning of Law 22
2.1 *The Origin of the Understanding of General Principles of Law* 22
2.2 *The Doctrine of Legal Positivism and General Principles of Law* 23
2.3 *The Doctrine of Natural Law and General Principles of Law* 23
2.4 *Contemporary Legal Theory Pertaining to Democratic States Based on the Rule of Law and General Principles of Law* 24
3 General Principles of Law and Legal Norms 33
4 Types of General Principles of Law 41
4.1 *Positivisation of General Principles of Law* 42
4.2 *Derived and Discovered General Principles of Law* 47
5 Conclusions 52

3 **The Axiological Meaning of General Principles of Law** 54
1 Meaning of General Principles of Law in the Variety of Sources of Law 54
1.1 *Significance of the Variety of Sources of Law in the Western Legal System* 54
1.2 *Normative Legal Regulation of Sources of Law in Latvia* 58
1.3 *Division of Sources of Law in Latvia* 60
1.4 *Hierarchy of Independent Sources of Law in Latvia* 65
2 Importance of the General Principles of Law in Drafting Normative Legal Acts 67
3 The Role of General Principles of Law in the Application of Legal Norms 80
4 Conclusions 87

4 The Functional Effect of General Principles of Law 88
1 Application of General Principles of Law 88
1.1 *Deriving, Discovering and Concretization* 89
1.2 *Solving of Mutual Collisions* 108
1.3 *Evaluative Subsumption* 115
2 The Impact of General Principles of Law on the Application of Written Legal Norms 123
2.1 *Collisions and Validity* 123
2.2 *Interpretation* 127
2.3 *Further Development of Law* 129
2.4 *Elaboration of Decision* 139
3 Conclusions 146

Bibliography 149
Index of Names and Subjects 163

Foreword

The development of laws and legal thinking had achieved incredible depth and detail by the time humanity entered the 21st century. Nevertheless, the very source of the binding force and validity of law continues to be conceptualised differently, depending on the school of legal thought and tradition that one shares or belongs to. Theoretizing about the nature of law is important and it belongs to the necessary and on-going process of reflecting and thinking on what kind of society we are and want to be. It is part of human history and of the future of ideas.

Dr Daiga Rezevska offers a new perspective on the idea of general principles as a source of law. It is a new perspective since, as the author explains, while thinking along with Hans Kelsen, Herbert L.A. Hart and Ronald Dworkin, she began to realise that the general theories of law do not sufficiently engage with particular legal arrangements, such as, for example, a Democratic legal order based on principles of Rule of Law and human dignity. In her book Dr Rezevska sets out to examine a particularly challenging proposition: since the ultimate goal of a Democratic legal order is to provide and ensure justice for all its citizens, the theory of legal positivism is insufficient in assisting us to conceptualize all the necessary legal tools to meet the challenges posed by pursuing this goal. She puts forward a thesis that she explains and justifies in the book that "natural law doctrine is a leading doctrine for understanding of the meaning of law" and conceptualizing the nature and functioning of law for the purposes of justice in a Democratic society. Dr Rezevska engages with the key notions of legal theory, such as Basic Norm (*Grundnorm*), system of beliefs and legal reason, and system of legal sources to explain the nature of general principles of law. All these ideas have been conceived to articulate that law and its application are valid and legally sound. The author takes stock of the work of those legal philosophers who developed the modern idea of general principles of law, beginning with Ronald Dworkin who is credited as a founder of this idea. She adds to it her perspective by contextualizing the importance of the idea for the purposes of transitioning from a totalitarian legal system, such as the one prevailing in the Republic of Latvia during the Soviet occupation, to a Democratic legal order which allowed Latvia to re-join the Western European legal tradition and become a member of the European Union in 2004.

The great merit of Dr Rezevska's work lies precisely in the practical testing of her theory against the experience of the transition from Communism to Democracy in Latvia and the tectonic shift in legal mind-set and practice that was necessary to fully achieve this transition. The theory of general principles of law, as developed in the book, inspired by the philosophy of natural law, represents a multi-layered thinking that connects the will of the Latvian people to have a Democratic legal order based on the principles of Rule of Law and human dignity, which will instruct the content of a Basic Norm as a source of general principles of law both as an independent source of law as well as a legal norm. Within the Latvian Democratic legal system the general principles of law have multiple functions. They are the ultimate standard of reference for the legislative process as well as ensuring that the legal system is coherent and comprehensive. Above all, and as explained by the Constitutional Court of Latvia, the general principles of law are engaged with the purpose of achieving justice when new legislative acts are adopted and when they are implemented. In other words, they are the measure of justice. Dr Rezevska substantiates and shows in her book that this theory of general principles of law has assisted Latvia to turn the page and move away from the Socialist legal tradition and its extreme normativism. While Dr Rezevska herself considers that her work is a work of legal theory and legal philosophy, which it undoubtedly is, it is important to point out that the book will also assist researchers in the transitional justice field because the book shows the importance of the ideas that are more suitable to conceptualise and guide Democratic processes so as to achieve the necessary transition and to do so with the ultimate aim to arrive at just solutions. A fundamental transformation of society requires that its legal theories are capable of assisting that transformation. The work of Dr Rezevska is unique in that it has been able to tackle precisely the question of the connection between the transformation of society and its legal theory.

Ineta Ziemele Ph.D. (*Cantab.*)
Judge, Court of Justice of the European Union
Professor, Riga Graduate School of Law (Latvia)

CHAPTER 1

Introduction

General principles of law are the beginning and the end of a legal arrangement; they determine the content of a legal arrangement as well as serve as a measure of its functionality. General principles of law are the sources of law and are also legal methods: they are applicable to resolve a case and at the same time they define the process of the application of a legal norm. This book comprises a study of a contemporary legal theory and legal method from the perspective of general principles of law within the legal arrangement of a particular State – that is, one which is Democratic and based on the Rule of Law. Thus, this is a theory which belongs to and covers this particular type of legal arrangement, and the claim is that the legal arrangement of a Democratic State governed by the Rule of Law can only exist in a proper way and fulfil the requirements imposed on it by a sovereign if this legal theory is followed.

Contemporary legal theory pertaining to Democratic States based on the Rule of Law has arisen taking into account the major legal theories. My[1] thinking draws on Kelsen, and Hart, and Dworkin, and as you will be able to see, they are my inspiration and form my basis for developing the legal thought further. These theories are general, they do not take into consideration the structure, the order of the State in which law operates, and although this makes them universal, at the same time it also makes them deficient for the legal arrangement of a Democratic State based on the Rule of Law, as this legal arrangement can only function in its full capacity and fulfil the requirements set by a sovereign if the leading understanding of law is a doctrine of natural law.[2] Why? Because the ultimate goal of the legal arrangement of a Democratic State based on the Rule of Law is *justice*, reaching a just and reasonable answer to each and every case, and in the centre of this State is *an individual*, a person, a human being with his/her *human dignity*. And that is simply not possible in conditions of legal positivism where the State and its power is the centre of everything and the system of laws is a closed system and the applier of legal norms can apply only those positive legal norms, which exist in this closed system to all of the

1 Further on I will address myself in a more scientifically neutral way as an "author". Here it did not feel right.

2 I will use terms "the law" and "law" to show the difference between written legal norms (the law) and all regulations valid in a given legal arrangement having the generally binding force as well as other sources of law (law).

 DOI:10.1163/9789004690516_002

factual cases which take place within this legal arrangement, but it is not possible to regulate on the written level all possible cases, legal relations arising among the members of a sovereign or ensure the protection of human dignity and justice with positive law only and without anything against which the action of the legislature would be checked.

Thus, this study covers the legal arrangement of a Democratic State based on the Rule of Law, where justice is an ultimate goal of the legal arrangement, natural law doctrine is a leading doctrine for understanding of the meaning of law, and a sovereign of the particular country has expressed their will to live in this specific kind of State (State order).

The Basic Norm[3] here in this study is an act of will of a sovereign (an unwritten legal norm) to live in a Democratic State based on the Rule of Law, determining both the procedure for the adoption of the legal norms within this legal arrangement as well as the content of these norms as the sovereign is before and above everything – before the State and above the legal arrangement. The will of the sovereign regarding the State order they want to live in can be detected in every given country. In the case of Latvia this act of the will of the sovereign was a proclamation of an independent Democratic Republic of Latvia which is governed by the Rule of Law – the Basic Norm of Latvia's legal arrangement – on 18 November 1918. Starting from this moment, the structure and the content of the legal arrangement is set by the sovereign's proclaimed Basic Norm from which the general principles of law are derived, and the sovereign themselves are subject to this Basic Norm and general principles of law. It means that from this moment on all the decisions taken by any of the branches of the State power must ensure the achievement of the ultimate goal of this legal arrangement – justice: "*The main goal of the legal arrangement of a democratic state based on the rule of law is to ensure justice.*"[4] "*It follows from the basic norm of Latvia as an independent, democratic and rule of law governed state that the constitutional value of the state is human dignity.*"[5]

Both Kelsen and Hart come to the conclusion that there has to be a point of reference, something against which the function of the legal arrangement can be measured and something that gives to those who apply legal norms confidence, or belief, or assurance that they are right, and that they are applying

3 I will use upper case for the term "Basic Norm" when talking about this specific Basic Norm – a Democratic State based on the Rule of Law.

4 Judgement of the Constitutional Court of the Republic of Latvia of 12 March 2020 in the case no. 2019-11-01, para 14. Available: satv.tiesa.gov.lv.

5 Judgement of the Constitutional Court of the Republic of Latvia of 12 November 2020 in the case no. 2019-33-01, para. 12.2. Available: satv.tiesa.gov.lv.

legal norms in a correct way. Something, on which "the system of beliefs"[6] of those who work with law is built. Here the legal reason comes into the theory, the answer to the question – but where we can find those unwritten legal norms? The assumption of the basic norm is a belief within the legal reason or consciousness of those applying legal norms about the authority and correctness. The basic norm makes those who apply legal norms safe and infallible when they are acting within its authority.[7] Contemporary legal theory pertaining to Democratic States based on the Rule of Law goes further and connects both of these ideas – the Basic Norm is created by a real act of will of a legal organ, but it is an unwritten legal norm, is itself witnessable, and at the same time it is presupposed in juristic thinking found in the legal reason of those who work with legal norms in a given legal arrangement. And again, this necessary further development of the notion of Basic Norm is because now it is connected with the State order of a Democratic State which is governed by the Rule of Law.

It could seem at first sight that this is all too good to be true and this is only a theory. But in the same way that chemists go to their laboratories to check how their theories work in reality, we lawyers go to the courts to check how our theories work in the reality of the legal arrangement. You will see in this book that the legal arrangements and the courts of the Democratic States based on the Rule of Law, including the "main laboratory" used here – Latvia's legal arrangement and the courts, the Constitutional Court of the Republic of Latvia (also the Constitutional Court or the Court) as well as the courts of general jurisdiction and administrative courts and their everyday practice – are an obvious and apparent proof that this theory is true, effective, and working:

> "The fourth paragraph of the Preamble to the Constitution stipulates that Latvia as a democratic, socially responsible state governed by the rule of law *is based on human dignity. The principle of a socially responsible state is a principle that has been derived from the basic norm of a democratic state governed by the rule of law*, which falls within the scope of Article 1 of the Constitution.
>
> *Human dignity as a fundamental right is unconditionally vested in each person*. From the principle of a socially responsible state based on human dignity follows the state's obligation to ensure a just social order, levelling

6 On international law as a belief system see: D'Aspremont J. *International Law as a Belief System* (Cambridge Studies in International and Comparative Law). Cambridge: Cambridge University Press, 2017.

7 Cf. Gardner J. *Law as a Leap of Faith*. Oxford: Oxford University Press, 2012, p. 9.

out the most significant social differences in society, fostering social inclusion and ensuring to each group of inhabitants the possibility to lead life that is worthy of human dignity (cf. Paragraph 18 of the Constitutional Court's judgement of 2 November 2006 in case no. 2006-07-01)";[8]

"It follows from *the basic norm of Latvia as an independent, democratic state governed by the rule of law,* that human dignity is a constitutional value of the state. Human dignity characterizes *a human being as the supreme value of a democratic state governed by the rule of law.* The value of each individual is the essence of fundamental rights. Human dignity must be protected both in relations between the state and an individual and in mutual relations between persons. In a democratic state governed by the rule of law, both the legislator when adopting legal norms and the entity applying legal norms must both protect and ensure human dignity (cf. see para.19.1 of the judgement of the Constitutional Court of 19 December 2017 in case no. 2017-02-03 and para.17.1 of the judgement of 25 June 2020 in case no. 2019-24-03). [...] The view that the dignity of one human being could be of lesser value than the dignity of another human being is incompatible with the principle of human dignity. The principle of human dignity does not allow the state to derogate from ensuring fundamental rights to a certain person or a group of persons. The stereotypes prevailing in the society may not serve as constitutionally justifiable grounds for denying or restricting fundamental rights of a certain person or a group of persons in a democratic state governed by the rule of law."[9] [author's emphasis]

---

8 Judgement of the Constitutional Court of 25 June 2020 in case no. 2019-24-03, para. 17.1. Available: satv.tiesa.gov.lv.

9 Judgement of the Constitutional Court of 12 November 2020, para. 12.2.; see similar concretization elements of content of the general principle of law – right to family life – in the Judgement of the Great Chamber of the European Court of Human Rights of 17 January 2023: *Fedotova and Others v. Russia*, applications nos. 40792/10, 30538/14 and 43439/14: "It [the Court] has also held, under Article 14 of the Convention, that traditions, stereotypes and prevailing social attitudes in a particular country cannot, by themselves, be considered to amount to sufficient justification for a difference in treatment based on sexual orientation (see *Khamtokhu and Aksenchik*, cited above, § 78). Thus, the Court has already rejected the Government's argument that the majority of Russians disapprove of homosexuality, in the context of cases concerning freedom of expression, assembly or association for sexual minorities. Like the Chamber (see paragraph 52 of the Chamber judgement), the Grand Chamber considers that it would be incompatible with the underlying values of the Convention if the exercise of Convention rights by a minority group were made conditional on its being accepted by the majority. Were this so, a minority group's rights to freedom of religion, expression and assembly would become merely

After Latvia regained its independence from Soviet occupation, for the first time in the legal arrangement of Latvia, conscious attention to the concept of general principles of law and their importance was paid in 1996 in an interview of the then judge of the European Court of Human Rights and now the President of Latvia, Egils Levits, in the newspaper "Diena" under the title "Between legal norm and legal reality".[10] The thesis expressed in this article on the problems of the transformation process of Latvia's legal arrangement in the field of application of legal norms inspired legal scholars to focus on the study of the legal phenomenon – general principles of law – that had been forgotten in the legal arrangement of Latvia for a long time due to the occupation and as a result of legal acculturation[11] during the Soviet era.

In the Soviet legal system, the diversity of the sources of law did not exist. Formally it was not recognized[12] by the legislator nor those applying legal norms. After regaining independence, the legal science in Latvia was the first to abandon the doctrine of legal positivism as the leading understanding of the meaning of law, prevailing for so many years during the occupation, and according to which the only source of law recognized was "the law" (in a broader sense, normative legal acts). There was not even a possibility that some supra positive principles of law could exist and be valid and at the same time be a criterion for the legitimacy of the legislative acts, and that the courts could directly apply these principles in cases of gaps in the law.

In the Soviet legal system, the concept of "principle of law" was understood differently, as a prescription of a declarative nature. The principles of law were not considered a source of law that could be applied directly, because the only source of law in the legal theory and practice of the Soviet period was the norm of the written law, while in Latvia before the occupation, the concept of

theoretical rather than practical and effective as required by the Convention", paras. 217, 218. Available: hudoc.echr.coe.int/eng#{%22itemid%22:[%22001-222750%22]}.

10 Levits E. Starp tiesību normu un tiesisko realitāti. Intervija. *Diena*, 1996. 10. oktobris.

11 On the meaning of acculturation see: Osipova S. Latvijas tautas tiesiskā apziņa un Latvijas valsts. *Jurista Vārds*, 2012, nr. 52; see also: Osipova S. Nacionālo tiesību nenacionālie avoti. *Jurista Vārds*, 2011, nr. 51.

12 The Soviet legal system is characterized by the so-called theory of fictions, that is, what happens in reality is one thing, but what is formally recognized is quite another. Likewise, with regard to the doctrine of sources of law, even though normative legal acts were recognized as the only sources of law (for example see: Plotnieks A. *Padomju sociālistiskās tiesības*. Rīga: Zvaigzne, 1975, 192.–193. lpp.), in fact, both scholars and law practitioners recognized and used other sources of law, such as jurisprudence in the form of binding Supreme Court Plenary Sessions decisions. Courts often referred to these decisions even in the operative (holding) part of the rulings. See: Sniedzīte G. Tiesību palīgavoti, piemērojot tiesību normas. *Jurista Vārds*, 2005, nr. 39.

"general principles of law" was known both theoretically, and also practically. In the twenties and thirties of the 20th century, several jurists within the legal arrangement of Latvia focused on the study of the problem of general principles of law, for example, Kārlis Dišlers,[13] Vasilijs Sinaiskis,[14] Lotārs Šulcs.[15] Already at that time, ideas appeared in their works that principles of law could have normatively binding force and that they should significantly influence the processes of adoption and application of written legal norms. However, these theories stopped at the formulation of the necessity and were not developed further, obviously because the normal course of development of the legal arrangement was discontinued due to the occupation.

In the Soviet legal system, general principles of law so significant to the Western legal system were completely foreign. For example, the principle of justice, the principle of proportionality, the principle of protection of legitimate expectations, the principle of the prohibition of arbitrariness, the principle of the justification of a decision, the principle of separation of power, the principle of private autonomy etc. were not known or applicable within the framework of the Soviet legal system.[16]

Therefore, starting the study on the general principles of law and trying to prove them as one of the types of the sources of law that exist in the restored legal arrangement of the Republic of Latvia, and even more so, that they should be used in the application of legal norms, was courageous. In 1997, the first scientific study on the general principles of law was published in Latvian on the understanding and significance of the general principles of law.[17] In this study, the meaning of general principles of law and their belonging to the sources of law were analysed, but they were placed in the group of supplementary sources of law.

The fact that after the restoration of independence, the legal arrangement of Latvia should return to the legal system of continental Europe was a logical and indisputable conclusion; however, the legal consciousness, which is based on a specific understanding of law, cannot change so quickly.[18] In 1997, the legal culture, which was still basically based on the positivistic understanding

13 Dišlers K. *Tautu pašnoteikšanās principa tiesiskais saturs*. Rīga: Latvijas Universitāte, 1932.

14 Sinaiskis V. Taisnības princips Latvijas civiltiesībās. *Jurists,* 1937, nr. 7/8; Sinaiskis V. Civillikuma principi un ģimenes tiesības. *Tieslietu Ministrijas Vēstnesis,* 1938, nr. 1.

15 Šulcs L. Dabisko tiesību jēdziens. *Jurists*, 1937, nr. ½.

16 See also: Levits E. Pārveidojot PSRS tiesiskās sistēmas mantojumu. *Likums un Tiesības,* 2002, 4. sēj., nr. 6 (34), 166.–167. lpp.; Briede J. Tiesiskās paļāvības aizsardzība – viens no administratīvā procesa principiem. *Cilvēktiesību Žurnāls,* 1997, nr. 5, 36. lpp.

17 Iļjanova D. Vispārīgie tiesību principi kā tiesību avots. *Latvijas Vēstnesis,* 1997, nr. 277/278.

18 Cf. Osipova S. 2012.

of law,[19] had developed so far in the legal arrangement of Latvia that legal professionals could accept the idea that alongside the written, positivized sources of law there may be another source of law (only as an additional argument to reinforce a ruling based on a written legal norm, though). Even more, this initial understanding was supported by the fact that several normative legal acts directly referred to the general principles of law in the text, and in a situation where the doctrine of legal positivism continued to be dominant and mainly determined the legal culture, such an argument was of undeniable importance, because it was often asked and the popular question of the law practitioners at that time was: "But where is it written?"

The Constitutional Court, which was established in 1996, adopted its first judgement[20] on 7 May 1997, and already in this first case the Court faced the well-known question: "But where is it written?" Namely, the main legal issue of the case which had to be resolved was whether the legislature, amending a specific section of a law, but not expressing its will in a written legal norm not to amend another section, which of course is not mentioned in the law on amendments, although such information can be found in the transcripts of the legislator's plenary session, for example, has thereby determined that this last section must remain in its current version while the relevant parliament is functioning, as required by Article 81 of the Constitution of the Republic of Latvia[21] (the Constitution) [*Latvijas Republikas Satversme*] in force at that time. The country's legal arrangement is what its constitutional court is. And the Constitutional Court of the Republic of Latvia was a modern, constitutional court of a Democratic State based on the Rule of Law. Already in its first judgement, the Constitutional Court referred to the general principles of law, concretizing them and recognizing as invalid the written legal norms, which were in contradiction with these sources of law.

Initially, the Constitutional Court, when applying general principles of law, did not link them to the written text of the Constitution,[22] but soon the Court

19 On the doctrine of legal positivism see more: Peczenik A. *On Law and Reason*. Dordrecht, Boston, London: Kluwer Academic Publishers, 1989, pp. 222–228; Liepa L. Pozitīvās tiesības. Grām.: *Mūsdienu tiesību teorijas atziņas*. Rīga: Latvijas Universitāte, 1997.

20 Judgement of the Constitutional Court of 7 May 1997 in case no. 04-01(97). Available: satv.tiesa.gov.lv.

21 The Constitution of the Republic of Latvia: the constitutional law of the Republic of Latvia. Adopted on 15.02.1922. Available: likumi.lv/ta/en/en/id/57980-the-constitution-of-the-republic-of-Latvia.

22 Judgement of the Constitutional Court of 7 May 1997.

began to mention Article 1[23] of the Constitution alongside the general principles of law, explaining that "a series of principles of the Rule of law, including the principle of separation of power and legality, follow from this article".[24] Later, the Court specified that the general principles of law derive directly from the concept of Democracy: "From the concept of a democratic republic contained in Article 1 of the Constitution, all state institutions have an obligation in their activities [...] to observe legality, separation of power [...] and other principles of the state based on the rule of law, including the principles of proportionality and protection of legitimate expectations."[25]

Until the loss of independence in 1940, both in legal theory and in practice, the general principles of law (principles of the Rule of Law) were perceived in Latvia as existing by themselves and were not linked to the text of the Constitution.[26] On the other hand, as already mentioned above, under the influence of the acculturation, many basic elements of the functioning of a Democratic State based on the Rule of Law had disappeared from the legal culture of those applying legal norms. Therefore, on the one hand, linking the general principles of law with Article 1 of the Constitution and the concept of Democracy can be considered as a sign of certain insecurity, but on the other hand, it was easier for the Constitutional Court and more comprehensible for the sovereign and those who apply legal norms to point to the predominance of the principles of law over written legal norms and the legitimization of adjudication based on the general principles of law.

The following years brought significant changes in the development of the understanding and meaning of the general principles of law. Thus, in 1999, a study on the understanding of the general principles of law and their functional significance in the legal arrangement of a Democratic State governed by the Rule of Law was published,[27] in which for the first time the general principles of law were ranked in the group of independent sources of law, indicating their generally binding nature, that is, proving that they are real legal norms valid for direct application. In 2000, a number of studies were published on

23 Judgement of the Constitutional Court of 11 March 1998 in case no. 04-05(97). Available: satv.tiesa.gov.lv.

24 Judgement of the Constitutional Court of 1 October 1999 in case no. 03-05(99). Available: satv.tiesa.gov.lv.

25 Sal.: Satversmes 1. panta komentārs. Grām.: Balodis R. (Zin.red.) *Latvijas Republikas Satversmes komentāri. I nodaļa. Vispārējie noteikumi.* Rīga: Tiesu namu aģentūra, 2014.

26 Pleps J. *Satversmes iztulkošana.* Rīga: Latvijas Vēstnesis, 2012, 163. lpp.

27 Iļjanova D. Vispārīgie tiesību principi un to funkcionālā nozīme. Grām.: *Mūsdienu tiesību teorijas atziņas.* Rīga: Tiesu namu aģentūra, 1999.

the concretization of the content of the specific general principles of law.[28] Furthermore, it was carefully pointed out that in the Western legal system, alongside the written sources of law, such sources of law as general principles of law are also recognized, "which may even have a higher rank than the constitution".[29]

In the following years, work continued proving that the general principles of law are real legal norms valid for direct application. Several articles were published on the understanding of legal norms in the legal arrangement of a modern Democratic State based on the Rule of Law, including the general principles of law as a legal norm.[30] This stage of the development of the doctrine of sources of law, during which it was still necessary to prove the generally binding force of the general principles of law and their place in the group of independent sources of law, ended in 2004 with the coming into force of the Administrative Procedure Law[31] [*Administratīvā procesa likums*], where in the fourth part of Section 1 it was recognized by the legislator that: "A legal norm is comprised of a legal act (part thereof) and general principles of law."

With the commencement of administrative courts and the entry into force of the Administrative Procedure Law, a wave of activation of the application of general principles of law began. Administrative courts raised the application of the general principles of law to the level of everyday work, and one of the most significant is the judgement of the Supreme Court Senate of 8 March 2007,[32] in which the court determined: "The state of Latvia is obliged to ensure

28 Briede J. Par samērīgumu administratīvajā procesā. *Latvijas Vēstnesis*, 2000, nr. 16; Briede J. Par tiesisko paļāvību administratīvajā procesā. *Latvijas Vēstnesis*, 2000, nr. 19; Briede J. Par vienlīdzību administratīvajā procesā. *Latvijas Vēstnesis*, 2000, nr. 25; Levits E. Samērīguma princips publiskajās tiesībās – *jus commune europaeum* un *Satversmē* ietvertais konstitucionāla ranga princips. *Likums un Tiesības*, 2000, 2. sēj., nr. 9 (13).

29 Levits E. Cilvēktiesības Eiropas Savienības tiesību sistēmā. *Likums un Tiesības*, 2000, 2. sēj., nr. 11 (15), 332. lpp.

30 Kalniņš E. Publiskas ticamības princips tiesu praksē. *Likums un Tiesības*, 1999, 1. sēj., nr. 2; Kalniņš E. Tiesību normas spēkā esamība un intertemporālā piemērojamība. *Likums un Tiesības*, 2000, 2. sēj., nr. 7 (11); Iļjanova D. Tiesību normu un principu kolīzija. *Likums un Tiesības*, 2000, 2. sēj., nr. 8 (12); Iļjanova D. Vispārējo tiesību principu aksioloģiskie un funkcionālie aspekti Latvijas tiesību sistēmas pārejas periodā. Grām.: *Tiesību transformācijas problēmas sakarā ar integrāciju Eiropas Savienībā*. Starptautiskās konferences materiāli. Rīga: LU, 2002; Iļjanova D. Vispārējo tiesību principu izpratnes izcelšanās vēsturiskā perspektīva. *Latvijas Vēsture. Jaunie un Jaunākie Laiki*, 2003, nr. 3 (51); Levits E. Par tiesiskās vienlīdzības principu. *Latvijas Vēstnesis*, 2003, nr. 68.

31 Administrative Procedure Law: the law of the Republic of Latvia. Adopted on 25.10.2001. Available: likumi.lv/ta/en/en/id/55567-administrative-procedure-law.

32 Augstākās tiesas Senāta 2007. gada 8. marta spriedums lietā nr. SKA-89/2007. Pieejams: tiesas.lv.

a fair balance between the individual's right to family life and the interests of society in the field of immigration control. The legislator is not always able to achieve such a balance by adopting legal norms, therefore the obligation to observe the balance also rests with the law applier, who evaluates each case individually. Thus, when issuing any type of administrative act, *including a mandatory administrative act, the institution must assess whether it does not disproportionately restrict the fundamental rights of a person.*" [author's emphasis] With this ruling, the court indicated that the legal arrangement of Latvia is the arrangement of a Democratic State based on the Rule of Law where the written legal norms are subject to the priority of the unwritten but generally binding general principles of law.

Now the period of transformation of the legal arrangement of Latvia can be considered as finished. Latvia is a Democratic State based on the Rule of Law belonging to the continental European legal system. The legal arrangement still shows some shortcomings, but they are mostly immanent to the legal arrangement of any Democratic country based on the Rule of Law. General principles of law have become an integral tool of the courts' daily work. They are recognized as sources of law of a generally binding nature both in legal doctrine and in the case law of the Constitutional Court, administrative courts, and courts of general jurisdiction.

The issue of general principles of law is relevant for Latvia also in connection with joining the European Union. The Court of Justice of the European Union, when developing the general principles of law, relies on the same criteria determining the content of these principles as the national law appliers of the Member States. In the case of European Union law, the "natural" scale of comparison is the national legal arrangements of the Member States.

In 1996, Egils Levits said that Latvia is in the process of transformation from the Soviet legal system to the Romano–Germanic legal system. In 2013, he concluded: "Latvia's [legal arrangement] has entered the "port of peace" – completely transformed (at the level of legislation, intellectual, state action) from the Soviet legal system to belonging to the Western European legal system and "connected" to the European Union legal system." In the opinion of Levits, this process has been successful in general, because in legal terms Latvia does not stand out negatively in any way among other European Union Member States; moreover, the national legal arrangement works without hindering the country's participation in this organization.[33]

33 Bīriņu domnīca – jau desmito gadu pēc kārtas. *Jurista Vārds*, 2013, nr. 32.

Commenting on the current situation, he concludes that Latvia currently belongs to the Western (continental European) legal system with a satisfactory functioning legal arrangement and as a moderately functioning Western-type Democratic State based on the Rule of Law. This should be considered a great achievement in such a short period of time and in specific conditions, because, as he himself admitted, in 1993, while participating in the restoration of the legal arrangement, he had very little confidence in the ability of lawyers trained in Soviet conditions to create a State based on the Rule of Law. Moreover, in another 20 years, Latvia will have completely forgotten its "specific" problems of the post-Soviet transition period, according to Levits.[34]

I am convinced that Latvia can celebrate this achievement mainly because of the legal doctrine on the theory of general principles of law that was so elaborated and clear, and thus the courts, based on this doctrine, were able to apply general principles of law to resolve the cases according to the requirements of the Basic Norm.

The main goal of this book is to prove that the general principles of law are legal norms – they are generally binding as of their nature and consist of legal content and legal consequences, respectively, they are valid for direct application and create subjective rights or impose legal obligations on a specific subject. Thereby, according to the value meaning of the normative essence in a legal arrangement – axiology – the general principles of law are in no way different from (written) legal norms. In the hierarchy of sources of law, the general principles of law have priority or prevail over the normative legal acts created by a legislator, also over the formal Constitution. As of their content general principles of law are regulations that: 1) express the highest values (reflecting a certain way of life) of the legal arrangement, its parts, or some institutions, etc. – human rights, 2) determine to the institutions that apply legal norms, how the eventually applicable legal norm should be searched for, examined, interpreted, etc. – legal methods, 3) as well as determine the systematization of the legal arrangement – for example, separation of power, hierarchy of normative legal acts.

Regarding the functional meaning or mechanism of functional effect in the legal arrangement, general principles of law differ from written legal norms, as they have a "dimension of weight". In all cases where there has been a conflict between the general principles of law and written legal norms, the general principles of law have priority over the written legal norm, which is in conflict with them, because the general principles of law are derived from the act of

34 Bīriņu domnīca – jau desmito gadu pēc kārtas. 2013.

sovereign's will – the Basic Norm of a Democratic State based on the Rule of Law – they reflect the spirit of the legal arrangement and determine its content.

Within the framework of this book, the legal arrangement is considered mainly deductively, that is, what it should be, based on the doctrine of natural law and the principle of a Democratic State based on the Rule of Law. A legal norm is now viewed not only in relation to a normative legal act, but also as a regulation that, in accordance with the general principles of law of the relevant legal arrangement, must regulate legal relations in a given country, regardless of whether the legislator has or has not been able to verbalize this norm properly. Therefore, the scope of the effect of the general principles of law in the legal arrangement of a Democratic State based on the Rule of Law is broad – it covers, is related to, and affects the entire process of drafting and adoption as well as application of legal norms (legal syllogism), every stage of it. The task of the book is to help the legislators to draft and adopt the written legal norms in accordance with the general principles of law, and the legal practitioners to comprehensively apply general principles of law in adjudicating cases within the legal arrangements of Democratic States based on the Rule of Law.

In the creation of this study, research in the field of general principles of law carried out by Latvian authors, for example, the author of this book,[35] the former President of Latvia Egils Levits,[36] Dr.iur. Kaspars Balodis,[37] Dr.iur. Jautrīte Briede,[38] Dr.iur. Aivars Līcis,[39] Dr.habil.iur. Edgars

35 Iļjanova D. 1997; Rezevska D. The Content of the General Principles of Law and Normative Legal Acts. In: *The Quality of Legal Acts and its Importance in Contemporary Legal Space.* International Scientific Conference, 4–5 October, 2012. Riga: University of Latvia Press, 2012, pp. 35–46; Rezevska D. Legal Methods in Latvia's Legal Arrangement and European Integration. In: *European Integration and Baltic Sea Region: Diversity and Perspectives.* Collection of Papers of International Conference held by the University of Latvia. Riga: The University of Latvia Press, 2011, pp. 222–234; Rezevska D. Tiesiskās paļāvības principa satura konkretizācija un attīstība judikatūrā. Grām.: *Apvienotā pasaules latviešu zinātnieku III kongresa un Letonikas IV kongresa rakstu krājums.* Rīga, 2011; Iļjanova D. Labas pārvaldības princips kā vispārējais tiesību princips: konkretizācija un piemērošana. Grām: Zin. red. Ozoliņa Ž., Reinholde I. *Laba pārvaldība.* Rīga: Zinātne, 2009, 137.–152. lpp.; Iļjanova D. 1999; Iļjanova D. 2002; Iļjanova D. 2003.

36 Levits E. 1996; Levits E. Tiesību normu interpretācija un Satversmes 1. panta *demokrātijas* jēdziens. *Cilvēktiesību Žurnāls,* 1997, nr. 4, 54.–77. lpp.

37 Balodis K. Labas ticības principa loma mūsdienu Latvijas civiltiesībās. *Likums un Tiesības,* 2002, 4. sēj., nr. 9 (37), 279.–286. lpp.

38 Briede J. 1997, 34.–39. lpp.; Briede J. 2000, nr. 25; Briede J. Par tiesisko paļāvību administratīvajā procesā. 2000; Briede J. Par samērīgumu administratīvajā procesā. 2000.

39 Līcis A. Vai tiesām jāievēro patiesības princips civillietās? *Likums un Tiesības,* 2000, 2. sēj., nr. 3, 80.–83. lpp.; Līcis A. Taisnīguma princips civilprocesā. *Likums un Tiesības,* 2001, 3. sēj., nr. 10 (26), 302.–306. lpp.

Meļķisis[40] was used and analysed. Likewise, works of jurists of other Western legal system countries, who had made a remarkable contribution to the development of the phenomena of the general principles of law. American jurist Ronald Dworkin[41] should be noted as the founder of the modern understanding of the general principles of law, and the inspirational legal theories of Hans Kelsen[42] and Herbert L.A. Hart.[43] Further, the doctrine of the general principles of law was developed within the legal science of Germany (Joseph Esser,[44] Robert Alexy,[45] Ulrich Penski,[46] etc.), France (Jean Boulanger[47]), Sweden (Aleksander Peczenik[48]), Spain (Manuel Atienza, Ruiz Manero),[49] as well as other countries belonging to the Western legal system.

The justification of the contemporary legal theory pertaining to Democratic States based on the Rule of Law in practice is shown by the case law of the courts of general jurisdiction, administrative courts, constitutional courts, jurisprudence of the European Court of Human Rights and of the Court of Justice of the European Union.

---

40 Meļķisis E. Likuma burts, likuma gars, Satversmes tiesa. *Latvijas Vēstnesis,* 1997, nr. 125; Meļķisis E. Kontinentālās Eiropas tiesību loks Rietumu tiesībzinātnieku skatījumā. *Juristu Žurnāls,* nr. 6, A211.–A217. lpp.; Meļķisis E. Tiesību normu abstraktums un tā sekas. *Juristu Žurnāls,* nr. 8, A234.–A240. lpp.; Meļķisis E. *Attīstības tendences dažos tiesību teorijas un prakses jautājumos.* Rīga: Latvijas Universitāte, 2000.

41 Dworkin R. *Taking Rights Seriously.* Cambridge, Massachusetts: Harvard University Press, 1977, 1978.

42 Kelsen H. *Pure Theory of Law.* Translation from the Second (Revised and Enlarged) German Edition by Max Knight. Berkeley and Los Angeles: University of California Press, 1967.

43 Hart H.L.A. *The Concept of Law.* Oxford: Clarendon Press, 1993.

44 Esser J. *Grundsatz und Norm in der richterlichen Fortbildung des Privatrechts.* 4. Aufl. Tübingen: J.C.B. Mohr (Paul Siebeck), 1990.

45 Alexy R. Zum Begriff des Rechtsprinzips. *Rechtstheorie,* Beiheft 1, 1979; Alexy R. *Theorie der Grundrechte.* Aufl. 1. Frankfurt am Main: Suhrkamp, 1986.

46 Penski U. Rechtsgrundsatze und Rechtsregeln. *Juristen Zeitung,* 1989, no. 3.

47 Boulanger J. *Principles généraux du droit et droit positif, Le droit prive français au milieu du 20e siècle.* Vol. I, 1950.

48 Peczenik A. Legal Rules and Moral Principles. *Rechtstheorie,* 1991, no. 11; Peczenik A. Principles of Law. The Search for Legal Theory. *Rechtstheorie,* 1971, no. 2; Peczenik A. 1989.

49 Atienza M., Manero J.R. *A Theory of Legal Sentences.* Dordrecht, Boston, London: Kluwer Academic Publishers, 1996.

1 Conclusions

Contemporary legal theory pertaining to Democratic States based on the Rule of Law is not a general theory of law but rather a theory which covers a legal arrangement of a Democratic State based on the Rule of Law, where justice is an ultimate goal of the legal arrangement, natural law doctrine is a leading doctrine for understanding of the meaning of law, and a sovereign of the particular country has expressed their will to live in this specific kind of State (State order) where in the centre of it is an individual, a person, a human being with his/her human dignity.

A Basic Norm within the contemporary legal theory pertaining to Democratic States based on the Rule of Law is an act of the will of a sovereign, which determines both the procedure for the adoption of the legal norms within this legal arrangement as well as the content of these norms. A Basic Norm is created by a real act of will of a legal organ, and it is an unwritten legal norm, and is presupposed in juristic thinking and found in the legal reason of those who work with legal norms in given legal arrangements.

CHAPTER 2

Understanding and Types of General Principles of Law

1 Definition

The word "principle" is used to describe different legal terms. We are talking about "principles of law",[1] "principles of natural law",[2] "basic regulations of law",[3] etc. This book is devoted to a study of the phenomenon of "general principles of law", which means a separate legal term, distinguished from other principles, which refers to a generally binding source of law, a legal norm. This legal term – general principles of law – has constantly gained importance in legal science and practice, and legislation both in Latvia and the world.[4]

To fully understand the concept of the general principles of law and the use of this concept, it should be analysed from two aspects. First, the concept of the general principles of law has to be examined in its grammatical (literal) meaning; and second, the concept should be analysed in its legal meaning.

In the literal meaning the term "principle" is defined as "the fundamental law, the main rule, statement",[5] "the fundamental truth".[6] And by "general" we understand "such that relates to everybody, everything, encompasses everything",[7] in this case it relates to the entire legal arrangement of the relevant country.

For the purpose of this study it is essential to understand first of all the complexity of law, which among other things includes both written and unwritten legal norms; and secondly, to understand how it actually works in a particular country, which is founded and based on the particular basic norm – to comprehend the difference and importance of various levels, spheres, systems of law and its relevance to other phenomena, which are in some way connected

1 For example, see Atienza M., Manero J.R. 1996; Peczenik A. 1971.

2 For example, see Bydlinsky F. *Juristische Methodenlehre und Rechtsbegriff.* 2. Aufl. Wien, New York: Springer Verlag, 1991.

3 For example, see Penski U. 1989.

4 *Allgemeine Rechtsgrundsätze* – in German; *principes généraux du droit* – in French.

5 *Latviešu valodas vārdnīca*. 2. izd. Rīga: Avots, 1998, 649. lpp.

6 Term "principle": *dictionary.com/browse/principle*.

7 *Latviešu valodas vārdnīca*. 2. izd. Rīga: Avots, 1998, 866. lpp.

 | DOI:10.1163/9789004690516_003

with law of the given country. Thus, *legal arrangement* is defined as the system, which comprises the broadest issues related to law in the relevant country – all legal phenomena of the relevant society, including questions of law (also the system of laws) and institutional questions. The legal arrangement encompasses all sources of law, all legal acts adopted (issued) or otherwise binding in the State and all institutions somehow involved in the application of law (both court and administrative institutions), as well as the totality of legal relations that have been established and exist in this system.

While a *system of laws* is just one part of the legal arrangement, which consists of legal norms (both written and unwritten legal norms), a *legal system* is the aggregate of legal arrangements of several countries with similar historical, geographical, political, religious or other characteristics. One of the established examples of legal systems is the Western legal system, which consists of the continental European legal system (the Romano-Germanic legal system) and the Anglo-American legal system. Other legal systems are also known, such as for example the Islamic legal system, the Soviet legal system, and others.

After the analysis of the law scholars' work related to the general principles of law, it must be concluded that there is still no common understanding among the authors how to use the notion of the general principles of law and what it includes. Yet one conclusion is evident, i.e., the concept of the general principles of law includes not only the grammatical understanding, but also *the dimension of legal understanding*. And in this legal understanding the concept of the "general principles of law" in comparison with the grammatical understanding is given also another – notional – capacity. Namely, these are principles that are derived from the Basic Norm, function in a State governed by the Rule of Law and are generally accepted either in a specific branch of law or in an entire legal arrangement.[8]

Respectively, in each legal arrangement, which is based on *the Basic Norm of a Democratic State governed by the Rule of Law*, there exist generally accepted[9]

8 For example, see Nedjati Z.M., Trice J.E., Dashwood A.A. *English and Continental Systems of Administrative Law.* Amsterdam, New York, Oxford: North Holland Publishing Company, 1978, p. 99, where the general principles of administrative law have been reviewed and Paine F.J. *Vācijas vispārīgas administratīvas tiesības. Vācijas Administratīvā procesa likums.* Rīga: Tiesu namu aģentūra, 2002, 50. lpp.; Larenz K. *Methodenlehre der Rechtswissenschaft.* Berlin, Heidelberg, New York: Springer Verlag, 1969, S. 460–473, where general principles of law that can claim validity not only in one branch of law, but in several if not all branches of law of the legal arrangement, include the principles of relativity and the most lenient means; Butāns M. Valsts atbildības izpratne (*Satversmes* 92. pants). *Likums un Tiesības,* 2000, 2. sēj., nr. 1 (5), 19. lpp., 2. vēre.

9 On the role of the feature "accepted" in the concretization of a general principle of law and its generally binding force see also Chapter 4.1.1.

fundamental statements, basic rules derived from this particular Basic Norm, and serving as the basis for the relevant legal arrangement – its general principles of law, which can be applicable in all the branches of law of the given legal arrangement as well as in only some or even one branch of law. So, for example, for a long time it was recognized[10] that in the Western legal system the principle of proportionality was applicable only in public, and not in private law;[11] nevertheless, it did not deprive this principle of the legal character of a general principle of law. The principle of impartial investigation is a general principle of law, functioning in an administrative procedure of a Democratic State based on the Rule of Law (see, for example, Art. 25^1 of the Law On Judicial Power[12] [*Par tiesu varu*]) while the principle of adversarial proceedings is a general principle of law functioning in the civil and criminal procedures (Art. 25 of the Law On Judicial Power). The fact that the relevant legal procedures should take place in these different ways is determined by the Basic Norm of – a Democratic State governed by the Rule of Law – from which the general principles of law are derived.

Thus, all general principles of law are *general* legal norms according to the characteristics of their legal content, therefore there cannot be "special" (less general) general principles of law.[13] Moreover, the general principles of law are all equally legally significant, they all have *the same legal force*.[14] Consequently, there is no automatic priority or hierarchical relationship between them, based on the connection of speciality or different legal force.[15] On the other hand, all written legal norms, as legal norms with lower legal force, are hierarchically subordinated to general principles of law as legal norms with higher legal force. In legal science, when denoting certain general principles of law, for example, the principle of democracy, principle of national state, socially

10 On the development of the scope of the content of the principle of proportionality, see Rezevska D. 2012, pp. 35–46.

11 Detailed on the nature and role of the principle of proportionality in public law in Europe and Latvia, see Levits E. 2000, 262.–270. lpp.

12 On Judicial Power: the law of the Republic of Latvia. Adopted on 15.12.1992. Available: likumi.lv/ta/en/en/id/62847-on-judicial-power.

13 On more general and less general legal norms see more Buls M. Vispārīgās un speciālās tiesību normas. *Likums un Tiesības*, 2003, 5. sēj., nr. 6 (46), nr. 7 (47), 183. lpp., 1. vēre.

14 The legal force of a written legal norm, or its place in the hierarchy of written legal norms of the particular legal arrangement, is determined by two factors: 1) the subject who is the creator of the legal norm and 2) the procedure by which the legal norm was adopted (or are amended). In the case of general principles of law, the subject that created them is a sovereign and their amendment is possible only by changing the Basic Norm.

15 On the collisions of general principles of law and the methods how to solve them, see hereinafter Chapter 4.1.2.

responsible state and the rule of law, the term "overarching principles of law"[16] is used; however, this notion of general principles of law is used only for the systematization purposes of a wide range of general principles of law without indicating any difference in legal force among them.

Therefore, the applier of legal norms, when applying the general principle of law in the process of application of legal norms, should consider to which branch of law the general principle of law is applicable because there can be cases when one and the same principle could be a basic rule of several branches of law; however, its content could be different, even though slightly.[17]

Finally, in order to clarify the concept under discussion, it should be analysed what principle is a principle of "law" because a branch of law or a legal arrangement may be related to various types of principles not belonging to law, but to other areas, for example, politics, morals, religion, etc.

Aleksander Peczenik offers the following list of features that help distinguish which principles are principles of law.[18] In addition, it is enough if the principle to be tested has at least one of the mentioned features in order for it to be recognized as a legal principle: 1) a principle is a legal principle if it is contained in a written normative legal act; 2) several principles are principles of law, if it is possible to deduce from them written legal norms that are in force; 3) a principle is a legal principle if it determines how new written legal norms should be created, and some part of them is also created according to this principle; 4) a principle is a legal principle if it determines how written legal norms should be interpreted, and some part of them is also interpreted according to

16 The specific political system of a state has its own identity, which is determined by the principles characterizing this system. They can be designated as overarching principles or structural principles of the state system. (Maurer H. *Staatsrecht I. Grundlagen, Verfassungsorgane, Staatsfunktionen*. 6. Aufl. München: C.H. Beck, 2010, S. 164.) The main principles of the political system of a State describe the nature of the state system but allow for various manifestations of it. At the same time, they distinguish it from other political systems – both from the systems of other countries and from the systems of the respective country that existed at a different time (or are planned in the future). Over time, starting with Aristotle and Plato, a typology of political systems of a State has been developed, which classifies them according to these structural principles (for example, Monocracy, Oligarchy, Democracy or Monarchy, Republic). See more Kusiņš G., Levits E., Liepa L., Mits M., Rezevska D., Ziemele I. *Par Latvijas valsts konstitucionālajiem pamatiem un neaizskaramo Satversmes kodolu. Konstitucionālo tiesību komisijas viedoklis un materiāli.* Rīga: Latvijas Vēstnesis, 2012, 60. lpp., nr. 105, 106. On the conceptual basis or core of the Constitution, see also Pleps J., Pastars E., Plakane I. *Konstitucionālās tiesības.* Rīga: Latvijas Vēstnesis, 2014, 55.–56. lpp.

17 On clarifying and finding the content of the general principles of law, see hereinafter Chapter 4.1.1.

18 Peczenik A. 1971, pp. 31–32.

this principle; 5) a principle is a legal principle if the result of its implementation will be (or already is) identical or at least causally or statistically similar to the result in the event that any written legal norms are implemented.

Although in this case the connection of principles with law is understood in a narrow sense, that is, according to the doctrine of legal positivism, because the existence or non-existence of the principles of "law" depends solely on their connection with written legal norms; however, recognizing that it is enough to have at least one of the features to consider the principle in question as a principle of "law", it is confirmed both that the principles of law can be unwritten (features 2–5) and that they bind both a legislator (feature 3), as well as the applier of legal norms (feature 4).

Summarizing the above, it must be concluded, that the clarification of the "legal" element of the concept of general principles of law is directly connected with the theories of origin of the general principles of law that will be analysed in the next section of this book. Namely, the principles will be of "law" if they are related to written legal norms and decisions or judgements of the appliers of legal norms (civil servants, judges)[19] or, to be more specific, principles that arise from the sources enlisted below (the Basic Norm, system of laws) and which the appliers of legal norms refer to and quote in their adjudications.

Certainly, in the legal science and practice of law the term "principles of law" is used in different meanings and denotes different forms of instructions. After reviewing the most significant and the most frequently quoted studies the following meanings of the "principles of law" can be enlisted:[20]

1) a principle as a very general instruction understood as a norm with very general characteristics of its legal content, for example the norm of the Civil Law[21] [*Civillikums*] referring to the form of legal transactions that may be written either as required by the law or pursuant to the voluntary agreement of the participants (Section 1482 of the Civil Law); thus this instruction is more general than those which refer to, for example, the form required for a specific type of contract (for example, a written form required for the contract for purchasing real estate);
2) a principle as an instruction comprising very general concepts or concepts with open-ended content, including general clauses;[22] these concepts need to be "value filled", for example, in determining whether a

19 See similarly MacCormick N. "Principles" of Law. *Juridical Review*, 1974, Vol. 19, p. 225.

20 See similarly Atienza M., Manero J.R. 1996, pp. 3–4.

21 Civil Law: the Law of the Republic of Latvia. Adopted on 28.01.1937. Available: likumi.lv/ta/en/en/id/225418-civil-law.

22 *Generalklausel* – in German.

possessor is in "good faith" (Section 910 of the Civil Law) or in concretizing the general clause "in the interest of state and public";[23]

3) a principle as a norm of a program (goal) or policy, that is, an instruction that defines the need to achieve a certain goal, for example, Section 2 (1) of the Environmental Protection Law[24] [*Vides aizsardzības likums*] provides that: "The purpose of this Law is to ensure the preservation and recovery of the quality of the environment, and also sustainable use of natural resources";
4) a principle as an instruction, which describes the highest values of a legal arrangement, its part or an institution etc. (reflects a certain way of living), for example, a norm of the Constitution which provides that "[a]ll human beings in Latvia shall be equal before the law and the courts. Human rights shall be realized without discrimination of any kind" (Article 91 of the Constitution);
5) a principle as an instruction which refers to institutions that apply legal norms and prescribe how the eventually applicable legal norm should be sought, interpreted, etc., for example, Section 9 (6) of the Law on Official Publications and Legal Information[25] [*Oficiālo publikāciju un tiesiskās informācijas likums*] provides that: "If a contradiction is detected between: 1) the legal norms of differing legal force, the legal norm of higher legal force shall be applied";
6) a principle as *regula juris*, i.e., a maxim of the legal science with a high degree of generalization which determines the systematization of a legal arrangement or a branch of law. Such principles as the hierarchy of external normative legal acts based on their legal force or the principle of separation of power belong to this group.

Different scholars of law, of course, provide a different number of possible meanings of the term "principles of law". But do all these listed meanings reflect general principles of law?

Meanings nrs. 1, 2 and 3 in the author's opinion only show that in a system of laws there exist normative instructions of a general character, which essentially are written (positivised) legal norms or parts thereof. Still, this enlisting of possible meanings helps to see the contrast and *to distinguish* from all other

23 Meļķisis E. Tiesību normu iztulkošana. *Likums un Tiesības,* 2. sēj., 2000, nr. 9 (13), 279. lpp.

24 Environmental Protection Law: the law of the Republic of Latvia. Adopted on 02.11.2006. Available: likumi.lv/ta/en/en/id/147917-environmental-protection-law.

25 Law on Official Publications and Legal Information: the law of the Republic of Latvia. Adopted on 31.05.2012. Available: likumi.lv/ta/en/en/id/249322-law-on-official-publications-and-legal-information.

instructions of a general character or probably other principles of law the one which is a "general principle of law", as by general principles of law one should understand meaning nrs. 4, 5 and 6.

Thus, by general principles of law one understands instructions that:

1) express the highest values of a legal arrangement, of a part thereof or of an institution, etc. (reflects a certain way of living); these are all natural rights and human rights as a result of the positivisation of natural rights (for example, the right to human dignity, the right to life, the right to freedom, the right to property, etc.) and the principle of justice as the ultimate goal of the legal arrangement of a Democratic State governed by the Rule of Law;
2) instruct the institutions, which apply the legal norms, on how the eventually applicable legal norm should be sought, interpreted, etc.; these are all legal methods[26] (for example, higher and lower critique of legal norms, interpretation or concretization of legal norms, further development of law, collision norms for resolving conflicts between legal norms, methods of argumentation of rulings, etc.);
3) define the systematisation of the legal arrangement or a branch of law; these are all other general principles of law that do not fit into any of the previous two categories but are related to the structure of the legal arrangement of a Democratic State based on the Rule of Law (for example, such as the principle of separation of power, the principle of the hierarchy of normative legal acts).

Thus, in order to check whether a provision, a principle of law is a general principle of law, a two-step test must be applied:

1) the direct relationship of the legal principle with the Basic Norm should be checked. A legal principle is only a general principle of law if it is directly derived from the Basic Norm – a Democratic State based on the Rule of Law; that is, such a principle can only function in its full scope of content and as a real, valid and directly applicable legal norm in the legal arrangement of a Democratic State based on the Rule of Law;[27]

---

26 See more on this in Chapter 3.3.

27 For example, the general principles of law – the right to human dignity, the right to freedom of expression and prohibition of censorship, principle of reasonable application of legal norms (interpretation), principle of separation of power – can function in their full scope and as a real legal norm valid for direct application only in the legal arrangement of a Democratic State based on the Rule of Law.

2) the content of the legal principle should be clarified: whether it is a principle of justice, a natural rights norm, a regulation, how to apply a legal norm, the legal method, or how to systematize the legal arrangement.

If *both* of the above factors are fulfilled, then the specific provision, principle of law is a general principle of law.

2 The Origin of General Principles of Law and Basic Groups of Meaning of Law

One of the basic elements that defines the characteristics of an object, value, etc. is its origin. The theories of origin of general principles of law are directly related to the most significant groups, doctrines of the meaning of law in the Western legal system, i.e., the doctrine of natural law and the doctrine of legal positivism.

2.1 *The Origin of the Understanding of General Principles of Law*

The origin of the understanding of the principles of law of the Western legal system as well as the understanding of law as such can be traced back to the times of ancient Greece and ancient Rome. Although the origin of the understanding of the general principles of law are from a doctrinal point of view related to the doctrine of natural law, one should, to be more precise, point out that over time to some extent general principles of law have turned into a third doctrine or the middle way between the doctrine of natural law and legal positivism, thus trying to solve the inherent and eternal dilemma between natural law and positivism,[28] between unwritten legal norms and written legal norms. Therefore, the basic postulates of natural law doctrine should be accepted as the main doctrine of origin of general principles of law but also representatives of legal positivism when facing the daily implementation of law needed to accept the existence of general principles of law and their influence on the process of application of legal norms.

The most interesting and the most important thing to note is that when the origin of the general principles of law is discussed then irrespective of the doctrine of law – natural law or legal positivism – representatives of both doctrines prove the character of the general principles of law as being *generally binding*.

28 See similarly Kaufmann A. *Rechtsphilosophie*. München: C.H.Beck'sche Verlagsbuchhandlung, 1997, S. 49 ff.

Generally binding means that:

1) the application of general principles of law with the help of coercive measures (mechanism) is ensured by state institutions and officials; that is, because of non-compliance with or violation of these principles adverse consequences take effect, and
2) they are related to an unlimited number of persons and can be applied to an unlimited number of all such kind of cases (in comparison with the "not generally binding", acts of application of legal norms, which are related to a certain physical person or legal entity and are binding only in respect of a specific case).

2.2 *The Doctrine of Legal Positivism and General Principles of Law*

The main idea that characterises the origin of general principles of law from the positivist understanding of law is that they arise from a positivised (written) system of laws – legal norms created by a legislator. Therefore, continuing the chain of logical argumentation, the representatives of the legal positivism doctrine indicate that something (general principles of law) that is derived from something of generally binding character (a system of written legal norms) should have the same characteristics as the original.

"Principles are normative regulations"[29] as contrasted to descriptive assertions. Consequently, the principles define "how it should be" and what is allowed, and not only describe the existing situation.[30]

Positivists consider that the existence and essence of legal principles can be justified only with positive law. They are thus something like a summary of the positive law and nothing more. In other words, they are a means to reflect the positive law.[31]

2.3 *The Doctrine of Natural Law and General Principles of Law*

Supporters of the doctrine of natural law consider that general principles of law arise from natural law, they exist already *before* the written legal norms created by a legislator and determine their content. Consequently, something (general principles of law) that determines the content of something (written legal norms) that essentially is generally binding, also should have this characteristic, should be generally binding, or only something that has the same or a higher ranking, force, status, etc. can define the content of something else.

---

29 Peczenik A. 1971, p. 29.

30 Sieckamnn von J.R. Logische eigenschaften von principien. *Rechtstheorie*, 1994, Band 25, Heft 2.

31 Cf. Peczenik A. 1971, p. 29.

From the point of view of the natural law doctrine the general principles of law are considered to be “the higher law”.[32] This means that the existence and application of the written legal norms created by a legislator, or the positive law, depend on their consistency with the general principles of law.[33]

In addition, natural rights itself, from the aspect of their internal structure and nature, are “real legal norms;”[34] therefore the general principles of law have a normative, generally binding character also because they result from unwritten legal norms of natural law.

2.4 *Contemporary Legal Theory Pertaining to Democratic States Based on the Rule of Law and General Principles of Law*

In order to understand the functioning of the legal arrangement of a modern Democratic State governed by the Rule of Law and its basis, it helps if one finds an answer to the question: is what the legislator determines the right thing to do because they determine it – omnipotence? Or does the legislator determine what it determines because it is right – that is, omniscience?[35] The choice of answer is directly related to the legal positivism or natural law understanding. Legal positivism represents the idea that law is binding because it is positivised, while the natural law school believes that law is positivised because it is binding.[36]

In the Soviet legal system, the understanding of a legal norm was closely related to the prevailing positivistic understanding of law, the basic postulates of which determine that law is a set of written (positive) legal norms adopted or issued by the State, a closed system; that “law” and “the law” – normative legal acts – are the same thing, because law can be found only in the normative legal acts; that it is impossible to morally evaluate law, just as it is not important to study the content and goals of law, as law is valid and exists because the legislator had adopted it and regardless of any moral considerations.[37] Consequently, the understanding of the legal norm was also related to the written normative legal act, which is the only source of law recognized in the Soviet legal system: “The source of law is an act of the state. […] Sources of law

32 David R. Sources of Law. In: *International Encyclopedia of Comparative Law.* Vol. II, Tübingen: J.C.B. Mohr, 1971, p. 140.

33 Stromberg T. *Inledning till den allmanna rattslaran.* Lund, 1970, p. 28; cited from: Peczenik A. 1971, p. 29.

34 See more on this in Chapter 2.2.4. Šulcs L. 1937, 24. sl.

35 Gardner J. 2012, p. 7.

36 Ibid.

37 See Hart H.L.A. 1997; Liepa L. 1997, 108.–112. lpp.

are the laws of the Supreme Council, decrees of the Presidium of the Supreme Council, government decisions and orders and other regulatory acts. Sources of socialist law are legal acts that contain legal norms. [...] Sources of law are the normative acts issued by the competent Soviet state bodies, adopted by the people in a referendum, as well as the normative acts issued by public organizations and sanctioned by the state";[38] and contained the legal norms: "Socialist legal norms are general rules of behavior adopted or sanctioned by the competent state bodies or under their delegation by public organizations, which express the will of the working people, regulate public relations and, in case of violation of the norms, provide for the responsibility of those who violate them."[39] As an essential feature of a legal norm in the two definitions discussed above appears a State institution that adopts or issues a legal act, which in turn contains legal norms, without the possibility that a legal norm can exist in an unwritten (non-positivised) form, regardless of the existing will of the State authorities, and the source of this legal norm is directly a person him/herself (the people, the sovereign).

On the other hand, the understanding of law based on the natural law doctrine, which is the leading doctrine for understanding of law in the legal arrangement of a Democratic State governed by the Rule of Law, unlike the doctrine of legal positivism, insists on the existence of a difference between the concepts of "*law*" and "*the law*" or "law" and "normative legal acts", "natural law" and "positive law", and ascertains the existence of natural and inalienable human rights in an unwritten form – natural rights exist before the State and independently of the State power. This understanding of law conceptually connects law and morality: natural law is legal norms by their structure and moral norms by their content.[40]

Lotārs Šulcs enumerates seven features that indicate that natural law consists of real legal norms by their structure, namely: 1) they regulate actions and not internal experiences; 2) they do not always take into account the motive of the action; 3) they have an imperative, attributive, nature – obligations correspond to a requirement; 4) their content changes depending on the time and place and 5) in case of their violation, legal consequences, which are ensured by the State's coercive mechanism, arise.[41]

38 Krastiņš I. *Valsts un tiesību teorija.* Rīga: Zvaigzne, 1985, 153.–154. lpp.

39 Ibid.

40 Šulcs L. 1937, 27.–28. sl.; on the features of law: Šulcs L. *Tiesības kā ētikas minimums.* Rīga: [B.i.], 1936, 73.–74. lpp.

41 Ibid.

All these features in general, and especially the fifth feature, indicate that natural law in the conditions of a Democratic State based on the Rule of Law has the basic feature of a legal norm – *generally binding force*. This means that in case of violation of the legal norm of natural law in a Democratic State based on the Rule of Law, the violator will suffer adverse consequences, while for the subject whose natural right has been violated it will be restored, and all of the above will be ensured by the State by activating a coercive mechanism, and this will happen regardless of whether this legal norm of natural law has already been partially[42] positivised or not, or it has existed in the system of laws in an unwritten form.

In modern legal theory, there is an opinion that two radically different and mutually incompatible understandings of a legal norm exist: the *hyletic* and the *expressive* understanding of a legal norm,[43] which are based on the understanding of natural law and legal positivism, respectively. According to the hyletic understanding, legal norms are conceptual units that *exist independently of language*; however, norms can also be expressed linguistically, that is, in sentences that have a prescriptive meaning. On the other hand, according to the expressive understanding, legal norms are commands, the result of a prescriptive use of language.

The study revealed in this book – contemporary legal theory pertaining to Democratic States based on the Rule of Law – is based on the basic postulate that in the conditions of a modern Democratic State governed by the Rule of Law, a legal norm is no longer viewed only in relation to a normative legal act, but as a regulation that, in accordance with the general principles of law of the legal arrangement determined by the will of the sovereign, should regulate legal relations in a given country, regardless of whether the legislator has been able to adequately verbalise this norm or not. The fact that the legal norm is

---

42 The norm of natural law can be positivised only partially; it is not possible for the legislator to express the entire scope of natural right in written form. The legislator provides only guidelines in the texts of normative legal acts on the content of general principles of law, which includes also natural rights. This content, in turn, is constantly improving along with the development of the legal arrangement (unlike the frozen text of the written legal norm, necessary amendments of which one must wait for in the hope of the legislative procedure) and it first manages to be fixed, formulated in the form of case law and legal doctrine.

43 Weinberger O. The Expressive Conception of Norms: An Impasse for the Logic of Norms. In: *Normativity and Norms. Critical Perspectives on Kelsenian Themes*. Oxford: Clarendon Press, 1999, p. 413; Alchourron C.E., Bulygin E. The Expressive Conception of Norms. In: Stanley L. Paulson (Ed.) *Normativity and Norms. Critical Perspectives on Kelsenian Themes*. Oxford: Clarendon Press, 1999, pp. 384–385.

not only the text of the written legal norm, which may or may not coincide with the article (section) of the normative legal act, is clearly proven by the understanding of general principles of law and their application in the conditions of a Democratic State based on the Rule of Law.

The next question that needs to be answered in order to understand the origin and nature of general principles of law, which is directly related to the concept of a legal norm in a Democratic State based on the Rule of Law, is the question of the true source of all law, including legal norms. Is the source of legal norms the legislator or is it the people, the sovereign?

Hans Kelsen in his work *Pure Theory of Law*[44] pointed out that all legal norms derive their legal force from the basic norm (*Grundnorm*), which is not a written norm, since even the formal Constitution derives its legal force from it. After all, it is only because of the basic norm that all positive law is valid. And the basic norm is neither correct, because positivised, nor positivised, because correct, as it is not positivised at all.[45] In the understanding of Hans Kelsen, the basic norm is a hypothetical assumption about the regulation that determines the procedure for the adoption of the first Constitution or a new Constitution in the event of a revolutionary break of the State system.[46] Its validity is the assumption of those who work with positivised law as valid law. What is this assumption – in Kelsen's words – the assumption that the historically first Constitution is legitimate.[47] The assumption of the basic norm is a belief in the legal reason or consciousness about the authority and correctness. The basic norm makes those who apply legal norms safe and infallible when they are acting within its authority.[48]

Kelsen regards the basic norm as not a "positive" one (which means for Kelsen that it is not a norm of positive law, i.e., created by a real act of will of a legal organ, but is presupposed in juristic thinking). Hence, he argues, it is "meta-legal".[49] And, since it enables anyone to interpret a command, permission or authorisation as an objectively valid legal norm, its legal functions are not in doubt. It is purely formal, is a juristic value judgement, and has a hypothetical character; yet it forms the keystone of the whole legal arch, it is

44 Kelsen H. 1967, p. 195.

45 Gardner J. 2012, p. 9.

46 See more on this Pleps J. Normatīvo tiesību aktu hierarhija: profesors *Hanss Kelzens* un mūsdienas (1). *Likums un Tiesības*, 2007, 9. sēj., nr. 2 (90), 49. lpp.; Morton P. *An Institutional Theory of Law. Keeping Law in its Place.* Oxford: Clarendon Press, 1998, p. 7.

47 Gardner J. 2012, p. 9.

48 Ibid., p. 15.

49 Kelsen H. 1967, p. 205.

at the top of the pyramid of norms of each legal order.[50] Kelsen believes that every jurist assumes this to be the basis of the legal order; and that it merely means that the legal order is as a whole effective (i.e., that people do in fact behave according to the norms of this order), and that it may be stated in the form that men ought to behave in conformity with the legal order only if it is as a whole effective. This seems to invoke either a totally unnecessary fictitious hypothesis, on the one hand, or on the other, a statement of fact, dressed up in the shape of a general norm. Moreover, the basic norm is propounded as the means of giving unity to the legal arrangement and enabling the legal scholar to interpret all valid legal norms as a non-contradictory field of meaning.[51]

But Kelsen also writes that it "looks that one could give as a reason for the validity of a norm the circumstance that it was established by an authority, human or divine [...] Only a competent authority can create valid norms; and such competence can only be based on a norm that authorizes the issuing of norms".[52] He recognizes that it is a static norm system, where the reason for validity and *content* of the system of norms is deduced from a norm presupposed as a basic norm and its content has to be assumed to be directly evident, which means that it follows from the reason while the creation of the norms is an act of will.[53]

Similarly to Kelsen's theory of the basic norm, Hart also believes that there has to be a rule which provides authoritative criteria for identifying valid law within a particular legal system. It also puts restrictions on legislative power as these restrictions are "parts of the rule conferring authority to legislate and they vitally concern the courts, since they use such a rule as a criterion of the validity of purported legislative enactments coming before them. Legislation, in these terms, which infringes such limitations is void."[54] This leads us to consider the rule of recognition. How then is the rule of recognition to be ascertained? Hart points out that such a rule is often not expressly stated but can be shown by the way in which particular rules ("primary" rules) are identified by courts and other legal officials. It is a form of social practice. Harris is led to the conclusion that the rule of recognition must be "an abstraction, a pure norm, arrived at inductively from observations of what lawyers do, but not itself witnessable."[55] Whatever its juridical status, Hart tells us that the rule

50 Cf. Freeman M.D.A. *Lloyd's Introduction to Jurisprudence*. London: Sweet & Maxwell ltd., 1994, p. 283.

51 Ibid., pp. 282–289.

52 Kelsen H. 1967, p. 193.

53 Ibid., p. 195.

54 Hart H.L.A. 1993, p. 69.

55 Freeman M.D.A. 1994, pp. 350–354; H.L.A. Hart. 1993, pp. 97–107.

of recognition is ultimate and as an ultimate rule it can "neither be valid nor invalid."[56] For Hart the only point is whether the rule of recognition is accepted as such by those who operate the system,[57] and this is the aspect important for this study as the courts have a central role in establishing the validity of the applicable legal norms by referring back to the basic norm or the rule of recognition.

Kelsen as a representative of legal positivism is clear about the fact that the basic norm is in no way connected with the requirement for the law to be just, as a legal order under the basic norm can be both just or unjust,[58] and it is true if we look at the legal orders in general. But this study covers the legal arrangement of Democratic States based on the Rule of Law, where justice is an ultimate goal of the legal arrangement, natural law doctrine is a leading doctrine for understanding law, and that is the act of the will of a sovereign of the particular country to live in this kind of a State, and from the moment of proclamation of their will the sovereign themselves are subject to the Basic Norm.

Thus, the source of the Basic Norm of a Democratic State based on the Rule of law is a *sovereign*. The content of the Basic Norm is the sovereign's will[59] – the real act of will of a legal organ; it's unwritten legal norm as it exists before the State but at the same time itself witnessable and found in the legal reason. Thus, the will of the sovereign determines the content of the Basic Norm, that is, in what type of country the sovereign wants to live. The Basic Norm of the legal arrangement of Latvia, for example, can be found in a formulated form in the Act of the People's Council of Latvia on the Proclamation of the Republic of Latvia of 18 November 1918,[60] but since the People's Council was not an elected, democratically legitimate body, on 27 May 1920, the Constituent Assembly of Latvia once again confirmed this choice by adopting the Declaration on the State of Latvia.[61]

---

56 Hart H.L.A. 1993, p. 109.

57 Ibid., p. 107.

58 Kelsen H. 1967, p. 217.

59 "The nation exists prior to everything; it is the origin of everything. Its will is always legal. It is the law itself. Prior to the nation and above the nation there is only natural law. To have a proper idea of sequence of positive laws, all emanating solely from the nation's will, the first in order of precedence will be constitutional laws [...] These laws are said to be fundamental, not in the sense that they can be independent of the national will" In: Sonenscher M. (Ed.) *Sieyès: Political Writings: Including the Debate Between Sieyes and Tom Paine in 1791*. Indianapolis, Cambridge: Hackett Publishing Company, Inc., 2003, p. 136.

60 Latvijas pilsoņiem!: Latvijas Tautas padomes Latvijas Republikas proklamēšanas akts. *Pagaidu Valdības Vēstnesis*, 1918, nr. 1.

61 Deklarācija par Latvijas valsti: Latvijas Satversmes sapulces deklarācija. *Likumu un Valdības Rīkojumu Krājums*, 1920, nr. 4. Skat. arī: Grigore-Bāra E., Kovaļevska A., Liepa

When the will of the sovereign is formulated in the form of a Basic Norm, the legal arrangement of the respective country *begins to be governed by the principles arising from the Basic Norm*, which in the case of a Democratic State based on the Rule of Law are *general principles of law*. Deciding and proclaiming to live in a Democratic State governed by the Rule of Law, the sovereign cannot influence the validity and content of general principles of law and is also subject to the provisions of these principles – according to another general principle of law, the principle of militant democracy derived from the Basic Norm.[62] If the sovereign determines with a basic norm some other State system and political regime in which they want to live, then other legal principles will operate in this regime, which determine the content and structure of the legal arrangement of that regime.[63]

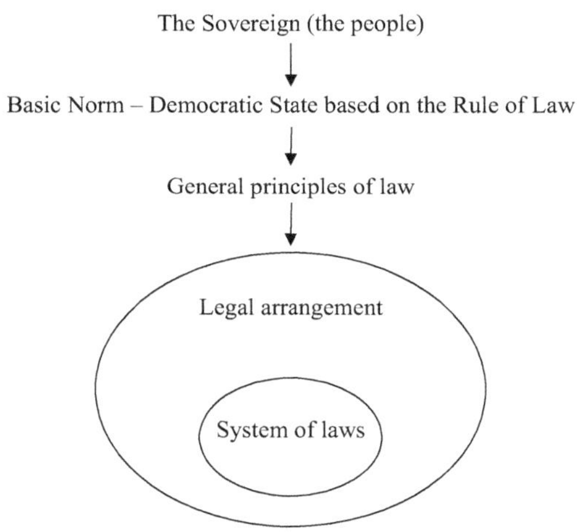

L., Levits E., Mits M., Rezevska D., Rozenvalds J., Sniedzīte G. 1. Latvija ir neatkarīga demokrātiska republika. Grām.: *Latvijas Republikas Satversmes komentāri*. Balodis R. (Zin. vad.) Rīga: Latvijas Vēstnesis, 2014, 147.–148. lpp.; Pleps J. 2007, 9. sēj., nr. 3 (91), 90.–91. lpp.

62 On concretization of the principle of militant democracy, for example, see the judgement of the Constitutional Court of 29 June 2018 in case no. 2017-25-01, para 13.3. Available: satv.tiesa.gov.lv; decision of the Constitutional Court of 27 May 2022, para. 18.4. Available: satv.tiesa.gov.lv; judgement of the European Court of Human Rights (Grand Chamber) of 16 March 2006: *Ždanoka v. Latvia*, application no. 58278/00, para. 100. Available: hudoc.echr.coe.int.

63 So, for example, the so-called "principle of leader" of an authoritarian State system is not acceptable for a democratic State but will work as a principle of law in the legal arrangement of an authoritarian State. Pleps J. 2007, 9. sēj., nr. 3 (91), 90. lpp.; Kalniņš E. 2000, 216. lpp. For example, on the principles of law of an authoritarian State system, see more Pleps J. Autoritāras valsts izpratne un pamatprincipi: Kārļa Ulmaņa režīms. Grām.: *Tiesību efektīvas piemērošanas problemātika*. Latvijas Universitātes 72. zinātniskās konferences rakstu krājums. Rīga: LU Akadēmiskais apgāds, 2014, 69.–76. lpp.

These principles then are the ones which determine both the substantive and structural elements of the legal arrangement in the given country; what legal norms must exist in the system of laws in order to resolve all the disputes arising in the legal arrangement.

From this sequence, it is obvious that the source of the entire legal arrangement, including the system of laws, is the sovereign, and the legislator is not an ultimate "authority" in determining the content of legal norms. The source of legal norms is the people or the sovereign, who have chosen to live in a certain State system and political regime, a Democratic State based on the Rule of Law, and thus divided (as according to the general principle of law, separation of power derived from the Basic Norm) the State's power between the legislative, judicial and executive branches, determining each of them to perform their tasks in the *interests of the sovereign*, so that it would be easier for the sovereign to organize their life.

The task of the legislator is to write down those legal norms, the content of which is determined by general principles of law arising from the Basic Norm and which exist and are valid in the system of laws, so that *all possible* disputes that may arise between members of the sovereign can be resolved according to the will of the sovereign. Contemporary legal theory examines the system of laws of a Democratic State based on the Rule of Law deductively – what it *should be*, based on the understanding of natural law and the Basic Norm, because *only a deductively derived system can be complete*.[64] This means that a system derived from something general, such as a system derived from the general principles of law, and not found inductively – from something singular, individual, such as a set of normative legal acts – can be complete. The fact that the system of laws itself is objectively, impartially complete,[65] namely, it includes all the written and unwritten regulations necessary to resolve disputes arising in the legal arrangement of a given country, is proven by the principle of the prohibition of legal obstruction by institutions and courts – the applier of legal norms does not have a right to refuse to adjudicate a case if there are no written legal norms. This principle is also positivised in Latvia, for example in Section 15 of the Administrative Procedure Law, Section 5 of the Civil Law, as well as in Section 1 of the Civil Procedure Law[66] [*Civilprocesa likums*], which guarantees a person's right to court protection.

---

64 Vīnzarājs N. Jēdzienu jurisprudence. *Tieslietu Ministrijas Vēstnesis*, 1937, nr. 1.

65 Kalniņš E. Tiesību tālākveidošana. Grām.: *Juridiskās metodes pamati. 11 soļi tiesību normu piemērošanā*. Rīga: Ratio iuris, 2003, 126.–205. lpp.

66 Civil Procedure Law: the Law of the Republic of Latvia. Adopted on 14.10.1998. Available: likumi.lv/ta/en/en/id/50500-civil-procedure-law.

However, such a task is objectively unfulfillable for a legislator. First, because the legislature is a group of people, and it is human nature to make mistakes. Even more so because written legal norms consist of a text, which in turn consists of words. Each word has multiple possible meanings, for example, a word can have its original (historical origin) meaning and a transferred or over time acquired meaning, or a word can have its broadest and narrowest meaning, or a word can have an ordinary and a legal meaning.[67] Different thoughts can be expressed with countless words and their combinations.

Secondly, the legal relations of the members of the sovereign are so numerous and dynamic that new relations constantly arise, which the legislator has not yet managed to regulate with the positive legal norms. But the general principles of law arising from the Basic Norm – the right to court protection and the principle of the prohibition of legal obstruction – state that the institution or the court may not refuse to adjudicate the case if there are no written legal norms. Therefore, according to the general principle of law of the separation of power there is a judiciary whose duty, according to the authority given by the sovereign, is, by applying legal methods (which are also general principles of law in a Democratic State based on the Rule of Law), to correct the mistakes of the legislator and find the legal norms existing in the system of laws and resolve the case without waiting for the legislature to adopt the written legal norm as a result of a long legislative process. In the event of a legislative mistake, taking into account the aspect of mutual interaction and control of the separate branches of the state power provided by the principle of separation of power (checking and balancing), it is the responsibility of the applier of legal norms to correct the written legal norm with the help of the application of relevant legal methods (for example, by applying the analogy, teleological reduction) by expanding or narrowing the legal content of the legal norm according to the will of the legislator (the plan of the law) and the norm's *ratio legis* (the teleology of the law).[68]

---

67 For example, the original and meaning gained later of the word "*muita*" contained in the previously valid Article 81 of the Constitution of the Republic of Latvia, or the ordinary and legal meaning of the word "*kukulis*". Cf. Rezevska D. 17. pants. Tiesību normu interpretācija un analoģija. Grām.: *Administratīvā procesa likuma komentāri.* Briede J. (Zin. red.) Rīga: Tiesu namu aģentūra, 2013, 269.–270. lpp.

68 For example, the sovereign must have wanted the legislature to determine that if, when donating blood to a blood donor centre, it is determined that the donor's blood contains a deadly virus, then this information must be communicated to the donor, as this is provided by such general principles of law as the right to health and the right to life. However, the legislator did not provide for such a norm in the written normative legal act, so the court had to find this norm already in another unwritten level of general principles of law. Or another example: the sovereign must have wanted the legislator to provide for the

The principle of separation of power in its developed content of contemporary concretization does not necessarily mean that the branches of the State power must be absolutely separated, but rather that there must be mutual control and limitations between them.[69] In Western democracies, the separation of power is not implemented strictly according to its ideal model. In general, only judicial independence from executive interference is strictly protected. Furthermore, by interpreting the laws and filling gaps in the laws, the judiciary participates in clarifying and supplementing the rights and obligations set forth in the normative legal acts. Thus, the judiciary also inevitably operates in the field of legislative functions.[70]

3 General Principles of Law and Legal Norms

Are the general principles of law legal norms? Would the fact that the nature of general principles of law is that they are generally binding, as was proved in the previous chapter, also mean that general principles of law are "real" legal norms? The term "real" is used here intentionally. In legal science, general principles of law are often called "false legal norms" or legal norms which are "not directly applicable".[71] This statement is based on the arguments that general principles of law in comparison with "real" legal norms would not provide for legal consequences that would take effect automatically after the required preconditions are fulfilled, and that general principles of law do not have a structure which is characteristic of the legal norms – they are not expressed in the form "if ..., then ...", respectively, they do not consist of legal content and legal consequences.[72]

---

possibility of home birth and how a child born at home is registered. But the legislator failed to make this regulation positive, and the court had to find the unwritten legal norm, which stipulates that every child has the right to a name, personal identification number, social benefit, etc. and it follows from the general principle of law of the protection of the best interests of a child, principle of justice, principle of equality and right to recognition as a person before the law.

69 Vildbergs H.J., Feldhūne G. *Atsauces Satversmei: mācību līdzeklis.* Rīga: Latvijas Universitāte, 2003, 4. lpp.

70 Skat. arī: Neimanis J. *Tiesību tālākveidošana.* Rīga: Latvijas Vēstnesis, 2006, 74. lpp.; Cipeliuss R. *Vispārējā mācība par valsti.* Rīga: AGB, 1998, 224. lpp.

71 For example, see Larenz K. *Richtiges Recht.* München: C.H. Beck, 1979, S. 23; Kalniņš E. Tiesību normu piemērošanas loģiskā shēma. *Likums un Tiesības,* 2. sēj., nr. 5 (9), 150.–151. lpp.; Kalniņš E. Tiesību normu piemērošanas loģiskā shēma. Grām.: *Juridiskās metodes pamati. 11 soļi tiesību normu piemērošanā.* Meļķisis E. (Red.) Rīga: Ratio iuris, 2003, 25. lpp.

72 Dworkin R. 1977, 1978, p. 25.

The following views on the nature and legal force of general principles of law can be found in legal writings: "A "principle" of law, one would assume, is something different from a rule (of law). When one refers to a rule, one often refers to a norm providing some rights or imposing some duties on the subjects of the law, which in turn can be invoked by physical and legal persons before the Courts. A principle of law is, on the contrary, a rule in the meaning of the rule-of-law, which represents an ideal of reason and/or of justice, which (accords with the permanent basis of human nature and) is presumed to form the basis of the very institution of law".[73] So the imperative attributive nature[74] of the general principles of law, as Lotārs Šulcs describes it, is called into question, namely, it is doubted that they could grant a person subjective rights or impose legal obligations.

In most studies on the subject of defining and comprehending the complicated notion of the general principles of law one of the main problem areas is the definition of characteristics and criteria for differentiating between the general principles of law and legal norms.[75]

The main question that this section will try to answer is: are these criteria for the separation of general principles of law and legal norms significant; do they prove that general principles of law are not legal norms or quite the opposite, that general principles of law are one of the types of legal norms?

Various authors find more or less the same differences between general principles of law and legal norms. Differences could be found in the types of origin, attitude to the idea of law, justification of significance as well as the degree of generalization, structure and the imperative, attributive character that are mentioned most often. The most important differences, namely, those which in the case of insufficient examination would indeed cause ambiguities in comprehending the relations between the general principles of law and legal norms are the latter three – *degree of generalization* or in other formulations, predicting the cases of application, *structure*, and the *ability to create subjective rights and legal obligations* – and therefore they will be analysed here.

The proposed thesis about the difference in the degree of generalization between general principles of law and legal norms is as follows: a legal norm

73 Harbo T-I. The Function of the Proportionality Principle in EU Law. *European Law Journal*, 2010, Vol.16, no. 2, p. 159.

74 Šulcs L. 1937, 27.–28. sl.; on the features of law: Šulcs L. 1936, 73.–74. lpp.

75 For example, see Dworkin R. 1977, 1978, Ch. 2, 3; Esser J. 1990; Alexy R. 1979, S. 59 ff; Alexy R. 1986, 3. Kap.; Penski U. 1989, no. 3; Boulanger J. 1950, pp. 50–75; Buchwald D. The Rule of Law: A Complete and Consistent Set of (Legal) Norms? *Rechtstheorie*, Beiheft 17, 1997, S. 157–160.

according to its degree of generalization is limited because it applies to certain activities or situations; a norm is formulated in respect of a certain legal situation, and it can be applied only in respect of this situation.[76] A principle, on the other hand, is general because it can be applied in an unlimited number of cases.

The degree of generalization as the main difference between a principle and a norm was clearly defined for the first time in the studies of Ronald Dworkin. That is why his theory, as the starting point for the discussions on principles of law in contemporary jurisprudence and on the separation of principles and norms, should be examined in greater detail.

According to Dworkin's theory the notion "principles of law" may be defined widely or narrowly.[77] In the wider meaning the principles include all general directives, which are not norms. If we look at the notion of the principle of law more narrowly, principles should be separated from aims. Aims (or policy) are related to the facilitation of social objectivity, improvement of the economic, political or social indicators of a certain society. A principle, in its turn, is orientated to the improvement of justice or social morals, and it should be respected not to ensure the economic, political or social situation, which is preferable, but because it is a requirement of justice, fairness or any other moral dimension.[78]

Dworkin considers that there is a "logical difference"[79] between general principles of law and legal norms, namely, the ways how they regulate the specific legal relations are different. Norms are applicable in the form of *all or nothing* – if the facts of the real (actual) life situation correspond to the characteristics defined in the legal content of the norm, then either the norm is valid and correspondingly the legal consequences provided in the norm take effect, or it is not valid, and therefore does not influence the result of the case. However, according to Dworkin principles do not provide for legal consequences, which would take effect automatically after the prescribed preconditions are fulfilled.

Every legal norm may have exceptions and theoretically it is possible to enumerate all exceptions, and the more exceptions are included, the more precise is the formulation of the norm. However, in the case of general principles of

76 So, for example, the legal norm that determines responsibility for not paying an income tax is applicable only in those cases when a person had a duty to pay the income tax but did not do it.

77 See Dworkin R. 1977, 1978, pp. 22–23.

78 See more Ibid.; Dworkin R. *A Matter of Principle*. Cambridge: Harvard University Press, 1985.

79 Dworkin R. 1977, 1978, pp. 24–25.

law even theoretically it is not possible to enlist all the probabilities when the principle would not be applicable because then we would have to enlist endless imaginary situations where it is obvious, even beforehand, that a certain principle cannot be related to them.

The example used for illustration is the famous 1889 case *Riggs v. Palmer* in the Court of New York where the court had to decide if the grandson mentioned in the last will was entitled to the property left by the grandfather if he had murdered his grandfather to inherit this property. In the judgement the court indicated that the valid written legal norms governing inheritance do not contain any limitations in respect of leaving the property to the murderer of the testator, however, "all laws as well as all contracts may be controlled in their operation and effect by *general, fundamental maxims* of the common law. No one shall be permitted to profit by his own fraud, or to take advantage of his own wrong, or to found any claim upon his own iniquity, or to acquire property by his own crime"[80] [author's emphasis].

Nonetheless, arguments offered by Dworkin for distinguishing general principles of law and legal norms on the basis of generalization can be disputed. First, can a legal norm be applied in all cases when the norm is valid and its legal content has been implemented in the actual situation, as considered by Dworkin? Of course not, and the answer to this question is provided by nobody else than Dworkin himself with the example of the *Riggs case*. Although there existed a valid legal norm which regulated the actual situation, i.e., when the last will had taken effect, after the death of the testator the legacy should be given to the legatee, it was not applied although it did not have a limitation in written form as one of the preconditions included in the legal content of the legal norm. This limitation then was found in and imposed by a general principle of law, which was included in the text of the legal norm as an additional characteristic of the legal content: "if the legatee does not profit from his wrongdoing, then has the right to receive the legacy." Thus, the application of a valid written legal norm depends on its consistency with general principles of law, and in fact the full or complete legal norm always consists of a written and an unwritten part where the written part of the legal norm is subject to the unwritten part found in the general principles of law.

In addition, the argument that in contrast with general principles of law, it is theoretically possible for a legal norm to enlist all exceptions, while for a principle even theoretically it is impossible to enlist all the probable situations, where the principle would not be applicable because then innumerable

80 Cf. Dworkin R. 1977, 1978, p. 23, ref. no. 10.

imaginary situations would have to be enlisted, actually does not present any difference. Would not an absolutely exhaustive list of all cases when a written legal norm is not applicable include the "innumerable imaginary situations" that this norm does not relate to at first sight?

The next characteristic that could be noted as a difference between general principles of law and legal norms and often is are their *structural differences*.

To ascertain what structural differences are and whether they really exist between legal norms and principles, it should be clarified what the structure of a legal norm is. But to define the structure of a legal norm, the notion, the understanding of a legal norm, should be analysed. In addition, we should consider that the understanding of a legal norm has developed and that nowadays in contemporary legal theory pertaining to Democratic States based on the Rule of Law we understand something different by a legal norm than in the beginnings of the development of the theory of general principles of law.[81]

So for an instruction to be recognized as a legal norm, it must comply with the substantial and the structural criteria of a legal norm.

First, discussing the concept of a legal norm it should be pointed out that a legal norm consists of words or text, which determine the required model of behaviour – should be, and it is directed to the establishment of certain legal consequences. A legal norm has three characteristic features:

1) it is generally binding;
2) its enforcement is ensured by the State courts or executive power by coercive measures;
3) it can be applied more than once.[82]

Therefore, every instruction which claims the status of a legal norm must correspond to the above-mentioned features. It is also important to note that in accordance with the statements of the doctrine of natural law these features do not include a certain form of an instruction, respectively, whether the instruction is expressed in writing (positivised), if it corresponds to the three above-mentioned characteristics – it is generally binding, applicable more than once and by compulsion – it is to be denoted as a legal norm.

Since a legal norm asks for certain legal consequences taking effect, it simultaneously provides for the preconditions for these consequences to take effect. Thus, structurally a legal norm consists of two parts: 1) legal content, which enlists all preconditions for the application of a norm and 2) legal

81 See in detail: Chapter 2.2.4.

82 Cf. Larenz K., Canaris C.W. *Methodenlehre der Rechtswissenschaft*. 3. Aufl. Berlin, Heidelberg: Springer-Verlag, 1995, S. 71; Kalniņš E. Tiesību normu piemērošanas loģiskā shēma. 2000, 148. lpp.

consequences, which take effect in the cases when the legal content is implemented in the actual case. Structurally, a legal norm follows the scheme: "If ..., then."[83]

A legal norm and a section (an article) of a law (or more widely, a normative legal act) are not identical notions. This means that there are three options:

1) the section of the law includes just a part of the norm;
2) the section of the law includes several norms;
3) in an ideal situation the section of the law includes a whole norm.

What then is a complete legal norm? A legal norm is an objective, logically closed, ideal unit, which consists of all the required and at the same time sufficient normative preconditions that are required for legal consequences to take effect. Objective in the meaning that, whether or not the legislator has succeeded to formulate in writing the features of the legal content according to their intentions, or the legislator has forgotten to regulate an actual case, although it follows from the legal arrangement that this case should have been regulated and it is regulated but due to the "failure" of the legislator, in another, unwritten normative level,[84] or the legislator has comprised the legal norm in one article, one normative act or in several articles or acts, it exists as a logically closed unit, which structurally consists of all the required and at the same time sufficient normative preconditions that are necessary for legal consequences to take effect.

The task of the applier of legal norms within the legal arrangement is to discover and clarify these required and at the same time sufficient normative preconditions to apply the relevant legal norm, it means to solve the actual case relating it to the legal consequences defined in the legal norm. At the same time, in case the legislator makes a mistake, the duty of the applier of legal norms is to correct the written legal norm with the help of the relevant legal methods (for example, analogy, teleological reduction) broadening or narrowing the content of the written legal norm according to the will of the legislator and *ratio legis* of the norm.

Thus, any instruction, which corresponds to the above-mentioned three characteristics and therefore is a legal norm with the function to regulate the sphere of existence "what is", structurally should consist of the legal content – if ..., and the legal consequences – then.

---

83 See Wank R. *Die Auslegung von Gesetzen.* München: Carl Heymanns Verlag KG, 1997, S. 5–12; Schmalz D. *Methodenlehre für das juristische Studium.* 3. Aufl. Baden-Baden; Nomos-Verlagsgesellschaft, 1992, S. 22; Kalniņš E. Tiesību normu piemērošanas loģiskā shēma. 2000, 149. lpp.

84 See Chapter 4.1.1.

By making such a conclusion all that remains is to answer the question: is it possible to express a general principle of law, for example, the principle of legal security, structurally in correspondence with the parts of a legal norm, respectively, is a general principle of law orientated to the establishment of legal consequences that take effect if certain preconditions are fulfilled or, in other words, is a general principles of law "a legal norm valid for direct application"? And the answer is affirmative.

The content and scope of general principles of law basically can be found in the legal doctrine and in the case law.[85] So, for example, the Constitutional Court in the judgement of 10 June 1998 in case no. 04-03(98), concretizing the principle of protection of legitimate expectations, has admitted that pursuant to this principle "*state institutions should be consistent in their actions related to the normative acts issued, should respect legitimate expectations that persons could have based on the relevant normative act*"[86] or, if reworded according to the scheme "if …, then …",

> *if* a state institution has issued normative acts (the legal content), *then* in its actions in relation to these acts [it] should be consistent and respect the legitimate expectations that persons could have on the basis of the relevant normative act (legal consequences).

Thus, general principles of law in any moment can be transformed into a "legal norm valid for direct application".[87] In addition, the written legal norm is also not automatically valid for direct application, that is, it must first be *interpreted* – the true content of the written legal norm must be clarified (also the structural parts of it (legal content and legal consequences) should be found – as they can be in different sections of the law or maybe even in the different laws), then it must be checked using methods of the lower and higher critique, if necessary, other legal methods must also be applied, and only then it is applicable. Like the general principles of law, in order to apply them in deciding a specific case, they must first be filled with content, *concretized*.[88]

A third possible distinguishing feature mentioned as existing between legal norms and general principles of law is the capacity to create subjective rights

---

85 For clarifying and concretizing the content of the general principles of law, see hereinafter Chapter 4.1.1.

86 Judgement of the Constitutional Court of 10 June 1998 in the case no. 04-03(98). Available: satv.tiesa.gov.lv.

87 See similar in Atienza M., Manero J.R. 1996, pp. 8–9.

88 See more on this Chapter 4.1.1.

and legal obligations. It is important to remember here that there is a difference between principles of law and general principles of law, and while the former (for example, the principles of programs or objectives) do not really have an imperative attributive nature, general principles of law as rules directly derived from the Basic Norm, which replace written legal norms, if the legislator has not managed to adopt them and make them in positive form, or replace such written legal norms that contradict or do not comply with general principles of law, create subjective rights and impose legal obligations.

For example, the above-mentioned principle of protection of legitimate expectations creates a subjective right for a person to bring a claim to a court in cases where the State authority has not been consistent in its actions in relation to the normative legal acts issued by it, and to demand protection of the legitimate expectations and even reimbursement of damages caused as a result of these inconsistent actions of the State. At the same time, this general principle of law imposes a legal obligation on the State, a specific institution thereof, to be consistent in its actions, because otherwise it will face negative consequences, which may manifest as restoration of the previous state and/or compensation for damages to the subject whose legal expectations were violated by the State's actions.[89]

Thus, general principles of law correspond to all the requirements defined for recognizing an instruction as a legal norm: they are generally binding as of their nature and consist of legal content and legal consequences, respectively, they are valid for direct application and create subjective rights or impose legal obligations on a specific subject. General principles of law are unwritten legal norms. Normative legal acts are written legal norms or the written part of legal norms. The full legal norm consists of a written and an unwritten part where the written part of the legal norm is subject to the unwritten part, which is determined by the Basic Norm of the legal arrangement.

Thereby, according to the value meaning of the normative essence in a legal arrangement, axiology, we can conclude that the general principles of law are in no way different from (written) legal norms. This gives ground for the next important conclusion: *generally binding instructions of the legal arrangement of a Democratic State governed by the Rule of Law may be expressed in*

---

89 More about the ability of the principle of protection of legitimate expectations to create subjective rights and impose legal obligations see Briede J. 10. pants. Tiesiskās paļāvības princips. Grām.: *Administratīvā procesa komentāri*. Briede J. (Zin. red.) Rīga: Tiesu namu aģentūra, 2013, 164.–170. lpp. Similarly on the principle of good governance see Iļjanova D. 2009, 137.–152. lpp.

two ways – they can be either written (positivised) legal norms or unwritten legal norms, general principles of law.[90]

Whether general principles of law differ from written legal norms in the aspect of functionality, according to the way in which general principles of law function in the legal arrangement will be analysed in the following chapters of the book.

4 Types of General Principles of Law

There are several criteria on the basis of which general principles of law could be divided. Therefore, legal science knows many quite different alternatives of dividing the general principles of law. So, for example, depending on who is the subject of the effect of general principles of law, these principles are divided into:

1) those that regulate the behaviour of the entire society;
2) those that regulate the regulatory activity of State authorities (creation and application of norms).[91]

The first group of this division includes those general principles of law that determine the highest values of society – justice, human rights – while the second group includes general principles of law – legal methods and principles of systematization of the legal arrangement.

Boulanger divides general principles of law according to the content criterion and offers the following classification of general principles of law (which are applied in France):[92]

1) political principles (*ordre politique*), such as equality before the law, the institution of civil marriage as the only legal form of marriage, the principle of individual freedom;
2) economic principles, such as protection of private property, freedom of agreement;
3) the principles of legal security (certainty) (*securite*), such as the inadmissibility of legislation with retroactive force, the laws must be observed;

90 Similar thoughts are also expressed in Peczenik A. 1991, p. 151; Atienza M., Manero J.R. 1996, p. 6. As unwritten legal norms in the legal arrangement of Democratic States based on the Rule of Law international and national customary legal norms also could be included.

91 Atienza M., Manero J.R. 1996, p. 5.

92 Boulanger J. 1950, pp. 50–75.

4) moral principles borrowed from the ideas of Christian morality: everyone must prevent losses caused by his/her fault, everyone must fulfill his/her legally given promise, fraud voids everything (e.g., a contract), no-one can get rich by causing damage to another;
5) the principles of the technical organization of law, such as there are no privileges without the law, the contract is concluded in principle by simple mutual agreement of the parties. These principles are found in the system of laws itself;
6) principles justification of which can be found in justice, such as the basis of the claim must be proven, no-one can transfer more rights to another than he/she has;
7) principles expressed in ancient sayings and proverbs.

This division, although it allows a transparent understanding of the content quality of certain general principles of law, does not reveal the comparative aspect in the study of these principles. Another possible division of general principles of law often used in the Romano-Germanic legal system is the division depending on whether the content (substance) guideline of the general principle of law is positivised (included in the normative legal act), or whether it is not formally determined in the text of the written legal norm, but the content of the general principle of law instead can be discovered from the existing normative legal acts, system of laws or even from the legal arrangement. The main task in this part of the study is to find out if, depending on whether the content guideline of the general principle of law is positivised or not, its functionality changes in the process of application of legal norms.

4.1 *Positivisation of General Principles of Law*

As was concluded previously, since a general principle of law according to its meaning and structure is a legal norm, then in the conditions of a contemporary Democratic State based on the Rule of Law within the understanding of natural law doctrine the form of a legal norm is not among its defining features, it means that a legal norm can exist and be valid in written (positivised) form or as an unwritten instruction. Regardless, the common legislative practice in the countries of the Romano-Germanic legal system shows that the legislator has a tendency to positivise the content guidelines of general principles of law.

Here it is very important to understand that general principles of law as unwritten legal norms already exist and are valid before a legislator, therefore a legislator, including a general principle of law in the text of a normative legal act, cannot thereby deprive it of its essence as of an unwritten legal norm. Thus, what a legislator positivises is, in fact, only a *content guideline* of the general principle of law, which is useful in an educational sense mainly to the appliers of legal norms. While the general principle of law itself still continues to exist and be valid in the legal arrangement as an unwritten legal norm and continuously evolves with the dynamics of the legal arrangement. The Constitutional Court has expressly stated that in its case law:

> A general principle of law *is binding directly* and there is *no need to include it in positive law*. Incorrect definition of the content of a general principle of law in positive law cannot change the content of this principle or exclude its fields of application. A general principle of law has a higher legal force than written legal norms, therefore the legislator cannot amend the content of the principle or limit its application.[93] [author's emphasis]

That is why it is essential to remember that a legislature can also make mistakes in the written texts of legal norms where they describe the content guidelines of general principles of law, and that does not change the real content of the general principle of law as in the hierarchy of legal norms, general principles prevail over the legislator's adopted written legal norms.[94]

> One of the examples where the legislature's text of the content guideline of the general principle of law positivised in the law was incorrect was the Law on the Procedure How the Acts of the *Saeima*, State President and the Cabinet of Ministers Get Adopted, Promulgated, Published, Take Effect and Being Valid [*Par likumu un citu Saeimas, Valsts prezidenta un Ministru kabineta pieņemto aktu izsludināšanas, publicēšanas, spēkā stāšanās kārtību un spēkā esamību*].[95] This Law among other things included several general principles of law which belong to the second group[96] of the principles, namely – those which define to the institutions, which apply the legal norms, how the norm is to be identified, tested, interpreted, etc. Here we find the general principles which speak to the application of the legal norms in a Democratic country based on the Rules of Law – the legal methods, prerequisites for their application, and

93 Decision of the Constitutional Court of 28 February 2007 on termination of proceedings in the case no. 2006-41-01. Available: satv.tiesa.gov.lv.

94 Cf. Chapter 3.1.4.

95 Par likumu un citu Saeimas, Valsts prezidenta un Ministru kabineta pieņemto aktu izsludināšanas, publicēšanas, spēkā stāšanās kārtību un spēkā esamību: LR likums. Nav spēkā. Pieejams: likumi.lv.

96 Cf. Chapter 2.1.

their content in terms of interpretation methods, norms on settling collisions, methods of argumentation, etc. Section 8 of this Law stated that if there was a contradiction between more general and less general legal norms, the more general legal norm was in force as far as the less general legal norm limited it. The legislature used the term "being in force", which means that the legal norm loses its validity and is no longer in force in the case of collision. However, it is wrong from the true and real content of the general principle of law determining the priority order between the colliding legal norms, as in this described situation one legal norm is not applicable, which means that it is still valid and in force, while a judge applies the other norm, which prevails in this particular case. The legal system consists of more and less general legal norms and it is a regular situation that these norms are colliding.

Or the legislature has used inappropriate wording to describe the content of the general principle of law in the Administrative Procedure Law which in Section 6 states the content guideline for the principle of equality: "In cases where there are identical actual and legal circumstances, an institution and a court shall adopt identical decisions (in cases where there are different actual or legal circumstances – different decisions) irrespective of the gender, age, race, skin color, language, religious beliefs, political or other views, social origin, nationality, education, social and financial status, type of occupation of participants to the administrative proceedings or other circumstances." A judge would never be able to apply the principle of equality following the wording of the written legal norm proposed by the legislature as there are no two cases with "identical actual and legal circumstances". The factual and legal circumstances of cases could be similar, but never identical.

In such States belonging to the Romano-Germanic legal system as Austria, Greece, Spain, Italy, Egypt, Switzerland[97] the content guidelines of general principles of law are included in the normative legal acts as a guarantee for filling in the gaps or deficiencies of the laws.

Thus, for example, Section 2 of the Swiss Civil Code prohibits the abuse of rights, while Section 281 of the Greek Civil Code similarly prohibits the use of rights that clearly violates the boundaries of good faith, good morals, or the social or economic purpose of the rights.[98] Paragraph 7 of the Austrian Civil

97 David R. 1971, p. 147.

98 David R. *Major Legal Systems in the World Today.* London: Steven&Sons, 1985, p. 151.

Code authorizes the judge to decide the case on the basis of "principles of natural law" if no answer to the dispute in question can be found in the provisions of the Code. Likewise, Section 6 (2) of the Spanish Civil Code refers to the general principles of law, and the Egyptian Civil Code, in the event of a deficiency in the law, requires a judge to refer to the principle of natural justice and equality [Section 1 (2)].[99]

As was noted earlier, the significance of general principles of law increases with the protection of human rights because courts are given wide powers to control how a legislator respects human rights. As human rights general principles of law are positivised in such international documents for the protection of human rights as the Universal Declaration of Human Rights[100] adopted by the United Nations Organization in 1948, the 1966 International Covenant on Civil and Political Rights[101] and the International Covenant on Economic, Social and Cultural Rights,[102] the European Convention on the Protection of Human Rights and Fundamental Freedoms,[103] etc. Thus, for example, the Basic Law of the Federal Republic of Germany (*Grundgesetz*) of 1949 repealed all earlier laws that contradicted the equality of women and men.[104] As a result, it was the courts that had to undertake the correction of the regulation of legal relations in family matters.

In France, general principles of law became an important source of law in the practice of the Constitutional Council (*Conseil constitutionnel*), when after 1979 it pointed out in several decisions unconstitutional legal acts that contradicted "the basic principles recognized in law (the laws) of the Republic and established in the preamble of the Constitution".[105] Thus, the duty of the legislator to respect these generally determined principles was established.

Starting with the 1950s in the Western European countries general principles of law develop also due to the integration processes. Especially the practice of

---

99 Lorenz W. General Principles of Law: Their Elaboration in the Court of Justice of the European Communities. *The American Journal of Comparative Law*, 1964, Vol. 13, p. 1.

100 Universal Declaration of Human Rights. Available: un.org/en/udhrbook/pdf/udhr_booklet_en_web.pdf.

101 International Covenant on Civil and Political Rights: International Convention. Available: likumi.lv/ta/en/starptautiskie-ligumi/id/705-international-covenant-on-civil-and-political-rights.

102 International Covenant on Economic, Social, and Cultural Rights: International Convention. Available: treaties.un.org/Pages/ViewDetails.aspx?src=TREATY&mtdsg _no =IV-3&chapter=4&clang=_en.

103 Convention for the Protection of Human Rights and Fundamental Freedoms: International Convention. Available: echr.coe.int/ documents/ convention_ eng.pdf.

104 David R. 1985, pp. 151–152.

105 See Szladits Ch., Germain C.M. *Guide to Foreign Legal Materials: French.* New York: Oceana Publications Inc., 1985.

the Court of Justice of the European Union has established the notion *principles of law common to the Member States.*[106] Since European Union law belongs to the common Western legal culture, then the general principles of law are a part of European Union law as well as indicated in Article 340[107] of the Treaty on the Functioning of the European Union,[108] acknowledging general principles of law as one of the sources of European Union law. Also, in relation to the integration processes in the Council of Europe and the European Union and due to the necessity to harmonize the legislation, collections of the content guidelines of common general principles of law are drafted according to branches of law, where these principles are not just enlisted, but with the purpose of achieving common understanding, quite often they are also explained in great detail. As a result, these general principles of law should ensure uniform practice of application in the Member States and improvement of the national systems of laws.[109]

Section 5 of the Civil Law states: "Where a matter is required to be decided in the discretion of a court or on the basis of good cause, the judge shall decide the matter in accordance with a sense of justice and the general principles of law." In the field of public law, the Law On Judicial Power contains such general principles of law as equality of persons before the law and the court and equality of parties (Sections 4, 24), presumption of innocence (Section 23), etc.

From the normative legal acts, it is important to pay attention to one of the bulkiest enactments most recently adopted by the legislator of Latvia – the Administrative Procedure Law. In this legislative act the legislator has referred to general principles of law several times:

106 See more in Lorenz W. 1964, pp. 1–29; on general principles of law as primary law of the European Union, see also Fogels A. Eiropas Savienība starptautisko un Eiropas Savienības tiesību skatījumā. *Likums un Tiesības,* 2003, 5. sēj., nr. 7 (47), 208. lpp.; Gatawis S., Broks. E., Bule Z. *Eiropas tiesības.* Rīga: Eirofakultāte, 2002, 72. lpp.

107 "In the case of non-contractual liability, the Union shall, in accordance with the general principles common to the laws of the Member States, make good any damage caused by its institutions or by its servants in the performance of their duties."

108 The Treaty on the Functioning of the European Union: European Union Treaty. Available: eur-lex.europa.eu/LexUriServ/LexUriServ.do?uri=CELEX:12012E/TXT:en:PDF.

109 For example, see *European Committee on Legal Co-operation, Project Group on Administrative Law. A Handbook: Principles of Administrative Law Concerning the Relations Between Administrative Authorities and Private Persons.* Strasbourg, Directorate of Legal Affairs, 1996; *Eiropas Savienības tiesību īstenošana Latvijā.* Alehno I. (Red.) Rīga: Latvijas Vēstnesis, 2003. See also Reich N. *General Principles of EU Law.* Cambridge: Intersentia Publishing Ltd., 2014, p. 161; Kennedy D. A Transnational Genealogy of Proportionality in Private Law. In: *The Foundations of European Private Law.* Brownsword R., Micklitz H.W., Niglia L., Weatherill S. (Eds.) Oxford: Hart Publishing Ltd., 2011.

1) by setting out their generally binding character:
"A *legal norm* is comprised of a legal act (part thereof) and general principles of law." (Section 1 (5));
2) by setting out the content guidelines of such important general principles of law as the principle of respecting the rights of a private person (Section 5), principle of equality (Section 6), principle of the rule of law (Section 7), principle of reasonable application of legal norms (Section 8), principle of the prohibition of arbitrariness (Section 9), principle of protection of legitimate expectations (Section 10), principle of lawful basis (Section 11), principle of democratic structure (Section 12), principle of proportionality (Section 13), principle of priority of laws (Section 14), principle of procedural equity (Section 14.^{1}), principle of objective investigation[110] (Section 107 (4));
3) at the same time, the Law provides that those general principles of law not referred to in this law "*which have been discovered, derived or developed within institutional practice or within jurisprudence as well as legal science shall also be applied in administrative proceedings.*" (Section 4 (2)).[111]

This means that we can add Latvia to those countries of the Romano-Germanic legal system, which in their normative legal acts not only provide for the possibility of application of the general principles of law, but also directly positivise the content guidelines of the general principles of law ensuring the written legislative basis for practical application of the general principles of law.

4.2 *Derived and Discovered General Principles of Law*

In many cases the content guidelines of general principles of law are not directly included in the normative legal acts, but general principles of law may be found – *derived from the Basic Norm*, other general principles of law or *discovered from the normative legal acts*[112] and they are becoming acknowledged

110 See more detailed in Bērziņš M. Objektīvās izmeklēšanas princips *Administratīvā procesa likumā. Likums un Tiesības*, 2003, 5. sēj., nr. 6 (46), 179.–182. lpp.

111 See similarly also Section 10 (11) of State Administration Structure Law [*Valsts pārvaldes iekārtas likums*] (The law of the Republic of Latvia. Adopted on 06.06.2002. Available: ikumi.lv/ta/en/en/id/63545-state-administration-structure-law).

112 "Derivate" means to create, also to infer from some basic category (Cf. *Latviešu valodas vārdnīca*. Rīga: Avots, 1987, 106. lpp.). The basic category from which principles can be *derived* is either the Basic Norm or other general principles of law, but not written legal norms, which are themselves the result of the expression of general principles of law. On the principles of democracy and the Rule of Law as overarching principles, from which the rest of the principles are derived, respectively, their branching, see Levits E. 1997,

as a source of law in the result of court practice. Thus, for example, the general principle of law *in dubio pro reo* (from Latin, doubts about the facts must be decided in favour of the defendant),[113] which is not directly formulated in normative legal acts, is generally applied throughout the judicial system of Democratic States based on the Rule of Law, determining that a person can be convicted only if the court is convinced of his/her guilt; if there is doubt about the guilt of the defendant, he/she must be acquitted.[114]

Likewise, no provisions regarding general principles of law as subsidiary sources of law in cases of gaps in the laws are to be found in the French Civil Code or in any other normative legal act of private law. The Civil Code does use the term "general principles" in several articles, for example in Article 1584: "In all cases, the purchase contract is governed by the general principles that apply to contracts", but in this case, as in others, this concept is not used in the sense in which courts apply the general principles of law; this is only a general reference to a group of norms that are defined somewhere in the code, but not as an subsidiary source of law.[115]

Public law in France, at least in respect to their general rules, is more judge-made law, work of the Council of State (*Conseil d'État*). Administrative law is not codified but consists of many separate laws, decrees and rules regulating specific governmental and civil service issues and paying less attention to the general principles of law. It was the task of the administrative courts to coordinate these various special rules and to discover general principles of law underlying them. Legal practice was the real source of doctrine here, because only it could distinguish permanent principles from occasional principles, create a hierarchy of normative legal acts, eliminate gaps or ambiguities in them based on general principles of law or justice. Thus, the decisions of the Council of State established a system of precedents based on written or unwritten traditional principles. However, looking from the historical perspective, it should be noted that for a long time the Council of State was very attentive. Referring to general principles of law, the Council of State, where possible, borrowed or

---

54.–77. lpp. On the other hand, from the texts of normative legal acts general principles of law can be *discovered*.

113 In Administrative Procedure Law, this principle (*in dubio pro civis* by extension) can be read within the scope of the principle of respecting the rights of a private person. See in more detail Višķere I. 5. pants. Privātpersonas tiesību ievērošanas princips. Grām.: *Administratīvā procesa likuma komentāri*. Briede J. (Zin. red.) Rīga: Tiesu namu aģentūra, 2013, 121.–125. lpp.

114 Banneberga Br. Pierādījumu nastas pārnešana? Mantas konfiskācija korupcijas gadījumos. *Likums un Tiesības*, 2001, 3. sēj., nr. 12 (28), 354. lpp.

115 See Szladits Ch., Germain C.M. 1985.

"attached" them to the written legal norms, or at least avoided to list the real source of its decision. Important changes in this approach occurred after the Second World War as counter reaction to the Vichy regime (*Régime de Vichy*) and actions taken against the recognition and respect of the basic principles of law due to purge proceedings. On 26 October 1945 the Council of State decided for the first time that "the general principles of law are applicable also in the cases where they are not prescribed in the text of legal norms".[116] Since then, there is an ever-increasing trend in France to use the general principles of law as basis for justification.

At that time a similar situation occurred also in Germany. It is related to the fact that the legal arrangement of Germany took over the legislation of the "Third Reich," which was not entirely revoked and formally continued to operate, and the question of validity was solved separately in respect of specific legal acts. The main role was assumed by the jurisdiction of the Federal Supreme Court, which followed the Radbruch formula: when the injustice of a law becomes unbearable, it has to give way to justice.[117] In the decision of 14 February 1968 the court states: "National socialist "law-governed" rules may not be recognized as valid law if they so obviously contradict the fundamental principles of justice that the judge who wishes to apply them instead of law will establish non-law."[118]

A decision of the Federal Constitutional Court of Germany stated: "Law is not only a set of written laws. As a counterweight to the positive rules of state power, there may also exist law outside of them that is capable of correcting written laws; the entire constitutional system as a conceptual entity serves as the source of this law; the task of judiciary is to find this law and include it in decisions."[119] In other words, the legal arrangement is legitimized by the unwritten principles of law, which serve as a guide for judges, who check their decision in accordance with the meaning of the legal arrangement, not with an individual written law.

The French Council of State adopted this position in order to subject the administration to unwritten rules that have a "legislative effect" and control the administrative branch and its rule-making power. To understand in which

116 See Szladits Ch., Germain C.M. 1985.

117 Radbruch G. Five Minutes of Legal Philosophy (1945). *Oxford Journal of Legal Studies*, 2006, Vol. 26, no. 1, pp. 13–15; Available: https://idv.sinica.edu.tw/philaw/Jurisprudence_Reading/Five%20Minutes%20of%20Legal% 20Philosophy%20(1945).pdf.

118 Dreier R. *Recht – Moral – Ideologie*. Frankfurt am Main: Suhrkamp Verlag, 1981, S. 189.

119 Ibid.

cases administrative judges refer to general principles of law, two examples can be shown.

> In the first case, an abuse of authority complaint was filed by a person who had been issued a permit to rent a newsstand, but that permit was later revoked by a special decision. The complaint was based on the fact that the interested person was not given the opportunity to defend himself against the administration's claims, although in this particular case no normative legal act obliged the administration to present the complainant with these claims raised against and listen to this person's objections. However, the Council of State decided that one of the general principles of law forbids the application of repressive means against a person without providing him/her with the right to defense, and annulled the special decision taken by the administration.
>
> In the second case, the Conservatory's Concert Society, acting within its rights, forbade the musicians not to attend rehearsals due to radio lessons. As a repressive measure, the Radio Broadcasting Service refused to continue broadcasting the concerts of the conservatory orchestra but continued to play the concerts of the orchestras of other symphonic societies. The Conservatory's Concert Society demanded that the administration of the Radio Broadcasting Service compensate for the losses. The government commissioner stated that the responsibility of the administration is not related to the violation of the contract, which did not exist at all, the law or the regulation. But the general principle of law obliges the public service to respect the equality of citizens or their associations. Thus, by using discriminatory means against the aforementioned society, which are not provided for by the law, the administration has committed a violation.[120]

Such practice, which has been defended in several cases in the opinions of the government commissioner and reflected in important written studies of the Council of State, allows to characterize the general principles of law in French public law as follows:[121]

1) there is a set of general principles of French public law, which sometimes are specifically analysed in decisions, but sometimes there is only a reference to them in general;

120 Cf. Iļjanova D. 1999, 102. lpp.

121 See Szladits Ch., Germain C.M. 1985.

2) these principles have the legal force of the supra law, and the courts must respect them and react to their violations in the same way as to the violations of written law;
3) these principles do not derive their force from the formal texts of laws, and they are applicable even in cases where these texts do not exist;
4) courts do not create these principles; they act according to them as objective norms and consider themselves bound by these principles as they are by the laws.

When you look at how many government acts and decisions have been annulled by the Council of State based solely on these general principles of law, there is no doubt about the functional effectiveness of non-positivised general principles of law in France.

The problem arises when we want to name these principles. They could be grouped according to the brunches of law from which the relevant principles are revealed. Thus, four groups of principles can be discerned in French public law:[122]

1) traditional principles of law based on the achievements of the French Revolution of 1789; such are the separation of power, equality of citizens, individual freedom, freedom of conscience;
2) principles established in private law and civil procedure and which the courts discovered from the relevant branches of law and applied in administrative law: the law does not have retroactive effect, responsibility for the damage caused, the need for a process before imposing a sanction, impartiality of a judge;
3) principles borrowed from the "nature of things" and necessary in certain social activities, for example, work of the civil service must be continued and uninterrupted;
4) principles borrowed from some minimum ethical requirements not reflected in the Declaration of 1789: the government acts in the general public interest, the requirements regarding the "honesty" of the government.

The Court of Justice of the European Union uses the general principles of law not only in the field of human rights, but also in other areas where the treaties cannot adequately meet specific needs, and first of all, the administrative procedure law of the European Union has to be mentioned here, the basic norms

122 Cf. Iļjanova D. 1999, 102.–103. lpp.

of which are formulated in the form of general principles of law developed by the Court of Justice of the European Union.[123]

5 Conclusions

General principles of law are those principles which are derived from the Basic Norm of Democratic States based on the Rule of Law, function in the legal arrangement of Democratic States based on the Rule of Law and are generally accepted in a specific branch of law or legal system.

General principles of law as of their content include regulations that: express the highest values (reflecting a certain way of life) of the legal arrangement, its parts, or some institutions, etc., determine to the institutions that apply legal norms, how the eventually applicable legal norm should be searched for, examined, interpreted, etc., as well as determine the systematization of the legal arrangement.

The system of laws objectively includes all those written and unwritten regulations necessary to resolve disputes arising in the respective legal arrangement. The legislator's task according to the principle of separation of power is to find these objective legal norms that exist in the relevant system of laws and regulate the actual cases occurring in the legal arrangement and enact them.

A legal norm is an objective, logically closed, ideal unit. It consists of all the required and at the same time sufficient normative preconditions that are necessary for legal consequences to take effect. It is objective in the meaning that, whether or not the legislator has succeeded to formulate in writing the features of the legal content according to its intentions, or the legislator has forgotten to regulate an actual case, although it results from the legal arrangement that this case should have been regulated and it is regulated but due to the "failure" of the legislator, on another, unwritten normative level, or the legislator has comprised the legal norm in one article, one normative act or in several articles or acts, it exists as a logically closed unit, which structurally consists of all the required and at the same time sufficient normative preconditions that are necessary for legal consequences to take effect.

The task of the applier of legal norms within the legal arrangement is to discover and clarify these required and at the same time sufficient normative preconditions to apply the relevant legal norm; this means to solve the actual

123 Cf. Levits E. Cilvēktiesības Eiropas Savienības tiesību sistēmā. 2000, 333. lpp.; For example, see the judgement of the European Court of Justice of 12 July 1957: C-7/56 *Algera and Others v. Joint Assembly*. Available: curia.europa.eu.

case relating it to the legal consequences defined in the legal norm. At the same time, in case the legislator makes a mistake, the duty of the applier of legal norms according to the principle of separation of power and principle of prohibition of legal obstruction is to correct the legal norm with the help of the relevant legal methods (for example, analogy, teleological reduction) broadening or narrowing the content of the legal norm according to the will of the legislator and *ratio legis* of the norm.

General principles of law correspond to all the requirements defined for recognizing an instruction as a legal norm. They are generally binding as of their nature and consist of legal content and legal consequences, respectively, they are valid for direct application and create subjective rights or impose legal obligations on a specific subject. Thereby, according to the value meaning of the normative essence in a legal arrangement – axiology – general principles of law are in no way different from (written) legal norms. The generally binding instructions of the legal arrangement of a Democratic State governed by the Rule of Law may be expressed in two ways – they can be either written (positivised) legal norms or unwritten legal norms: general principles of law.

General principles of law are unwritten legal norms. Normative legal acts are written legal norms or the written part of legal norms. The full legal norm consists of a written and an unwritten part where the written part of the legal norm is subject to the unwritten part, which is determined by the Basic Norm of the legal arrangement.

The texts of the normative legal acts, which describe the content of the general principles of law are not complete; these are only the guidelines to their content positivised by a legislator while the general principle of law itself still continues to exist and be valid in the legal arrangement as an unwritten legal norm and continuously evolves with the dynamics of the legal arrangement. The content of general principles of law changes with the development of the legal arrangement and legal relationships immediately, while the written legal norms are not suitable for such rapid change. Consequently, the legislature's adopted written legal norms are always objectively incomplete as opposed to the unwritten legal norms, the content of which does not depend on the lengthiness of the legislative process.

CHAPTER 3

The Axiological Meaning of General Principles of Law

With the regaining of independence in Latvia and the transformation of legal arrangement general principles of law have acquired immense significance in the work of the legislator, and in the court practice[1] although understanding about them and their application, especially initially, has not always been easy.[2] However, over time and as a result of the development of the legal arrangement, general principles of law have largely become an everyday work of the courts and the legislature.

1 Meaning of General Principles of Law in the Variety of Sources of Law

1.1 *Significance of the Variety of Sources of Law in the Western Legal System*

Looking at the theory of sources of law (the theory on the types of sources of law, and more specifically on one of them, general principles of law) in a certain State, we should first clarify to which legal system the legal arrangement of the State belongs. Historically, there are at least three different approaches to the problem of the principles of law – namely, the traditional (Islamic), the Romano-Germanic and the Anglo-American.[3]

In the traditional legal system, the concept of "principles of law" as such is not yet fully formed, although there is a complex of basic ideas that are actually principles of law. So, for example, in Muslim law, eternity, immutability,

1 On the axiology of general principles of law in the countries of the Western legal system, see also Cipeliuss R. Par tiesisko apsvērumu racionālu strukturēšanu. *Likums un Tiesības,* 2000, 2. sēj., nr. 4 (8).

2 Regarding the initial insufficiency of knowledge about the principles necessary for the functioning of the legal arrangement of a Democratic State based on the Rule of Law, cf. also Ziemele I. Mazākumgrupu tiesiskās aizsardzības nodrošināšana Latvijā: dažas mācību stundas Eiropai. *Likums un Tiesības,* 2001, 3. sēj., nr. 10 (26), 290. lpp.; Čepāne I., Meiere S. Patvaļīgā būvniecība, Satversme un vispārīgie tiesību principi. *Latvijas Vēstneša* pielikums *Jurista Vārds,* 2003, nr. 36 (294).

3 See Iļjanova D. 1997; Iļjanova D. 1999.

 | DOI:10.1163/9789004690516_004

universality and inviolability of divine norms of Sharia can be considered as such. Today, in several Eastern Muslim countries (Egypt, Pakistan, etc.), Sharia or its principles are considered the basic source of legislation.

In the countries of the Romano-Germanic legal system (especially in France), "general principles of law" have developed as a source of law (especially in administrative law).

In the countries of the Anglo-American legal system, cases were initially decided on the basis of common sense in the case of gaps in the law. Later, this principle was replaced by the concept of natural justice, which was developed in the courts. Justice as a legal category has a dual meaning in English law. In chancellery courts, equity served as a means to correct the decisions of lower courts, while the principles of natural justice were the basis for deciding the case in the situations of gaps in the law.[4]

The main difference indicated in respect of the general principle of law as a source of law in the Romano-Germanic legal system and Anglo-American legal system is that the basic sources of these legal systems differ – the legislative acts and precedents. Respectively, the laws in the Anglo-American system are viewed only as norms rectifying a specific situation and not as a possible source for general principles of law. Therefore, the law is not interpreted strictly, and in the cases when there is no rule, which would provide a specific regulation in a given case, the gap is immediately filled in with the principles and norms developed by the common law judges.[5] Actually the process of legal thinking of the appliers of legal norms when turning to the sources of law to solve a specific case is different – in the Romano-Germanic legal system it is deductive (the basic source is an abstract legal norm, which is consulted to solve a specific case), and in the Anglo-American legal system it is inductive (the basic source is a certain ruling in a certain case, a precedent that is used to solve similar actual cases).[6]

The period of transformation of the legal arrangement of Latvia can be considered as finished. Latvia is a Democratic State based on the Rule of Law, and although its legal arrangement still shows some shortcomings, they are mostly

4 See more in Iļjanova D. 1999, 91.–92. lpp.

5 Ferrari Fr. General Principles and International Uniform Commercial Law Conventions: A Study of the 1980 Vienna Sales Convention and the 1988 Unidroit Conventions. *RDU*, 1997, no. 3, pp. 457–458.

6 On the differences between the Romano-Germanic and Anglo-American legal systems and the impossibility of their merging see Legrand P. European Legal Systems Are Not Converging. *The International and Comparative Law Quarterly*, 1996, Vol. 45, no. 1, pp. 52–81.

immanent in the legal arrangement of any Democratic State based on the Rule of Law.[7]

For such a successful transformation to have taken place and for the further development of the legal arrangement to strengthen it, that is, for legal norms to be properly implemented or applied, one needs clarity about the sources of law existing in the relevant State. Therefore, in Latvia now the doctrine of the sources of law has become one of the topical issues of the legal theory. It is evident that legal science is giving up the positivist approach, which reigned for so many years when the only source of law was "the law" (normative legal acts) and it was out of the question that there could exist some supra-positive principles of law, which could act as the criterion for the legitimacy of the legislative acts, and which could be applied directly in the case of the gaps in the laws.

Describing the theory of the sources of law of the Romano-Germanic legal system is not that easy because, firstly, in each national legal arrangement, this issue is complex and often causes discussions, and secondly, the way in which a specific issue is resolved may differ depending on the branch of law and be to a certain extent dependent on the understanding of law and personal views of an individual lawyer, and, thirdly, the theory of the sources of law changes historically, as it is related to the leading philosophical trends of the relevant time.[8]

The countries of the Romano-Germanic legal system are called "written law countries", which means that one of the primary and main sources of law here are the acts adopted or issued by the legislature or administrative institutions. However, the theory of the sources of law has developed over time, and as one of the primary sources of law of the modern Romano-Germanic legal system are now mentioned general principles of law,[9] which are identified and formulated by the courts, also found in guidance of the general spirit of the written law.[10]

"Determining precisely the nature of general principles of law and their place among the sources of law is undeniably a very delicate undertaking."[11]

---

7 About Latvia's situation at the beginning of the transformation of the legal arrangement and belonging to the so-called mixed legal system see Levits E. 1996.

8 See David R. 1985.

9 See Glendon M.A., Gordon M.W., Osakwe Chr. *Comparative Legal Traditions*. St.Paul.: West Publishing co., 1985.

10 Aarnio A. *The Rational as Reasonable*. Dordrecht, Boston, Lancaster, Tokyo: D. Reidel Publishing Company, 1987, pp. 86–87; West A., Desdevises Y., Fenet A., Gaurier D., Heussaff M.C. *The French Legal System. An Introduction*. London: Fourmat Publishing, 1992, pp. 43–65.

11 See Szladits Ch., Germain C.M. 1985.

This is the opinion expressed not to shed doubt on the importance of general principles of law, but to show their meaning and significance. Even if they are not formally recognized as sources of law in some countries of the continental European legal system, courts often base their decisions on general principles of law, referring to them in their motivations in the same way that they usually refer to the statutory provisions.

Thus, for example, in France, where the concept and application of general principles of law are one of the most developed amongst the countries of the continental European legal system, and where the legal control of autonomous regulations (*règlements autonomes*) is based solely on these general principles of law,[12] in legal science it is recognized that two systems of sources of law actually exist, namely, the official and the actual system of sources of law.

Officially, French law is entirely written law, created only by the legislature, not by the courts. Legal norms can be found only in the Constitution, the laws and regulations. Judges interpret legal norms, but do not create them. The operation of a court's judgement is strictly limited within the specific case in which it was adopted.

But in reality, this system of sources of law is a fiction.

The law itself obliges the judge to adopt a judgement even when the law is unclear, insufficient and incomplete, thus forcing the judge to replace the legislator. Many legal norms that are not formulated in the law in France (for example, *nemo auditor*, without hearing the parties or "no-one may unjustly prosper by causing damage to another") are nevertheless applied in civil cases, even though the judge is very much bound by the principle: there is no legal norm without a normative legal act. Finally, it is very well known that if the court, and especially the highest court instance, finds and applies a norm thoughtfully, long-term and uniformly, then it determines the judicial practice and, if not formally in the legal sense, then in reality it becomes mandatory. Thus, in French civil law, an important part of legal norms is created by a judge, not to mention administrative law, where even the most important norms have no other origin.[13]

A very similar situation has also developed in Germany, where it is now widely recognized that various general principles of law and legally significant judgements are one of the sources of law, and they provide the rules used in the application of normative legal acts. These principles are applied in all branches of German law. Many of these had developed in the legal arrangement due to

---

12 See more Hübner U., Constantinesco V. *Einführung in das französische Recht.* München: Verlag Beck C.H., 1994, S. 14.

13 Cf. Szladits Ch., Germain C.M. 1985.

the reception of Roman law, but currently the most extensive source of general principles of law is the Basic Law, and the most important of these principles derive from the requirements of its Article 20. The most significant is the requirement that Germany is a State based on the Rule of Law (*Rechtsstaat*) and this determines the existence of many other general principles of law. Often, the legislature and the government adopt judges' judgements in the form of normative legal acts, thereby normatively strengthening the principles of law established by the courts over the years.[14]

In the countries of the Romano-Germanic legal system, general principles of law indicate that the law is subject to the requirements of justice according to its understanding in a specific era and at a specific moment in time, and that this legal system today is already more "law of lawyers" than just a system of the written legal norms.[15]

1.2 *Normative Legal Regulation of Sources of Law in Latvia*

The specific types of sources of law within a legal arrangement are determined by two factors:

1) the normative legal regulation provided by the legislator, and
2) a group of factors independent from the legislator related to the features of the specific legal system and legal arrangement.

In the legal arrangement of Latvia, the legislator has provided legal regulation for the application of different sources of law, including general principles of law.

These are some of the most important norms that indicate the existence of certain types of legal sources:

Section 1 of the Civil Law: "Rights shall be exercised and duties performed in *good faith*."

Section 2 of the Civil Law: "Rights based on *custom* may neither set aside nor vary law. Rights based on custom are applicable in the cases specified by law."

Section 5 of the Civil Law: "Where a matter is required to be decided in the discretion of a court or on the basis of good cause, the judge shall decide the matter in accordance with a *sense of justice* and the *general principles of law*."

Section 22 of the Civil Law: "Where Latvian law allows the application of the *law of a foreign state*, the substance thereof shall be determined in accordance with the procedures laid down in the laws."

14 Foster N.G. *German Law and Legal System*. Cardiff: Blackstone Press Ltd., 1993, pp. 58–59.
15 See Glendon M.A., Gordon M.W., Osakwe Chr. 1985.

Section 5 of the Civil Procedure Law: "(1) Courts shall try civil cases in accordance with *the laws* and *other regulatory enactments, international agreements* binding upon the Republic of Latvia, and the *legal norms of the European Union.* (5) If there is no law governing the contested relation, a court shall apply a law governing similar legal relations, but if no such law exists, a court shall act according to *general principles* and *meaning of law.* (6) Upon applying legal norms, a court shall take into account the *case law.*"

Section 97 of the Civil Procedure Law: "(1) A court shall assess the evidence according to its own convictions which are based on evidence that has been thoroughly, completely, and objectively examined, and according to *judicial consciousness* based on the *principles of logic, scientific findings,* and observations drawn from every-day experience."

Section 3 of the Law On Judicial Power: "(2) Every person is guaranteed the right to have their rights and obligations or validity of the accusations brought against them determined on the basis of full equality by publicly examining the case before an independent and impartial court and meeting all *requirements of fairness.*"

Section 32 of the Constitutional Court Law[16] [*Satversmes tiesas likums*] "(2) *The Constitutional Court judgement and the interpretation of the relevant legal norm* provided therein shall be obligatory for all State and local government authorities (also courts) and officials, as well as natural and legal persons."

Section 1 of the Administrative Procedure Law: "(4) A legal norm is comprised of a legal act (part thereof) and *general principles of law.* (7) A provision of international law is comprised of *international agreements binding on Latvia, customary international law, and general principles of international law.*"

Section 10 of the State Administration Structure Law: "(1) State administration shall be governed by *law and justice.* [...] (3) State administration shall act in the public interest. Public interest shall include also *proportionate* observance of the rights and lawful interests of private individuals. (5) State administration shall comply with the *principle of good administration* in its activities. This principle shall include openness with respect to private individuals and the public, the protection of data, the fair implementation of procedures within a reasonable time period and other regulations the aim of which is to ensure that State administration complies with the rights and lawful interests of private individuals. (9) State administration shall be organized in conformity with the *principle of subsidiarity.* (11) State

16 Constitutional Court Law: The Law of the Republic of Latvia. Adopted on 05.06.1996. Available: likumi.lv/ta/en/en/id/63354-constitutional-court-law.

administration shall, in its activities, also comply with the *principles of law not referred* to in this Section which have been discovered, derived and developed in institutional or court practice as well as in jurisprudence." [Emphasis added by the author.]

Thus, summarizing the normative legal regulation given by the legislator for the existence of different types of sources of law in the legal arrangement of Latvia, it can be concluded that these sources of law are: normative legal acts, including normative agreements (international agreements), customary law, legal doctrine, case law, and, of course, also general principles of law.

1.3 *Division of Sources of Law in Latvia*

As in the legal arrangement of a Democratic State based on the Rule of Law and belonging to the legal system of continental Europe, normative legal acts are not the only source of law in Latvia, but even not the only source of law, which contains legal norms. This means that in the legal arrangement of Latvia there exist and are recognized other sources of law that contain legal norms which are generally binding and compulsory, and therefore in the cases to which they refer mandatorily applicable. The question about what sources of law currently exist in Latvia, i.e., how the law applier should substantiate and justify the act of the application of legal norms, and what is the division and mutual hierarchy of these sources of law – the question about the *national doctrine of the sources of law* – is one of the central and topical issues in every legal arrangement.

The doctrine of sources of law[17] in the legal arrangement of one particular country could be characterized by several criteria. First, the country's doctrine of sources of law is *national*, that is, it is *original* to each legal arrangement. This means that the names (titles) of the types of sources of law, which form the basis of this doctrine, are specific, original, found in the legal reason within the framework of the legal arrangement of this country. This also means that notwithstanding that several legal arrangements are similar, either by belonging to a given legal system, or by the fact that they are based on the same basic norm, or that several legal arrangements have the same leading understanding of law, the titles of the types of sources of law will not be the same, they even

17 See more on the meaning of national doctrine of sources of law and its development in Latvia in: Rezevska D. Nacionālās tiesību avotu doktrīnas attīstība gadsimta laikā. Grām.: *Tiesības un tiesiskā vide mainīgos apstākļos*. Latvijas Universitātes 79. starptautiskās zinātniskās konferences rakstu krājums. Rīga: LU Akadēmiskais apgāds, 2021, 281.–288. lpp.

could be not similar at all. That is why the doctrine of the sources of law of a specific country is national or original.

The next criterion that characterizes the national doctrine of sources of law is that it is *belonging* to a specific legal system. This means that the particular sources of law included in the division of sources are similar to the sources of law in those legal arrangements that belong to the same legal system.

The third feature of the national doctrine of sources of law is that it is *reflective*. It reflects the basic norm and the leading understanding of law of the given legal arrangement. Namely, the doctrine of the sources of law, even though it is in the framework of the same basic norm as in another country, is different depending on the leading understanding of law, because the leading understanding of law is directly related to the sources of law that can be applied in the legal arrangement, their diversity and mutual importance. This, in turn, brings us to the fourth feature of the national doctrine of sources of law, namely, that it is *changing*. It develops along with the development of the legal arrangement. Over time, new sources of law, types of sources of law, and new possible criteria underlying the classification or division of sources of law and titles of types of sources appear in the national doctrine of sources of law. However, the opposite direction is also possible, when certain sources of law, becoming insignificant as a result of the development of the legal arrangement, lose their place in the doctrine of sources of law.[18]

The national doctrine of sources of law is *dimensional*. This means that it can include several classifications of sources of law based on different criteria, as is the case with the Latvian doctrine of sources of law, which includes the classification of sources of law based on the criterion of binding force, and the criterion belonging to the continental European legal system. In addition, it also includes a list of specific sources of law. Namely, from the doctrine of the sources of law alone, it is possible to learn a large number of elements of the specific legal arrangement and even its general characteristics, or information about this legal arrangement: what is the basic norm on which the legal arrangement is based?; what is its leading understanding of law?; what are the types of sources of law?; and what are the specific sources of law that are valid and applicable in this legal arrangement, including what are the titles of the types of normative legal acts in this legal arrangement: what names has the legislator chosen to call specific normative legal acts? For example, in Latvia,

18 For example, the question could be asked whether national customary law is still a source of law in nowadays still applicable.

they are, among others, the Constitution, the law, regulations of the Cabinet of Ministers, and binding regulations of municipalities.

All the above indicates that the national doctrine of sources of law is closely related to the general principle of law – *the principle of diversity of sources of law*. The principle of diversity of sources of law is the legal method applicable in the second stage of the process of application of legal norms – the search for the eventually applicable legal norm – and at the same time the general principle of law in the legal arrangement of a Democratic State based on the Rule of Law. It determines that, in order to achieve a just decision in each and every case in accordance with the Basic Norm, the applier of legal norms must rely on several types of sources of law.

In the early stages of the transformation of the legal arrangement of Latvia from the Soviet to the Romano-Germanic legal system, it was crucial to understand how significant it was for a successful transformation to understand the types of the sources of law recognized and applicable in the countries of the continental European legal system. The difference regarding the sources of law between these two mentioned legal systems already exists in the very concept of the source of law, or in the understanding of what the source of law is.

In the Soviet legal system, sources of law are exclusively normative legal acts, legal norms adopted or sanctioned by the State. This created a situation where many actual cases were not resolved in court, under the pretext that there is no legal norm that determines how such a case should be resolved, or they were resolved by applying existing written legal norms, which in fact regulated different factual compositions, not resolving the case according to the principle of justice. Thus, any possibility for the judge to creatively search for a solution to the problem that would provide a just and reasonable answer in each specific case was limited or even completely excluded.

So, for example, in books on Socialist legal theory, we can read: "The source of Soviet socialist law is a state act. [...] The most important types of sources of Soviet law are determined by the law. Such acts include the laws of the Supreme Council, decrees of the Presidium of the Supreme Council, decisions and orders of the Council of Ministers, orders and instructions of state committees, ministries and special departments, decisions and orders of the council of workers' deputies and its executive committee. The system of sources of law consists of internally unified acts that are under mutual subordination."[19]

Thus, a myth was created about so-called diversity of the sources of law, although there was only one source of law: a normative legal act.

19 Plotnieks A. *Padomju sociālistiskās tiesības*. Rīga: Zvaigzne, 1975, 192.–193. lpp.

However, in the Western legal system, including the Romano-Germanic legal system, the factual variety of sources of law exists. Here *all the factors that should be considered in the application of law and which help to adopt a just decision* are recognized as sources of law, thus admitting that a variety of sources of law is an undeniable precondition for making a just decision. It is the variety of sources of law (and not a single source of law) that will ensure maximum impartiality of the applier of legal norms, because the decision will be tested "all-around", and so the only right, just and reasonable decision in the relevant case will be found and adopted.

As was mentioned before,[20] the legislator plays a role in determining what sources of law exist in the given legal arrangement, but alongside normative legal regulation on the types of sources of law, there are several other factors that determine what sources of law exist in a given country, for example:

1) belonging to a certain legal system;
2) stage of historical development of the legal arrangement;
3) the leading understanding of law in the State;
4) specific branch of law, etc.

Considering the above-mentioned factors, which determine the sources of law and the normative legal regulation of the types of sources of law, there exist several types of sources of law in Latvia now, and according to the nature of the source of law they can be divided into two groups:[21]

1) *independent* sources of law or sources of law of generally binding force;
2) *supplementary* sources or sources of law without generally binding nature.

This division of sources of law is based on an important criterion – generally binding force. This means that independent sources of law, in contrast to supplementary sources of law:

1) consist of legal norms, so they are compulsory and binding;
2) each of the independent sources of law can be applied independently to support the operative (holding) part of a legal decision, which means

20 See Chapter 3.1.2.

21 See similary Jelāgins J. Tiesību pamatavoti. Grām.: *Mūsdienu tiesību teorijas atziņas*. Rīga: Tiesu namu aģentūra, 1999; another title for the division – primary and secondary sources of law – can be found in the book *Ievads tiesībās* by Jānis Neimanis (Rīga: zv. adv. J.Neimanis, 2004, 72.–73. lpp.), however, in order not to confuse the types of sources of law of the European Union, where the division of primary and secondary sources of law is based on criteria other than the generally binding nature of the source of law, when designating the types of sources of national law of Latvia based on this criteria, it is recommended to use the title of the division: "independent sources" and "supplementary sources of law".

that every independent source of law may on its own substantiate an act of the application of legal norms.

In their turn, supplementary sources of law do not have a generally binding nature and they can be used only for the argumentation of a legal decision (argumentation or motivation part). Similarly, for the argumentation (motivation part) of the decisions independent sources of law can, and even should be used.

Hence, *independent sources of law* in the legal arrangement of Latvia are:

1) general principles of law;
2) generally binding interpretations of legal norms by authorized courts (the Constitutional Court, regarding national legal norms; the European Court of Human Rights, regarding the legal norms of the Convention for the Protection of Human Rights and Fundamental Freedoms; the Court of Justice of the European Union, regarding European Union law);
3) normative legal acts;
4) customary law,

and *supplementary* sources of law are:

1) case-law (judicature);[22]
2) legal doctrine;
3) *travaux préparatoires* – materials used in the process of drafting of normative legal acts;
4) dissenting or concurring opinions of judges etc.

Taking into account the fact that the countries of the Romano-Germanic legal system are "written law" countries, and that the applier of the legal norm will first turn his/her attention to and look for the eventually applicable legal norm

22 On the development of the use of the term "judicature" in the Latvian language within the legal arrangement of Latvia see Levits E. Ģenerālklauzulas un iestādes (tiesas) rīcības brīvība. Funkcijas likumā, piemērošana konkrētā gadījumā, kontrole augstākā iestādē un tiesā. *Likums un Tiesības,* 2003, 5. sēj., nr. 6 (46), nr, 7 (47), 166. lpp., 17. vēre. However, during the development of the understanding of case-law – judicature – as a source of law, there has been also an idea that, taking into account the special importance of the judicature as a source of law for judges, to separate it from other supplementary sources of law and, bring it closer to the independent sources of law, placing it in the group of so-called "mandatory sources of law". About this in detail see Sniedzīte G. *Tiesnešu tiesības. Jēdziens un nozīme Latvijas tiesību avotu doktrīnā.* Rīga: Latvijas Vēstnesis, 2013. An even more radical opinion regarding the placement of that part of the case-law, which is a generally binding interpretation of a legal norm given by the Constitutional Court, the European Court of Human Rights and the Court of Justice of the European Union, in the group of additional or subsidiary sources within the independent sources of law see Rezevska D. Judikatūra kā tiesību avots: izpratne un pielietošana. *Latvijas Republikas Augstākās Tiesas Biļetens,* 2010, nr. 1, 28.–31. lpp.

in the normative legal acts, the independent sources of law can be divided even further and in a more detailed way, namely:

1) basic sources of law, respectively, normative legal acts, and
2) additional or subsidiary sources of law, general principles of law and customary law.

Thus, general principles of law are an independent, generally binding source of law, which can be applied in the legal arrangement of Latvia, and in any Democratic State based on the Rule of Law, not only for the argumentation of a decision (in the motive part) but also to substantiate the operative (holding) part of a decision.

1.4 *Hierarchy of Independent Sources of Law in Latvia*

The issue of the hierarchy of sources of law is topical in relation to the role and meaning of the general principles of law in a legal arrangement. There is no need to prove that the independent sources of law prevail over the supplementary sources of law. This is provided already by the generally binding nature of the independent sources of law, which is not a feature of the supplementary sources of law, respectively, supplementary sources of law do not consist of legal norms. The question to ask is: what is the mutual hierarchy of the generally binding sources of law, the independent sources of law? To put it more precisely for the purposes of this study: what are the hierarchical relations between the general principles of law and normative legal acts, leaving untouched the question of the place of national customary law in the hierarchy of independent sources of law, which could largely depend on the specific branch of law?[23] While at the same time it is reasonable to conclude that generally binding interpretations of legal norms by authorized courts prevail over normative legal acts as legislators are bound by the results of these interpretations and have to take them into account when drafting new written legal norms.

Regarding the hierarchy of the sources of law in other countries of the Western legal system, the hierarchical enumeration of Swedish sources of law provided by Peczenik is comprehensive.[24] He hierarchically divides the sources of law of Sweden into three basic groups:

1) binding sources of law: must-sources;

---

23 Thus, for example, the importance of national customary law in commercial law and criminal law could differ, because the role of customary law in commercial law is incomparably greater than in criminal law. But, as has already been mentioned, this is not an issue to be resolved within the scope of this work.

24 Peczenik A. 1989, pp. 319–321.

2) guiding sources of law: should-sources;
3) permitted sources of law that could be applied: may-sources.

This hierarchical division is based on the criterion of significance of sources of law, which determines that some sources of law are generally binding, while others are not. These generally binding sources of law – for example, normative legal acts, customary law, contracts – are must-sources, while the others are only such sources of law that could be applied, for example, legal literature (doctrine), draft laws – may-sources. However, in addition to generally binding sources of law, there are also sources of law in the legal arrangement that enjoy a certain authority, which is by no means less than the authority of generally binding sources of law. These are sources that guide legal practice, such as, for example, precedents and legislative preparatory materials, so they should be applied – should-sources.[25]

The hierarchical relation is based on the criterion of legal force. Respectively, the element having higher legal force prevails over the other. Legal force is determined by two factors:

1) origin of the object, and
2) procedure by which the relevant object was adopted or amended.

On the basis of the postulates of natural law, in the previous chapters of the book, among other things, it was concluded that the general principles of law derive from the Basic Norm of the legal arrangement of a Democratic State based on the Rule of Law, which is an act of will of the sovereign, that they exist independently and before the legislator, function in the conditions of a Democratic State governed by the Rule of Law and serve as a supra-positive criterion of legitimacy for the written legal norms – i.e. the action of the legislator. Thereby, the legislator's action has to correspond to the general principles of law, and this means that the legal norms created by the legislator have to comply with the general principles of law. This leads to the conclusion that general principles of law have *priority or they prevail over* the normative legal acts created by a legislator, including also over the formal Constitution.[26]

---

25 Cf. Peczenik A. 1989, pp. 319–328.

26 Similar opinion has been expressed: Jelāgins J. 1999, 80. lpp., 154. vēre: "it should be remembered that the principle of supremacy of the constitution in a *state based on the Rule of Law* [author's emphasis] is not absolute. In the theoretical aspect, it manifests itself by opposing the norms of the written constitution and the general principles of law. Spanish lawyer J. Lorca-Navarrete believes that objectively existing principles of law stand above and outside the law. And even the most perfect legal technique cannot sufficiently reflect these principles. [...] This principled position is fixed in Paragraph 1 of the Declaration of 4 May 1990, which recognizes the priority of the basic principles of international law over the norms of national law. Only the constitution in the material

This understanding of the hierarchy of sources of law as analysed by Egils Levits, admitting that in the Western legal system side by side with the written sources of law also such sources of law are recognized as the general principles of law "which can have even higher rank than the constitution"[27] is chosen also by the Court of Justice of the European Union. The 1957 Treaty of the European Economic Community did not include a catalogue of human rights,[28] but ignorance of human rights is unthinkable in a legal arrangement governed by the Rule of Law. Therefore, in its jurisprudence the Court of Justice of the European Union had to develop the human rights norms in the form of general principles of law. The Court considered that Article 220 of the Treaty Establishing the European Economic Community authorised the Court to develop such general principles of law because they, similarly to the written law (normative legal acts), are included in the notion "lawfulness" in the meaning of Article 220: a normative legal act, which contradicts the general principles of law cannot be considered "lawful".[29]

What happens to those normative legal acts that contradict general principles of law (they lose their validity automatically, are recognized as null and void, etc.) will be analysed further in Chapter 4.

2 Importance of the General Principles of Law in Drafting Normative Legal Acts

The significance of general principles of law in the countries of the Romano-Germanic legal system is represented not only in the process of application of legal norms but also in the drafting of normative legal acts.[30] Procedurally,

sense, or the constitutional order, which also includes the *unwritten general principles of law* [author's emphasis], could claim the status of absolute supremacy."

27 Levits E. Cilvēktiesības Eiropas Savienības tiesību sistēmā. 2000, 332. lpp.

28 The Charter of Fundamental Rights of the European Union was adopted on 7 December 2000 and became legally binding on 1 December 2009 with the entry into force of the Treaty of Lisbon. The Charter sets out a broad catalogue of fundamental rights, such as freedom of expression and the protection of personal data, which reflect Europe's common values and its constitutional heritage. (Available: eur-lex.europa.eu/legal-content/EN/TXT/?uri=CELEX:12012P/TXT).

29 Cf. Levits E. Cilvēktiesības Eiropas Savienības tiesību sistēmā. 2000, 332. lpp.

30 The discussion about the influence of general principles of law both on the work of the legislator and on the work of those applying legal norms within the legal arrangement took place already in the first half of the last century. See Šulcs L. 1937, 19.–21. sl. On the requirements of legal technique, which result from the principle of good legislation, in the development of normative legal acts see Rezevska D. Legislation in Latvia.

the legislation process is governed by the general principle of law, the principle of good legislation derived from the Basic Norm and formulated by the Constitutional Court in the form of the generally binding legal norm for the first time in the Western legal system[31] in its judgement of 6 March 2019.[32]

> "The branches of power of a democratic state based on the Rule of Law, including the legislature, must strive to increase the people's trust in the state and law, as well as the understanding of the democratic process. Adherence to the principle of good legislation contributes to the achievement of this goal."[33]
>
> "The principle of good legislation does not guarantee a specific result desired by one person or a group of persons, however, its observance gives everyone confidence that the relevant issue has been democratically discussed, that is, different opinions have been expressed and analysed, and the best possible balance between different conflicting rights and interests has been sought and achieved in accordance with the values contained in the Constitution and the general principles of law."[34]
>
> "In accordance with the principle of good legislation, the legislator is obliged to evaluate the conformity of the legal norms provided for in the draft law with the legal norms of higher legal force, including the Constitution, international and European Union legal norms, and to harmonize the legal norms provided for in the draft law with the legal norms already existing in the system of laws. In addition, the legislator must ensure that in the legislative process the views of all interested parties are recognized as much as possible and objections to the legal framework provided for in the draft law are heard directly or indirectly. The legislator

---

Chapter 17. In: Karpen U., Xanthaki H. Eds. *Legislation in Europe: A Country by Country Guide*. Oxford: Hart Publishing, 2021, pp. 283–298. On the nature and scope of good legislation as a general principle of law see also Pleps J. The Principle of Good Legislation. In: *The Quality of Legal Acts and its Importance in Contemporary Legal Space*. Materials of the International Scientific Conference. Riga: University of Latvia Press, 2012, pp. 16–26.

31 Valsts Prezidenta Egila Levita uzruna konstitucionālo tiesību ekspertu domnīcā Satversmes tiesā. 13.12.2019. Pieejams: president.lv/lv/jaunums/valsts-prezidenta-egila-levita-uzruna-konstitucionalo-tiesibu-ekspertu-domnica-satversmes-tiesa.

32 Judgement of the Constitutional Court of 6 March 2019 in case no. 2018-11-01. Available: satv.tiesa.gov.lv. Detailed analysis of the process of derivation and concretization of the principle of good legislation see in Chapter 4.1.1.

33 Judgement of the Constitutional Court of 6 March 2019, para. 18.1.

34 Judgement of the Constitutional Court of 23 April 2019 in case no. 2018-12-01, para. 24.1. Available: satv.tiesa.gov.lv.

can ensure the hearing of the interested persons by also hearing the representatives of the relevant groups of persons."[35]

From the point of view of the content of the drafted written legal norms the legislator bases the normative legal acts on these principles, and also refers to them in the texts of these acts.[36] In this case, it is taken into account that the law has its limits, that every case cannot be regulated by written legal norm, and the appliers of legal norms, based on the principle of justice, are given the opportunity to refer to natural rights (for example, Section 7 of the Civil Code of Austria), or to refer to general clauses of good morals and public interest in the application of legal norms.

Especially in the postmodern systems of laws, legislation develops toward the so-called open-ended written legal norms, that is, written legal norms containing the content guidelines of general principles of law are adopted, or a judge or other applier of legal norm is left with the possibility to choose to act on its own – to apply the norm to a specific case, considering the various circumstances.[37]

The legislator also includes in the text of the law frequently used, content-rich, but briefly formulated concepts that include the features of as many activities as possible – general clauses,[38] which are understood as a normative concept of law that has to be filled with a certain content.[39] Thus, the legislator avoids the potential burden of detailed features in the text of the norm, while at the same time not limiting the scope and extent of application of the content contained in the general clause, which in turn is determined by the general principles of law of the given system of law.[40]

Thus, general principles of law have to be taken into account by the legislator in the creation of normative legal acts. Otherwise, the normative legal act

---

35 Judgement of the Constitutional Court of 13 November 2019 in case no. 2018-22-01, para. 17. Available: satv.tiesa.gov.lv.

36 As concluded in Chapter 2.4.1. these are only content guidelines of the general principles of law, while general principle of law itself still continues to exist in the legal arrangement as an unwritten legal norm and its content continuously evolve alongside with the dynamics of the legal arrangement.

37 See more Unger R.M. *Law in Modern Society*. New York: The Free Press, 1977; about "over-regulation" as one of the most typical mistakes of the legislator see Levits E. 2003, 163. lpp.

38 See Chapter 2 and on the difference of general clauses from the general principles of law see Chapter 4.1.1.

39 Krūmiņa V., Skujiņa V. *Normatīvo aktu izstrādes rokasgrāmata*. Rīga: Valsts kanceleja, 2002, 14.–15. lpp.

40 See *Rechtsworterbuch*. München: C.H.Beck, 1994.

created by the legislator has a constitutionality problem taking into account the hierarchy of sources of law proved in the previous chapter acknowledging that normative legal acts have to correspond to the general principles of law.

Following the conclusions of the previous chapter, general principles of law as of their content can be divided into three groups including regulations that: 1) express the highest values (reflecting a certain way of life) of the legal arrangement, its parts, or some institutions, etc. – human rights, 2) determine to the institutions that apply legal norms, how the eventually applicable legal norm should be searched for, examined, interpreted, etc. – legal methods, 3) as well as determine the systematization of the legal arrangement – separation of power, hierarchy of normative legal acts, for example. Thus, in drafting new regulations legislators are obliged to follow, to take into account, the contents of these various general principles of law and accordingly draft and adopt new written legal norms as legitimacy – constitutionality – of these legal norms depends on their compliance with general principles of law. In a case of no compliance written legal norms are not applicable and have to be declared as null and void, which in the situation of centralized constitutional control is done by the constitutional review institution, usually a constitutional court.

Regarding the compliance of written legal norms with general principles of law belonging to the first group – human rights norms – the Constitutional Court has stated, that, first of all, the principle of human dignity has to be taken into account drafting the legal norms in a Democratic State based on the Rule of Law. Most often the Court also deals with the principle of justice, the right to equality, the right to fair trial, the right to property, for example:

> "The basis of the legal [arrangement] is the obligation of *all branches of state power* in their activities to *respect human rights and other general principles of law*."[41]
>
> "*From the basic norm of a democratic state based on the rule of law follows the state's obligation* in its activities to observe the principles of a democratic state based on the rule of law including the principle of human dignity."[42]
>
> "The requirement included in Articles 1 and 109 [right to social security] of the Constitution to ensure that a person can live a life that corresponds to *human dignity* is the *positive obligation of the state*. In order

41 Judgement of the Constitutional Court of 8 June 2022 in case no. 2021-40-0103, para. 13.3.2. Available: satv.tiesa.gov.lv.

42 Judgement of the Constitutional Court of 16 July 2020 in case no. 2019-25-03, para. 11.1. Available: satv.tiesa.gov.lv.

to assess whether the state has fulfilled this obligation, it is necessary to check whether: 1) the *legislator has taken measures to provide individuals with the opportunity to exercise social rights*; 2) these measures *have been taken properly*, that is, individuals have been provided with the opportunity to use their social rights at least to a minimum extent; 3) the *general principles of law have been observed*."[43]

"The *main goal* of the legal arrangement of a democratic state governed by the rule of law is *to ensure justice*."[44]

"Equality is *derived from the general principle of justice*, which is a fundamental value of a democratic state governed by the rule of law. It is recognized that the *right to equality is a fundamental right to be protected and binding on the legislator*."[45]

"The *protection of fundamental human rights is one of the most important duties of a democratic state governed by the rule of law*. The state must provide effective protection to every person whose rights or legal interests are violated. Therefore, ensuring a person's *right to a fair trial* is a mean of achieving this goal, because the protection of other fundamental rights of a person also depends on the proper provision of this right."[46]

"Ensuring *access to the court* is a way for a person to exercise the protection of his/her rights and legal interests and to achieve *justice – the ultimate goal* of the legal arrangement of a democratic state based on the rule of law."[47]

"In cases where the *state has an obligation* to take measures for the implementation of the rights contained in Article 92 [right to fair court] of the Constitution, the Constitutional Court assesses whether the state has fulfilled this obligation. In addition, if this obligation requires the development and *adoption of regulation of a specific content*, the Constitutional Court evaluates the content of this obligation and whether the legislator has fulfilled his obligation properly, including *in compliance with the general principles of law*."[48]

---

43 Judgement of the Constitutional Court of 25 June 2020, para. 17.4.

44 Judgement of the Constitutional Court of 12 March 2020, para. 14.

45 Judgement of the Constitutional Court of 15 December 2022 in case no. 2021-36-01, para. 12.1. Available: satv.tiesa.gov.lv.

46 Judgement of the Constitutional Court of 20 April 2012 in case no. 2011-16-01, para. 9. Available: satv.tiesa.gov.lv.

47 Judgement of the Constitutional Court of 23 February 2022 in case no. 2021-22-01, para. 10. Available: satv.tiesa.gov.lv.

48 Judgement of the Constitutional Court of 25 March 2022 in case no. 2021-25-03, para. 12. Available: satv.tiesa.gov.lv.

> "When restoring the legal [arrangement] of independent Latvia, the legislator, observing the principles of the rule of law, was obliged to take measures to compensate the damages caused by the previous regime and to *restore justice* as much as possible. However, the legislator, when choosing the means of land reform, had *to achieve as fair balance* as possible between the conflicting interests of various members of society."[49] [All inserts and emphasis by the author.]

Peczenik considers these principles used by the legislator in the legislative process of drafting new written legal norms "general principles of law belonging to the so-called group of principles of justice, whose initial principle reads as follows: essentially similar objects should be treated similarly" and derivates of this:

a) essentially similar human activities should be regulated similarly;
b) no one may profit or gain benefit from wrongdoings that they have committed;
c) everybody has to be treated according to his/her merits and his/her wrongdoings;
d) *communis error facit jus* – a general error gives rise to rights: if the interpretation of a legal norm is generally accepted and widespread, even if it is wrong, it still gives rise to rights if the refusal of this interpretation makes more harm than good;
e) essentially similar individuals should be treated alike in as many respects as possible;
f) the one whose condition improves as a result of an action must bear the expenses of that action.[50]

The word "object" here means "anything". Objects are not only persons, actions and cases, but also legal norms. It is also important to pay attention to the feature "essential". Although there are no identical objects, which often serve as an excuse for both the legislator and the applier of legal norms, that the application of the principle of equality cannot be demanded, since there are no absolutely identical cases, things, persons, etc., there are nevertheless essentially similar objects. In order to find out whether the similarity of the objects is essential, the features of the respective objects should be compared. If the

49 Judgement of the Constitutional Court of 25 March 2003 in case no. 2002-12-01, para. 1 (arg. part). Available: satv.tiesa.gov.lv.

50 Cf. Peczenik A. 1971.

essential characteristics of both (several) objects are similar, then the objects are essentially similar.[51]

In the drafting of written legal norms, the legislator has to take into account also legal methods as general principles of law. The Constitutional Court regarding this obligation of the legislature, has concluded, for example:

> "The task of the principles [included in] Article 1 of the Constitution is to ensure that other legal norms, including those contained in the Constitution, are *applied correctly* and that their application, as well as the result of application, *fully meet the requirements of a state governed by the rule of law*."[52]
>
> "When implementing the delegation set by the legislator, the [government] executes the legal norm adopted by the legislator, therefore the [government] in this process is obliged to use *such legal methods that respect the check and balance existing in the division of state power*. Namely, the Cabinet of Ministers, being aware of and using the *diversity of legal sources*, must perform not only a *grammatical, but also a systemic, historical and teleological interpretation* of the delegating norm. This follows not only from the principles of the rule of law and the separation of power as the basis of the existence of a democratic state based on the rule of law, but also from the principle of a rational legislature."[53] [All inserts and emphasis by the author.]

The Constitutional Court has provided the legislator with several elements of the concretization of legal methods: principles of intertemporality, which have to be taken into account in the process of legislation.[54] The question of the

---

51 On the comparison of essential features as precondition for the application of analogy more see Vīnzarājs N. 1937, 69.–71. lpp.

52 Judgement of the Constitutional Court of 16 December 2005 in case no. 2005-12-0103, para. 24. Available: satv.tiesa.gov.lv.

53 Judgement of the Constitutional Court of 28 September 2020 in case no. 2019-37-0103, para. 29.3. Available: satv.tiesa.gov.lv.

54 See more on this in Rezevska D. The Temporal Effect of Legal Norms and Case Law of the Constitutional Court of the Republic of Latvia. In: *The Materials of the 8th International Scientific Conference of the Faculty of Law of the University of Latvia, 21–22 October 2021.* Rīga: LU Akadēmiskais apgāds, 2021, pp. 43–51; on intertemporality issues in general see Krons M. Intertemporālo tiesību mācība un Civillikuma trešais pants. *Tieslietu Ministrijas Vēstnesis,* 1938, nr. 1.

intertemporality of the written legal norms[55] arises in the situations when a legislator has decided to adopt a new legal norm which regulates the same legal relations as the old legal norm. The temporal effect of a written legal norm (force of a legal norm) can be manifested in time as: 1) future force, 2) immediate force, and 3) retroactive force. In turn legal facts can be: 1) past facts (*facta praetaria*) – facts started and ended before the new norm entered into force, 2) pending facts (*facta pendentia*) – facts started before the new norm entered into force and still continuing after its entry into force, and 3) further facts (*facta futura*) – facts started after the new norm had entered into force.[56] According to the principles of intertemporality, the legislator is always free to determine further temporal effect for a written legal norm, which then will be applicable to the future facts. It is when the legislator decides to determine the immediate or even retroactive temporal effect to the new, written legal norm that the issue of the compliance of this decision with the principle of protection of legitimate expectations arises. This question is the question of constitutionality of a legal norm based on its temporal effect and as such could be brought before the constitutional court.

According to the general principles of intertemporality, retroactive temporal effect of the legal norm always is an exception either in public or private law, while immediate effect is rather an exception in private law. What does it imply from the perspective of the principle of good legislation and protection of legitimate expectations? It means that the burden of arguments given and discussed by a legislator during the legislation process is directly connected with the decision to determine the immediate or retroactive temporal effect to the new legal norm.[57]

It could be concluded in fact that intertemporal law involves two sets of rules: basic rules and constitutional rules. The basic rules are used to determine whether the legislator wanted the new legal norm to be applied retroactively while constitutional rules implicated by the intertemporal law set limitations on the power of the legislator to impose retroactive effect.[58] Basic rules then

---

55 On intertemporality issues of unwritten legal norms (rules of customary international law) see: Wheatley S. Revisiting the Doctrine of Intertemporal Law. *Oxford Journal of Legal Studies*, 2021, Vol. 41, no. 2, pp. 484–509.

56 See also on this: Kalniņš E. 2000, 214.–220. lpp.; Onževs M. *Tiesību normu laika aspekti tiesiskā un demokrātiskā valstī*. Rīga: Latvijas Vēstnesis, 2016, 38.–39. lpp.

57 Regarding this, see also: Onževs M. Atpakaļejoša un tūlītēja spēka noškiršana praksē. *Jurista Vārds*, 2021, nr. 30.

58 McCreary J. M. Retroactivity of Laws: An Illustration of Intertemporal Conflicts Law Issues Through the Revised Civil Code Articles on Disinherison. *Louisiana Law Review*, 2002, Vol. 62, no. 4. Available: digitalcommons.law.lsu.edu/lalrev/vol62/iss4/16.

would be such legal methods as interpretation and transitional provisions of the normative legal acts while constitutional would be the principle of protection of legitimate expectations, which is derived from the principle of legal security. The former legal methods would be applied to clarify what was the goal of the legislator in terms of the temporal effect of the new legal norm, the latter to determine whether the issue of legitimacy or constitutionality exists.

Thus, the exceptional character of the retroactive effect of a new written legal norm does not mean a legislator will never be able to set this effect for a legal norm, but it means that the legislator is obliged, according to the principle of good legislation, to state reasonable and well-grounded arguments to justify such a decision from the perspective of the principle of protection of legitimate expectations providing as well a reasonable transitional period and compensatory mechanism. The same applies regarding the immediate temporal effect for the legal norm with the only difference in the amount of necessary justification, which is largely connected with the assessment of the principle of proportionality. The ultimate issue though is the complexity of identifying the retroactive effect of a legal norm, which in legal doctrine is widely recognized as one of the most complex legal methods. Retroactive effect can be identified by the doctrine of: 1) retroactive effect of legal consequences, 2) finished legal relations, and 3) acquired rights.[59]

> For example, in case no. 2020-30-01[60] the applicant contested the constitutionality of the legal norm included in the transitional provisions of the law on Compensation for Damage Caused in Criminal and Administrative Violations Proceedings. The norm stated that a person who was entitled to compensation for damage caused to him or her by an unlawful or unreasonable action of an institution, the prosecutor's office or court before the entry into force of this Law and for which no legal proceedings are opened in the courts of general jurisdiction had the right to submit an application for compensation for damage within six months from the moment of occurrence of the legal basis for compensation for damage.
>
> The applicant argued that according to the old norm he had the right to claim compensation for non-pecuniary damage within the 10-year limitation period, while now the term in his case was reduced to around the time frame of four months. The Court started its assessment by determining the type of the temporal effect of the contested norm and stated that

59 Onževs M. 2016, 147.–184. lpp.

60 Judgement of the Constitutional Court of the Republic of Latvia of 5 March 2021 in the case no. 2020-30-01. Available: satv.tiesa.gov.lv.

it has *an immediate temporal effect*, and at the same time concluded that the legislator has the right to adopt amendments in the laws that have immediate effect. Consequently, it is permissible to extend the adopted legal regulation also to such legal relations which were pending (*facta pendentia*). However, the Court stressed that when adopting a legal norm, *the legislator must always ascertain its impact on the existing legal relations. It is essential that in such a case the legislator provides for a lenient transition period or appropriate compensation – these are preconditions set for a legal norm with immediate temporal effect* (*but even more – for a legal norm with a retroactive effect*) *which arise from the principle of protection of legitimate expectations*.

The Court further concluded that the applicant had legitimate expectations according to the old norm and that it does not follow from the legislative materials and the content of the contested norm that the legislator would have assessed, in relation to non-pecuniary damage, how long a reasonable transition period should be for a person to reschedule his actions from a 10-year period to a much shorter period. Thus, the Court concluded that the legislator, when determining the period for the transition to the new legal regulation, *has not comprehensively and fully ascertained* the impact of the contested norm on the already existing – pending legal relations. Thus, this regulation does not comply with the principle of protection of legitimate expectations and does not ensure the protection of person's right to adequate compensation for non-pecuniary damage.

The Court stated that the situation when a person's legal position is deteriorated *without appropriate justification or assessment* does not ensure the *principle of protection of legitimate expectations* and does not provide for a reasonable transition to the new legal regulation. Such a situation is not justified by the public interest in ensuring legal stability.

From the perspective of the application of legal method of identifying whether the retroactive effect of a contested legal norm can be detected, the Court has not found in this situation that the contested legal norm would either have had retroactive effect of legal consequences, nor that it would have intervened in the finished legal relations, nor has taken away any acquired rights. Namely, the period of formal validity of the contested norm coincides with the period of its temporal effect (force over time).

While in case no. 2020-23-01 the Court stated that the legislator has to take into account the principle of the retroactive effect of the rule which is favourable to a person in public law: "The principle of the *retroactive effect of a norm which is favourable to a person in criminal law* is derived

> from the principle of the rule of law, as this principle also includes that each punishable act must be subject to a punishment that the legislator considers appropriate at the time of determining the punishment. Therefore, the principle of retroactive effect of a rule which is favourable to a person in criminal law states: if there are differences between the law in force at the time when the criminal offence was committed, which provides for criminal liability, and the law adopted after the criminal offense was committed, then courts must apply the law which provides for more favourable consequences to the accused. The principle of the retroactive effect of a rule which is favourable to a person in criminal law should be applied by weighing and balancing it in the specific situation and circumstances in connection with other general principles of law in force in a democratic state based on the rule of law, including the principle of justice, as well as observing other provisions of the Constitution and international law."[61]

These elements of the principle of intertemporal effect are also called semi-logical[62] general principles of law, like:

1) law does not regulate the past, or inadmissibility of retroactive effect and the derived principles;[63]
2) the retroactive effect is admissible in the public law if it improves the condition of the subject;
3) the retroactive effect is admissible if it is necessary for the interest and security of a Democratic and Rule of Law governed society.

The third group of general principles of law, which must be taken into account in the drafting of written legal norms are system principles, which determine the systematization of a legal arrangement. One of the main general principles of law of this group is the principle of separation of power.[64]

In the Soviet legal system, this principle was not respected as in the case of the continental European legal system. The functions of the legislature, judiciary, and executive in the creation of legal norms were not clearly distinguished either in the written legal norms or in the practice of the applying of legal norms. Thus, for example, the executive authorities issued instructions, which

61 Judgement of the Constitutional Court of 19 February 2021 in case no. 2020-23-01, para. 21.4. Available: satv.tiesa.gov.lv.

62 Cf. Peczenik A. 1971.

63 Cf. Iļjanova D. 2002, 99. lpp.

64 Cf. Levits E. Normatīvo tiesību aktu demokrātiskā leģitimācija un deleģētā likumdošana: teorētiskie pamati. *Likums un Tiesības,* 2002, 4. sēj., nr. 9 (37), 262. lpp.

in reality in the process of application of legal norms had a higher force than the laws (so-called reverse hierarchy).

The fact that the principle of separation of power plays an important role in the legal arrangement of Latvia is also indicated by the judgements of the Constitutional Court,[65] which analyse the meaning and content of this principle. Thus, for example, the Court while analysing the content of the principle of separation of power, regarding the legislator's duties to draft and adopt written legal norms, has stated:

> "The *legislator has an obligation arising from the principle of separation of power* to treat the judiciary in such a way as to ensure mutual balance between the three branches of state power. Among other things, this attitude of the legislator towards the judiciary *must be reflected in the legal regulation* of judges' compensation."[66]
>
> "In order to ensure a more efficient implementation of state power, it is permissible to deviate from the requirement that the legislator must completely decide all issues himself. This efficiency is achieved by the *legislator deciding the most important issues in the legislative process* but delegating the development of more detailed rules and technical norms necessary for the implementation of the law to the [government] or other state institutions. Such an arrangement not only makes the legislative process itself more efficient, since the legislator does not have to deal with solving technical issues, but also allows a faster and more adequate response to the need for amendments to the regulatory framework. In addition, the [government] or other authorized state institutions are often more competent than the legislator in the drafting of technical norms, and the decision-making process in these institutions is not so complicated."[67] [All inserts and emphasis by the author.]

One of the most visible examples of the violation of the principle of separation of power was the regulation inherited from the Soviet legal system, which

65 For example, see Judgements of the Constitutional Court starting from the time of its foundation: of 7 May 1997 in case no. 04-01(97), of 11 March 1998 in case no. 04-05(97), of 10 June 1998 in case no. 04-03(98), of 9 July 1999 in case no. 04-03(99), of 1 October 1999 in case no. 03-05(99). Available: satv.tiesa.gov.lv.

66 Judgement of the Constitutional Court of 26 October 2017 in case no. 2016-31-01, para. 21.1. Available: satv.tiesa.gov.lv.

67 Judgement of the Constitutional Court of 21 November 2005 in case no. 2005-03-0306, para. 7. Available: satv.tiesa.gov.lv.

determined the binding nature of the Supreme Court's Plenary Session's decisions, which "supposedly" were applicable only towards the courts. Thus, for example, the second part of Section 49 of the Law On Judicial Power determined: "The Plenary Session adopts explanations binding on the courts on the application of the laws."

What proves that the decisions of the Supreme Court's Plenary Session were generally binding for an unlimited number of legal subjects, and not only for courts?

First, if the courts are bound by the decision and do not have the right to deviate from it (respectively, a higher instance court will overrule the judgement of a lower instance court if it is (even reasonably) contrary to the decision of the Supreme Court's Plenary Session), then this decision has a generally binding nature. Secondly, if the decision has a general binding nature, then it applies to everyone who is involved in the court proceedings, so not only to the court, but also to the plaintiff, defendant, third parties, etc., respectively, to an indefinite number of persons. The next conclusion: if the decision applies to every individual, how legitimate is the institution that adopted it, and does this institution – the Supreme Court's Plenary Session – have to be delegated to have legislative rights, that is, the right to adopt generally binding legal norms?[68]

68 Similar analysis see in the judgement of the Constitutional Court of 4 February 2003 in the case no. 2002-06-01: "The Latvian court practice confirms the mandatory nature of the binding interpretations of the Plenary Session's decisions. The courts, when reaching judgements, rather often apply the instructions (directions) of the Plenary Session's decisions as generally binding legal norms [...]. Sometimes the court of a higher instance amends or repeals the decisions, reached by the courts of lower instance, if they are unconformable with the interpretations of the Plenary Session's decisions. For example, the Supreme Court Senate Department of Criminal Cases repealed the judgements of the Riga Regional Court Division of Criminal Cases and the Supreme Court Chamber of Criminal Cases because it held that "the appellate instance court had erroneously interpreted Item 11 of 19 December 1994 Republic of Latvia Supreme Court Plenary Session's Decision No. 7 "On Application of Law in Cases on Endangering Movable Property of Another, when Committing Robbery or Theft" [...]. Other state institutions also approximate their resolutions with the provisions of the Plenary Session's decisions. Thus materials of the application No. 204 (2002) submitted to the Constitutional Court testify that the officials of the Prosecutor General's Office and the Ministry of Justice, when giving an answer to applications of a certain person, have taken into consideration the interpretation of Article 56 of the Criminal Law, which has been expressed in 23 July 1999 Plenum Plenary Session's Decision No.7 "On Application of Several Norms in Criminal Matters Connected with the Taking Effect of the Criminal Law". Sometimes the Plenary Session's Decisions incorporate such instructions, which cannot be regarded as concretization of generally binding legal norms. For example, Item 4.7 of the already mentioned Plenary

By their very nature, decisions of the Supreme Court's Plenary Session are summaries of the case law. On the other hand, case law in the continental European legal system is only a supplementary[69] source of law, that is, it does not have a generally binding character, so these summaries do not consist of legal norms.

On 31 October 2002 the parliament amended Section 49 of this Law and expressed it in the following wording: "Plenary Session shall discuss current issues of interpretation of legal norms", thereby correcting the long-standing violation of the principle of separation of power.

3 The Role of General Principles of Law in the Application of Legal Norms

The application of legal norms, just like the drafting of normative legal acts, is the area of the legal arrangement where the axiology of general principles of law is reflected.

The fact that general principles of law significantly influence decision-making in a case was the main statement of Dworkin's original theory. Dworkin considers that in the analysis of the notion of the principle of law it is important to separate it from the notion of the "aim" thus making it possible to differentiate argumentation based on aims from argumentation based on principles.[70]

The argument that there are unwritten rights, supra-positive norms, which are the ideal of positive law and on which positive law must be based, is a

---

Session's Decision No. 7, establishes: "If the accused person is hiding in another state and his/her hunt is announced, then the criminal liability limitation is terminated by forwarding the official request to the accused person." However, Section 56 of the Criminal Law to which the above interpretation of the Plenary Session's Decision is given, does not envisage such a reason for terminating criminal liability limitation period. Thus, in practice the Plenary Session's decisions have been applied not only as a supplementary source of law but – like the generally binding normative acts – have also acquired the status of an independent source of law. [...]. Thus, the challenged norm, which authorized the Supreme Court Plenary Session to pass binding on the courts decisions on application of laws, is at variance with the principle of separation of power and limits independence of judges (courts). [...]. Thus, the court decisions, which have been taken by applying binding to the courts Supreme Court interpretations, may come into collision with the principle of fairness (justice), which is incorporated into Article 1 of the Constitution." Available: satv.tiesa.gov.lv.

69 See Chapter 2.1.3.

70 Dworkin R. 1977, 1978, pp. 22–28; Chapter 3.

long known concept of natural law. From that follows the next conclusion: if rights are guaranteed already before the decision of an authority, then the relevant institution cannot have the competence to violate these rights. This idea is based on the assumption that human rights may only be based on norms (thus, on general principles of law) that refer to each person individually, and not on common social goals required by a bigger or more authoritative part of society. Therefore, human rights have an individual character (here the principle of human dignity and a human being as the highest value and the centre of a legal arrangement emerges). This leads to the conclusion that the operation of courts protecting these rights is based on rules, legal norms adopted by a legislature, and if there are no such norms, then on the general principles of law. The court decisions in these cases are based on "arguments of principle" and not on "arguments of policy". "[J]udicial decisions must be taken to be justified by arguments of principle rather than arguments of policy."[71]

Further analysis of this opinion leads to several conclusions. One of those is related to the idea of division of power in decision-making between a legislator and a court. Decisions that create or fulfil the aims of the society are adopted by a legislator. Thus, the legislator is guided by the policy arguments. Whereas the activities of the court are connected with either rules or general (possibly even not yet formulated) principles of law. Thus, court activities are based on principle arguments. This opinion in respect of division of power is developing and becoming the foundation of the decision-making theory. The court is and it should be bound by principles. The opinion in respect of the decision-making theory is based on the assumption that human rights, which are based on principles, already "exist" before the decision is taken. From the aspect of legal order and legal argumentation the individual rights have an absolute priority over the "collective" social aims. The principle arguments in a system of laws have an absolute priority over the arguments of aims (policy).[72]

This theory by Dworkin is not accepted without questioning and it has been criticized in respect of the statement about the absolute priority of individual rights over the social objectives as the legal order tends to develop in the direction of goal-oriented law.[73] Also, in the countries of the Romano-Germanic legal system there is a universally acknowledged opinion that injustice can be admitted in some cases as a fee for the social order, and lawyers of this system disapprove of decisions which might be socially unjust.[74] Strict application

71 See Dworkin R. 1977, 1978, p. 115.

72 Ibid., pp. 96–97.

73 *Scandinavian Studies in Law*. Stockholm: Almqvist & Wiksell International, 1991, p. 283.

74 See David R. 1985, p. 150.

of legal norms without regard to the social aim and the injustice caused as a result (*summum ius summa iniuria*, in Latin) has never been the ideal of the Romano-Germanic legal system.

Thus, it does not mean that aims could not be considered in the application process of the legal norms, as the principle of higher critique, for example, demands that if the written legal norm imposes a restriction on the fundamental rights of a person, then for the written legal norm to be legitimate or constitutional the restriction has to be adopted in order to achieve a legitimate aim (for example, protection of the rights of other persons or protection of the Democratic state order). Hence, individual rights can be and are subject to limitations imposed by written legal norms adopted by a legislature in order to ensure the achievement of a legitimate social aim, but in the legal arrangement of a Democratic State based on the Rule of Law this has to correspond with general principles of law, such as for example, the principle of proportionality.[75]

When talking about the role of general principles of law in the process of the application of legal norms first it has to be remembered that all legal methods themselves are general principles of law.[76] General principles of law are real, directly applicable (generally binding) legal norms, and they consist of the structure immanent to legal norms: legal content (If ...,) and legal consequences (then ...). It also means that legal methods as the general principles of law create subjective rights and impose legal obligations. Justice is the ultimate goal of the legal arrangement based on the Basic Norm of a Democratic State governed by the Rule of Law.[77] It is possible to achieve justice and to reach a fair and reasonable result in every case only if the legal methods are applied in the process of the application of legal norms. Therefore, the legislator does not have any freedom to exclude these instructions from the field of generally binding regulations on how a judge has to work in applying legal norms. For example, the legislator cannot adopt a normative legal act stating that judges will no longer apply an interpretation method when deciding cases, as that would contradict the principle of justice: it is not possible to reach a just and reasonable decision in every case if the written legal norm is not first interpreted. That applies of course to all legal methods. Thus, even if a legislator

75 On mutual collisions of general principles of law thereof limitations on individual rights and legal methods of how they are solved see Chapter 4.1.2.

76 See Chapter 2.1.

77 As has been clearly, and multiple times, confirmed and emphasized by the Constitutional Court. Compare, for example: Judgement of the Constitutional Court of 12 March 2020, para. 16.

would adopt such a rule – cancelling the application of legal methods by the legal norms' appliers – that would be in contradiction with the principle of justice and would be declared null and void within the constitutional review procedure.

Legal methods are unwritten legal norms of a Democratic legal arrangement based on the Rule of Law, they are valid and exist before the legislator and the legislator cannot abolish them. A little bit more complicated at first sight could be the question how legal methods – if they are the general principles of law, which means that they are unwritten legal norms – can have the structure of a legal norm and can create subjective rights and impose legal duties (the imperative attributive character of any legal norm). And the answer is: first they have to be concretized, filled with content like any other general principle of law. For example, the general principle of law, the legal method of interpretation in its concretization states: "If an applier of legal norm (Feature 1 (F1) of the legal content), if written legal norm (F2), if applies it (F3), then uses literal, historical, systemic, and teleological methods of interpretation in order to reach just and reasonable decision in a case." The legal duty is imposed on the applier of a legal norm, while subjective right to appeal the adopted unjust decision if the interpretation method is not applied (or applied incorrectly) is given to a person. The legislator also has given the content guideline for this general principle of law – legal method of interpretation, naming it "principle of reasonable application of legal norms" in Section 8 of the Administrative Procedure Law: "In applying the legal norms, an institution and a court shall use the basic methods of the interpretation of the legal norms (grammatical, systematic, historical, and teleological methods) in order to achieve the most equitable and useful result (Section 17)." Nevertheless, even if such a written legal norm would not be adopted by the legislator or if the legislator would decide to repeal this written legal norm, the general principle of law – the legal method of interpretation – would still be valid as an unwritten legal norm in a legal arrangement based on the Basic Norm, derived from the principle of justice and the principle of the right to fair trial, as it exists and is a valid legal norm within the system of laws already before the legislator.

Thus the role of the general principles of law in the process of application of a legal norm can be observed either 1) in the absence of the written legal norm, which solves the case (and by absence is meant also the situation when the written legal norm is adopted by a legislator, but it is not legitimate (constitutional), it does not give a just and reasonable answer to the case), and 2) when general principles of law accompany the entire process of the application of a legal norm, even if the written provision exists, is valid and legitimate, as, for example, all legal methods to be applied in the application process (methods of interpretation, further development of law, methods of resolution of collisions, methods of legal reasoning, etc.) in order to achieve a just result in a case are general principles of law.

The entire process of the application of legal norms can occur in four different ways:

1) *intra legem* (*secundum legem*): staying within the limits set by the text of the written legal norm (which includes interpretation of the written text of the legal norm);
2) *praeter legem*: application, which stays "next to" the text of the written legal norm (includes the method of filling with the content any open-ended legal concepts such as general clauses);
3) *extra legem*: overstepping the limits set by the text of the written legal norm (which includes analogy and teleological reduction); and
4) *contra legem*: application of a legal norm "contrary to the law", "against the law", though *contra legem* but *intra ius,* which means that the true legal norm found by a court in the given legal arrangement is contrary to the wording of the positive law but corresponds to the whole legal arrangement and stays within the *ratio iuris* of the legal arrangement and according to the Basic Norm proclaimed by the sovereign.

While the process of the application of a legal norm involves the following steps with corresponding legal methods:

1) inquest of facts: construction of factual content (establishing of the raw material of the facts; selecting the legally significant facts);
2) finding the eventually applicable legal norm: the principle of diversity of sources of law;
3) examining the eventually applicable legal norm: lower critique, principles of intertemporality, transitional provisions, higher critique, the principle of the hierarchy of legal norms;
4) finding the real content of the eventually applicable legal norm: interpretation (literal, systemic, historical, and teleological sub-methods; mixed theory of the aim of interpretation of legal norms (which stipulates that the legal norms should be interpreted in accordance with the will of the legislator to the extent that this does not contradict the text of the legal norm (its objective meaning)[78]), *argumentum e contrario*, concretization;
5) resolving the collisions of the written legal norms and principles: collision norms (for example, *lex superior derogat legi inferiori, lex specialis derogat legi generali, lex posterior derogat legi priori, lex posterior generalis*

78 Wank R. 1997, S. 37–38.

non derogat legi priori speciali), hierarchy of the collision norms, weighing and balancing of general principles of law;

6) further development of law: analogy, teleological reduction, *argumentum a fortiori* (*argumentum a maiori ad minus*, i.e., the argument "from larger to smaller", and *argumentum a minori ad maius*, or the argument "from smaller to larger");
7) subsumption: regular subsumption, evaluative subsumption, creation of the chain of value judgements;
8) elaboration of the decision: methods of argumentation, principle of prohibition of arbitrariness by a court, and necessity to justify a decision.

Alongside the general principles of law, which are derived from the Basic Norm, and which provide a legal basis for the application of all legal methods in order to find a just solution for each and every case, the judgement of the Constitutional Court of the Republic of Latvia of 4 January 2005, case no. 2004-16-01[79] could be regarded as a general authorization for the courts of the general jurisdiction and administrative courts to apply legal methods. It says: "Application of legal norms, which comply with the Constitution, includes finding the right legal norm and adequately interpreting it; assessment of inter-temporal and hierarchic applicability, use of appropriate judicature as well as further development of the law." By this statement the Constitutional Court once more announced the authorization to the courts of general jurisdiction and administrative courts that in the legal arrangement of a Democratic State based on the Rule of Law they are obliged to apply all legal methods to reach a just and reasonable decision. In fact, only application of *contra legem* stays still as a prerogative of the Constitutional Court, which is the only one that can declare the illegitimate written legal norm as null and void.

The other two groups of the general principles of law – human rights and systematization of legal arrangement principles – influence the entire process of the application of the legal norms as well and have to be taken into account by the applier of legal norms in order to reach a just and reasonable answer to the case. Thus, for example, continuing to consider the role of the principle of separation of power in the application of legal norms in connection with previous court case law, which was based on the binding nature of the decisions of the Supreme Court's Plenary Session as then determined in the Law On

79 Judgement of the Constitutional Court of 4 January 2005 in the case no. 2004-16-01, para. 17. Available: satv.tiesa.gov.lv.

Judicial Power, the case reviewed in the Supreme Court Senate on 20 August 1996 is worth looking at.[80]

> Persons A and B stole rabbits from a rabbit hutch, and the court convicted the guilty persons under the fourth part of Section 139 of the Criminal Code of Latvia for stealth theft involving breaking into another storage. The Supreme Court Senate overturned the sentence, concluding that since the rabbit hutch was made of wire mesh, it is neither a room nor another storage, but, as it follows from the argumentative part of the judgement, a fenced section of the territory, which does not correspond to the concept of "other storage", therefore the offense cannot be qualified as the above-mentioned crime.
>
> In its decision, the Senate determined that the explanation of the terms: "premises" and "other storage" referred to in the fourth part of Section 139 of the Criminal Code of Latvia is given in the Supreme Courts' Plenary Session's Decision "On the Application of the Law in Cases of Threats to Someone Else's Property When Committing Theft or Robbery".
>
> According to the Plenary Session, "other storage" was a place or territory separated from the surrounding environment, intended for the storage of material assets, such as mobile car shops, tanks, luggage compartments of vehicles, containers, safes, railway wagons, but to the keeping of livestock and poultry according to the Plenary Session's Decision the term "premises" should applied, which is a building, construction or part thereof enclosed by building structures (walls, ceiling, floor and roof) and intended, among other things, for keeping livestock and poultry. On the other hand, the fenced sections of the territory are intended for the cultivation of some production (e.g., cereals) or livestock grazing (e.g., enclosures, etc., which do not consist of building structures). At this point, the Plenary Session "unfortunately" had not mentioned anything about the attribution of rabbit hutches to one or the other concept. The Supreme Court Senate apparently believed that, taking into account the low value of the stolen rabbits, the offense should be requalified from the fourth part of Section 139 to the less harsh second part, but chose to argue with the Decision of the Supreme Court's Plenary Session – since the rabbit hutch was made of a wire mesh, then the court held that it is not a building structure with walls, ceiling and floor, so it does not meet the

80 Lieta nr. SKK-205. Grām.: *Latvijas Republikas Augstākās tiesas Senāta spriedumi un lēmumi 1996*. Rīga: Latvijas Tiesnešu mācību centrs, 1997, 606.–608. lpp.

concept of "room". Due to the explanation given by the Supreme Court Senate regarding the term used in the Decision of the Supreme Court's Plenary Session, the question arises: what would the court do if the hutch would have been made of boards and not of a grid, and whether the hutch is really meant for grazing rabbits (as the purpose of the fenced areas of the territory, which according to the Supreme Court Senate, was this rabbit hutch, explained in the Supreme Court's Plenary Session's Decision is livestock grazing)?

4 Conclusions

General principles of law are an independent source of law – a real, directly applicable legal norm that can be used to justify a decision in a specific case (the operative (holding) part of the decision).

In the hierarchy of sources of law, general principles of law have priority or prevail over the normative legal acts created by a legislator, also over the formal Constitution.

The axiology of general principles of law is expressed in the legislation process as well as in the process of the application of legal norms. The principle of good legislation determines the procedural requirements for the legislation process while other general principles of law have to be taken into account by the legislator when drafting the contents of the written legal norms. The role of the general principles of law in the process of application of a legal norm can be observed either 1) in the absence of the written legal norm, which solves the case (and by absence is meant also the situation when the written legal norm is adopted by a legislator, but it is not legitimate (constitutional), it does not give a just and reasonable answer to the case), and 2) when general principles of law accompany the entire process of the application of a legal norm, even if the written provision exists, is valid and legitimate – as, for example, all legal methods to be applied in the application process (methods of interpretation, further development of law, methods of resolution of collisions, methods of legal reasoning, etc.) in order to achieve a just result in a case are general principles of law.

CHAPTER 4

The Functional Effect of General Principles of Law

1 Application of General Principles of Law

The functional meaning of general principles of law or the mechanism of functional effect finds expression in two forms. First, the general principle of law itself may appear as an applicable legal norm, which is either derived from the Basic Norm (a Democratic State based on the Rule of Law) or other general principles of law or is found, discovered in the written legal norms based on a general principle or principles of law. It should be pointed out that these are very rare cases, not only in the court and administrative practice of Latvia but also in the legal practice of the countries of the Western legal system, when a specific decision is substantiated solely with a general principle of law (usually some written legal norm containing the content guideline of the general principle of law is shown as a basis for the holding part of the judgement; in the case of Latvia it is quite usually the principle of a Democratic State based on the Rule of Law found in Article 1 of the Constitution). Of course, this is related to a certain insecurity of the appliers of legal norms as work on the application of general principles of law requires great intellectual effort and practical competence, as well as being related to the still high, though not always publicly recognized impact of the doctrine of legal positivism on the legal thinking, the understanding of law of the appliers of legal norms.

What is crucial in the application of general principles of law is the professional's ability to derive them from the Basic Norm, other principles of law, to discover them in written legal norms, as well as to concretize the general principle of law, i.e., to specify its content. When the general principle of law is derived or discovered and concretized, collision with other general principles of law always occurs in its application process. Solving this collision appears by way of "weighing" of the principles. In accordance with the scheme of the legal syllogism, the application of general principles of law always occurs in the form of evaluative subsumption.[1] This means that legal syllogism does not consist of two premises (the Major Premise, specifying that each legal content has definite legal consequences, and the Minor Premise or subsumption,

1 Cf.: Larenz K., Canaris C.W. 1995, S. 95; Kalniņš E. Tiesību normu piemērošanas loģiskā shēma. 2000, 152. lpp.

 | DOI:10.1163/9789004690516_005

where the features of the factual content are compared to the features of the legal content, and a conclusion is drawn whether or not the legal content has been implemented in the actual content) but consists of three premises, the third of which is the legal norm found by a court.

Second, the functional effect mechanism of the general principles of law finds expression in the process of application of another, a written legal norm,[2] for example, by influencing the understanding of the content of the legal norm, as well as the solving of collisions and drafting of the judgement.

If in Chapter 2 it was concluded that general principles of law are real and directly applicable legal norms by their value or axiology in the legal arrangement, then the main question examined in this chapter is whether the way of functional impact of general principles of law on the legal arrangement differs from that of the written legal norms.

1.1 *Deriving, Discovering and Concretization*

If written legal norms do not provide an answer in the given case because none of the norms is directly applicable in the relevant actual circumstances, which may be extraordinary, new or unexpected, then the logical and objective answer that would ensure coherence, uniformity and order of the legal arrangement and public security has to be sought in another normative level, i.e., on the level of general principles of law. Written legal norms shall be considered as expressions of general principles of law. A judge him/herself does not have to try to create them and is not inventing those principles. It is not the task of a judge.[3] Even more – that would be in a contradiction with the Basic Norm and principle of separation of power. On the contrary, a judge's duty is *to find* these principles that already exist in the system of laws in the form of unwritten legal norms. His/her task is to adjudicate cases by applying all sources of law, which are required in order to find the just and reasonable answer to each case according to the general principle of law – the diversity of the sources of law; and in order to give sufficient and comprehensive justification according to the principle of prohibition of arbitrariness and the principle of the necessity of justification; and to substantiate the judgement – to base it on a legal norm in accordance with the legal syllogism.

What, then, are the stages of the doctrinal method to discover general principles of law? According to Julio C. Cueto-Rua it consists of six steps.

2 See Chapter 4.2.

3 See Cueto-Rua J.C. *Judicial Methods of Interpretation of the Law*. Louisiana: The Publications Institute Paul M.Hebert Law Center, 1981, p. 122.

The first step is that the legal norms adopted by a legislator, which refer to the specific field of legal regulation are analysed in order to discover their common and homogeneous elements.

The second step is the elimination of redundancies, peculiarities, inconsistencies and legislative errors.

The third step is to filter out, based on common and homogeneous conceptual elements, an abstract assumption or norm.

The fourth step is to seek a higher degree of generality by trying to discover the genus (class) to which the homogeneous and common concepts belong.

The fifth step is the starting point for deduction, based on the basic principles thus obtained. Several concepts are being developed. Logic performs a creative function. It creates new concepts that refer to new facts or to unexpected elements of a case that have no similar ones.

The sixth step is the application in two ways of concepts obtained through deduction:

1) to clarify the words or provisions used by the legislator, which were unclear or undefined; this is achieved by elaborating on concepts that are in logical connection and accordance with the general principles of law of the system of laws, and
2) to provide a logically normative basis for a judgement that was not possible to be based on some written legal norm.

It is also recognized that this sixth step is the most difficult and has to be performed with great care, as the judge may encounter the "dangers" associated with the extensive nature of the deductive process. Definitions of general principles of law provide a very broad logical basis for deduction. It is possible to extend the process and cover a wide variety of situations in a logical way, and the risk is obvious. A high degree of coherence and unity can be achieved while harming justice and other legal values. It will be up to the judge to determine how far he/she will go. Logic itself does not create any limits. The judge then tries to "control" logic with experience and intuition, and to create a boundary beyond which he/she can no longer reason based on logic, because if the judge would be logical to the end, justice, solidarity, cooperation, peace and other values, which a judge is expected to maintain may be ignored or destroyed.[4]

This process of the *discovery* of a general principle of law from the texts of the written legal norms described by Cueto-Rua is different from the *deriving* of general principles of law from the Basic Norm, which is a deductive process. Here, in the discovery process of the finding of a principle, this happens

4 See more Cueto-Rua J.C. 1981, pp. 124–125.

inductively and only the concretization part starting the fifth step is based on deduction. This way of discovering a general principle of law would be more acceptable for a judge with the prevailing meaning of law based in the legal positivism doctrine; however, if the result of the discovery and further the content obtained by the concretization is later verified according to the Basic Norm and is compatible with it, it could give valid and useful guidelines for the content of a general principle of law as well.

The Constitutional Court has derived general principles of law since its foundation; however, it has developed its approach since the early days of its operation. Initially, the Court derived general principles of law from the text of Article 1 of the Constitution which states: "Latvia is an independent democratic Republic."[5] Then, the Court continued to develop its approach and indicated that general principles of law are derived not from the text of Article 1 of the Constitution but rather from the notion of the Democratic Republic included in Article 1.[6] The next step of the development of the approach was when the Court reasoned that general principles of law emerge from the fundamental values established in Article 1 of the Constitution.[7] Finally, in 2016, the Court evolved its approach, referring to the true source of general principles of law, the Basic Norm proclaimed by the sovereign, thus stating: "The principle of the protection of legitimate expectations *derived from the Basic Norm – democratic state based on the Rule of Law* [author's emphasis], and embodied in the scope of Article 1 of the Constitution protects only those rights which are based on legal, justified and reasonable expectations, which are the core of this general principle of law."[8]

As mentioned earlier, the discovery and derivation of "new"[9] general principles of law are not a frequent phenomenon; however, it can be found in the legal arrangement of Latvia. One of the most significant developments in this

5 See for example: Judgement of the Constitutional Court of 20 April 1999 in case no. 04-01(99), para. 1.2.1. Available: satv.tiesa.gov.lv.

6 Judgement of the Constitutional Court of 24 March 2000 in case no. 04-07(99), para. 3. Available: satv.tiesa.gov.lv.

7 Judgement of the Constitutional Court of 15 March 2010 in case no. 2009-44-01, para. 15. Available: satv.tiesa.gov.lv .

8 Decision of the Constitutional Court of 21 October 2016 on termination of proceedings in case no. 2016-03-01, para. 13. Available: satv.tiesa.gov.lv.

9 Here, the term "new" should of course be understood conditionally because general principles of law as objective legal norms specific to the given legal arrangement exist in an unwritten form, waiting for the occurrence of the actual circumstances necessary for their application, regardless of whether they have been positivised by a legislator or whether the applier of the legal norms has already discovered and derived them.

regard, deriving the "new" general principle of law from the Basic Norm, is considered to be the judgement of the Constitutional Court of 6 March 2019[10] where the general principle of law – the *principle of good legislation* – was derived. The Court's case law is unique in this regard within the European legal space[11] as it is for the first time that this principle is formulated as a general principle of law, a generally binding legal norm prevailing over all of the written legal norms, with a concrete core and peripheral content of its scope.

Thus, the principle of good legislation has become one of the most recently acknowledged general principles of law, which has found its refined concretization through the case law of the Court. The development was gradual. First, on 12 April 2018, for the first time during its existence, the Court recognized the two laws contested in the case as not adopted in due process.[12] Both of these laws were declared incompatible with the Constitution. In this judgement, the Court offered a view to the legislative process, which corresponds to the Basic Norm – a Democratic State based on the Rule of Law – but did not yet formulate the notion of the general principle of good legislation. The Court based the assessment of a legislative process on the necessity to ensure justice. In the judgement, the Court highlights that "the main purpose of the law is to ensure justice". The Court also accentuates that the legislative process must not only comply with the formal requirements laid down in regulatory enactments but must also promote the people's trust in the State and law. The Court emphasises that the legislative process nowadays does not exist for the convenience of the legislator but serves as an effective mechanism by which public trust in adopted laws and the legislator itself can be promoted. The Court has pointed out that "the legislator must ensure a legislative process that promotes trust in the state and law, namely, the conviction that the chosen solution is fair".

10 Judgement of the Constitutional Court of 6 March 2019.

11 The European Union, its Member States, as well other Democratic States based on the Rule of Law under different common forums of course have paid close attention to the necessity to improve the quality of the legislative process under better law-making, good regulation programs (see for example: Interinstitutional Agreement between the European Parliament, the Council of the European Union and the European Commission on Better Law-Making of 13 April 2016. Available: eur-lex.europa.eu; Rule of Law checklist of the European Commission for Democracy through Law (Venice Commission) of 11–12 March 2016. Available: venice.coe.int; OECD Recommendation of the Council on Regulatory Policy and Governance of 22 March 2012. Available: oecd.org/gov/regulatory-policy/49990817.pdf; OECD Guiding Principles for Regulatory Quality and Performance of 2005. Available: oecd.org/fr/reformereg/34976533.pdf), but the principle of good legislation was not yet formulated as one of the general principles of law.

12 Judgement of the Constitutional Court of 12 April 2018 in case no. 2017-17-01, paras. 21.3., 22.2., 22.3. Available: satv.tiesa.gov.lv.

And the Court here starts to outline the content of the principle of good legislation: 1) the legislator has to provide proper analysis as well as justification for the constitutionality of a possible regulation, *inter alia* in the context of the established case law of the Court in this matter; 2) in order to adopt a just legal norm, the legislator has to make such an assessment by itself, and not after, but before any restriction on fundamental rights is imposed.[13]

The next level of concretization of the principle of good legislation was reached by the Court in the case where the judgement was delivered on 6 March 2019. The Court for the first time formulates in the text of the judgement the principle of good legislation and displays that it has derived it from the Basic Norm and the principle of the Rule of Law.[14]

The Court concretizes the content of the principle of good legislation using different types of sources of law (generally binding (independent) sources, but mostly, supplementary) such as: 1) generally binding interpretations of legal norms by authorized courts – of the Court itself, of the Court of Justice of the European Union, of the European Court of Human Rights; 2) legal doctrine – national and international doctrinal legal writings (commentaries to the Constitution of the Republic of Latvia, monographies, collected articles), recommendations of national and international bodies for the improvement of the legislative process (Constitutional Law Commission of the President of the Republic of Latvia, Venice Commission), dissenting opinion of the judges of the European Court of Human Rights; 3) *travaux préparatoires*, and 4) normative legal acts – national and European Union legal acts.[15]

It states very precisely the elements of the content of the principle of good legislation, namely, in order that the legislative process could be recognized as being in compliance with the principle of good legislation:

1) the legislator must assess the compliance of the envisaged legal norms with the legal norms of a higher legal force (including European Union legal norms and taking into account the principle of sincere cooperation it has to assess the compliance of the intended provisions also with that European Union law which has entered into force but has not yet become applicable) and their compatibility with the system of laws according to the principle of a rational legislator, as well as assess the compliance of the intended regulation with the established case law of the Court in the matter;
2) the intended legal framework should, where appropriate, be based on explanatory studies;

13 Judgement of the Constitutional Court of 12 April 2018, para. 21.3.

14 Judgement of the Constitutional Court of 6 March 2019, para. 18.1.

15 Ibid., para. 18.

3) according to the principle of sustainable development the legislator in adopting legal norms, especially in cases where fundamental rights are restricted, has to base its decision in the social impact assessment study of the planned legal framework and consider the measures necessary for the implementation and enforcement of this legal framework;
4) the legislator has to assess the risks expressed by the specialists in the field and take timely actions to eliminate the possible risks;
5) the legislator must inform the public in a timely manner and appropriately about the intended legal framework, and as far as possible, directly or indirectly, involve the public in the legislative process and have consultations with stakeholders;
6) it has to be made possible for the members of the legislator to participate in an open debate;
7) the objections about the draft expressed by the State President using the suspensive veto rights have to be considered in a manner, which corresponds to the principle of inter-institutional loyalty and the principle of *bona fide*.[16]

Furthermore, the Court stated that these requirements are the main, but not the only elements of the principle of good legislation *derived from the principle of the Rule of Law and the Basic Norm.* Among other things, they are of the utmost importance as they make it possible to understand why the restriction of fundamental rights set by the legislator in a Democratic State based on the Rule of Law is permissible. These requirements must be respected in determining any restriction on fundamental rights.[17] In this case, similarly as in case no. 2017-17-01, the Court found violation of several of the elements of the principle of good legislation. Thus, the violation of this unwritten legal norm – a general principle of law: the principle of good legislation – was recognized as essential. If such violation had not occurred the decision adopted by the legislature would be different: the core content of the principle of good legislation, and the Court declared the contested legal norms as not adopted in due process and not in compliance with the principle of good legislation and thereby incompatible with the Constitution.

The courts of general jurisdiction also discover and derive general principles of law in cases when the court has to justify the judgement, the justification of which lacks a written regulation given by the legislator.

16 Judgement of the Constitutional Court of 6 March 2019, paras. 18.1., 18.2., 18.3., 18.4.

17 Ibid., para. 18.1.

Thus, for example, Riga city Zemgale District Court, while considering an application for turning the execution of the judgement, faced the lack of a written regulation.[18] Section 634 of the Civil Procedure Law stated: if an executed judgement is overruled and after a new trial of the case, a judgement is adopted rejecting the claim, everything recovered from the defendant for the benefit of the plaintiff after the overruled judgement has to be returned to the defendant. The factual situation was that, pursuant to a court judgement that had not yet entered into force and was in favour of the defendant, a writ of execution was erroneously issued, and costs of legal assistance were recovered from the plaintiff in favour of the defendant. However, later during the case review, the erroneously issued writ of execution, by which the amount of money was recovered from the plaintiff in favour of the defendant, was annulled.

Analysing Section 634 of the Civil Procedure Law, the Court recognized "that it is not directly applicable to solving the situation, because, firstly, the executed court judgement was not overruled and an opposite judgement was not adopted instead, secondly, the applicant has not been a defendant, but a plaintiff.

At the same time, the court acknowledges that there is no provision in the Civil Procedure Law that would directly provide legal regulation for the repayment of the amount recovered in a situation where, by mistake, that is [...] after a court judgement which has not entered into force yet, a writ of execution is issued, and a certain amount of money is recovered. Taking into account the mentioned circumstances, the court recognizes that it is reasonable to apply the principle included in Section 634 of the Civil Procedure Law for solving the situation indicated in the application – *everything that was recovered (received) without a legal basis by a court decision must be returned to the party from whom the amount was unreasonably recovered* [author's emphasis]."

The Riga Regional Court, while considering a side complaint regarding the above-mentioned court decision, recognized that "the court *correctly* [author's emphasis] recognized that the law does not have a provision that would directly provide a legal regulation for the repayment of the recovered amount in a situation where, by mistake, after an invalid court judgement, a writ of execution is issued and after that a collection is made. Part 5 of Section 5 of the Civil Procedure Law stipulates that

18 Rīgas pilsētas Zemgales priekšpilsētas tiesas 2002. gada 6. februāra lēmums lietā nr. 2-00987/98. Nav publicēts.

> in the absence of a law regulating the disputed relationship, the courts shall apply the law regulating similar legal relations, but in the absence of such a law, they shall be guided by the general principles and meaning of the law.
>
> Due to the above, it must be recognized that the court of first instance has resoled this case *correctly* [author's emphasis] applying the principle – everything that was recovered (received) without a legal basis by a court decision must be returned to the party from whom the amount was unreasonably recovered, included in the Section 634 of the Civil Procedure Law."[19]
>
> Similarly, the refusal of the plaintiff's representative's request to determine the easement of the use for the room is based solely on the general principles of law – the right to property and the principle of proportionality: "The request of the plaintiff's representative at the court hearing to determine the easement of use for room "A" in favour of the plaintiff is not justified, because [...] the determination of the easement, taking into account the materials of the case, from which it is evident that the plaintiff herself is able to build the entrance to the disputed room, would be contrary to the *principle of property rights law that the owner's property rights are limited to the smallest extent possible* [author's emphasis].[20]

In order to apply a general principle of law for adjudicating a specific, actual case, it is necessary to determine the content of the general principle of law. Unlike the written legal norms, the contents and true meaning of which are determined by way of interpretation, by applying interpretation methods, a general principle of law requires *concretization*[21] to determine its content. The difference here lies in the object of interpretation, which is a text: *interpretation is a textual method* and written legal norms are expressed in a written textual form. General principles of law, however, are unwritten legal norms, which first need to be filled with content, that is, concretized. Therefore, in order to express a general principle of law (for instance, the principle of equality or the principle of legal certainty) in the structure of a legal norm, firstly, it needs to be concretized, by expressing it textually.

Concretization or the process of filling general principles of law with content is neither a simply deductive process, i.e., may be concluded from the

---

19 Rīgas apgabaltiesas 2002. gada 13. maija lēmums lietā nr. CA-2736/02, C-31 184994. Nav publicēts.

20 Ibid.

21 Cf.: Larenz K. 1979, S. 23.

Basic Norm, because each concretization presents the further-going meaning, requiring additional considerations, nor a simply inductive process, where a general principle of law may be obtained from the positive law, because the peculiarities related to positive law – historical situation or special considerations of the legislator – are included there. On the one hand, a principle allows for variable concretization every time *in its periphery*, but on the other hand, this concretization always develops *within the basic meaning of the principle, its core*.[22] Thus each concretization reached for a general principle of law partially has just the meaning of an example that enhances the content of the principle. Hence, these examples may never be provided completely.[23]

As is analysed in legal doctrine, international courts and tribunals use two means to ascertain the content of the general principles of law: 1) using previous decisions; 2) in their absence, or if they choose not to rely on those decisions, with the help of comparative law, by appealing to legal doctrine as well.[24] The comparative law method suggests using the so-called "representative legal system" approach by applying principles of law, which are common to the major legal systems of the world and are suitable for transposition into the international legal system. This process of transposition is inductive by its nature where a principle found underlies rules in many national legal systems, while discounting the national differences of detail or procedure and isolating the basic uniform principle, which is common to all.[25]

---

22 In this way, general principles of law differ from general clauses, which are also concepts with an undefined content, or open-ended legal concepts, but the result of concretization of general clauses can be completely different in each case. Thus, for example, the general clause "on the basis of special meritorious service for the benefit of Latvia" contained in Section 13 of the Citizenship Law [*Pilsonības likums*] (The law of the Republic of Latvia. Adopted on 22.07.1994. Available: likumi.lv/ta/en/en/id/57512-citizenship-law) can be filled with a different content in each specific case – in one case the special merits will manifest as ensuring the stability of the economic system, in another good sporting successes that have brought Latvia's name to the world, etc. While a general principle of law, such as the principle of equality for example, will always mean the same thing within its basic meaning or the core, namely that "like shall be treated alike", for example see Vainovskis M. Nodokļu krimināllietu aktuālā problemātika un atšķirības tiesu praksē. *Likums un Tiesības*, 4. sēj., nr. 2 (30), 61. lpp. About general clauses as the "extreme" form of concepts with indefinite content (open-ended concepts) and differences in their concretization in more detail see Levits E. 2003, 165.–166. lpp.

23 Cf. also Larenz K. 1979, S. 43–44.

24 Fabian O.R. *General Principles of Law in the Decisions of International Criminal Courts and Tribunals*. Leiden: Martinus Nijhoff Publishers, 2008, p. 45; Redgwell C. General Principles of International Law. In: Vogenauer S., Weatherill S. Eds. *General Principles of Law. European and Comparative Perspectives*. Oxford and Portland: Hart Publishing, 2017, pp. 15–18.

25 Redgwell C. 2017, p. 16.

Another method of "finding the right – just and reasonable – answer for a case" is mentioned as well: when judges turn to their intuition to determine general principles of law, and usually do not disclose the methods by which they are derived, discovered and concretized, and even rarely refer to comparative law research – normative acts, customary law or case law (judicial and administrative).[26]

The approach defended in this book is that judges refer to their *legal reason*[27] to find the content of general principles of law. This is why the personality of a judge, the previous life and professional experiences, legal consciousness, the leading meaning of law possessed by a judge are some of the factors which complement and fill the notion of legal reason. The previous development of a legal arrangement, the sources of law – generally binding, such as generally binding interpretations of legal norms by courts authorized to do so, normative legal acts, customary law – as well as supplementary – case law, doctrine, *travaux préparatoires*, separate (dissenting, concurring) opinions of judges etc. – are the starting points for the developing further of the content of general principles of law.[28]

The main methodological guideline that a judge should keep in mind when concretizing a general principle of law is that those principles have to be oriented to a *reasonable and just solution*. A reasonable and just solution is the one which corresponds to the Basic Norm. Moreover, in the determination of the content of the relevant principle the method of comparison and typification[29] ("belonging to the same type") is used when the case to be solved is compared with other similar cases, which have already been solved in the court practice based on certain principles. In this way, the relatively undetermined contents of the principles are constantly refined and concretized in the court practice in respect of definite cases or groups of cases, and as a result a general principle of law, an unwritten legal norm, has found its core content while the peripheral content of course is broadening and developing alongside with the development of a legal arrangement, and thus can be applicable to next and new, but similar, life situations in the future.

Thus, it should be stressed that the process of concretization should not be regarded as something uncertain or subjective as it should be accompanied by the wide and extensive legal reasoning showing arguments for and against a

26 Fabian O.R. 2008, p. 47.

27 Chapter 1; Chapter 2.2.4.

28 Rezevska D. *Vispārējo tiesību principu nozīme un piemērošana*. Rīga: D.Rezevskas izd., 2015, 100. lpp.

29 Cf.: Larenz K., Canaris C.W. 1995, S. 113; Kalniņš E. 1999, 82. lpp.

given decision as one of the main characteristics of a general principle of law is its (general) acceptance:[30] only those prescriptions, which are concretized correctly, rightfully and correspond to the Basic Norm will gain a generally binding character and therefore will be regarded as general principles of law as they will be accepted by those applying the legal norms.

The content of a general principle of law basically can be found:

1) in case law (judicature), and
2) legal doctrine.

However, with the legislator's work progressing, at least within the content guideline of the basic meaning of a general principle of law, it can also be found in:

3) normative legal acts.[31]

The source of the concretization is not only the case law of the judiciary of Latvia, but, of course, also judgements of the European Court of Human Rights and the Court of Justice of the European Union,[32] and the case law developed in other countries of the Western legal system may help to determine the contents of the general principles of law as well.[33]

> Thus, for example, the Constitutional Court has concretized several general principles of law, including using the case law of other courts. Regarding the concretization of the general principles of law – human rights, the Court has stated: "The fundamental rights contained in the international human rights treaties and the Constitution form a unified entirety in the legal arrangement of Latvia."[34]
>
> For example, the judgement of the Court of 4 February 2003 specified the *principle of a fair trial*: "Article 92 of the Constitution stipulates that everyone can defend their rights and legal interests in a fair court. The right to a fair trial involves several interrelated aspects, but two of them are relevant in the context of this case:
>
> first, a "fair court" as an independent and impartial judicial authority that examines the case. In this aspect, the mentioned concept can

30 See Ch. 2.1.

31 See Chapters 2 and 3.

32 Translation of selected judgements of the European Court of Human Rights into Latvian see *Eiropas Cilvēktiesību tiesa. Spriedumu izlase 1.* Mits M. (Red.) Rīga: Latvijas Vēstnesis, 2003.

33 Similarly, legal doctrine includes all the authoritative doctrinal insights and studies found in the Western legal system.

34 Decision of the Constitutional Court of 27 May 2022 on termination of proceedings in case no. 2021-34-01, para. 18.3. Available: satv.tiesa.gov.lv.

be concretized in connection with both the principle of separation of power and the principle of independence of judges (court) established in Article 83 of the Constitution;

secondly, a "fair trial" as a due process in accordance with the Rule of Law in which the case is heard. In this aspect, the concept of "fair trial" can be concretized in connection with the principle of justice, which derives from Article 1 of the Constitution."[35]

The *principle of a fair trial* has been concretized in several judgements of the European Court of Human Rights. So, for example, the Court has established that "the right to a fair trial is not absolute. It may be limited to the extent that it is not deprived of its essence" and that "the right to appeal may be limited by the law, if the limitation in relation to the rights provided for in the first part of Article 6 of the Convention is established by the law, the limitation has a legitimate aim and the limitation is proportionate to the legitimate aim".[36]

The *principle of equality* was concretized in the judgement of the Constitutional Court of 10 January 2003: "The principle of equality, which follows from the first sentence of Article 91 of the Constitution, prevents state institutions from issuing such legal norms that, without a reasonable basis, allow different treatment of persons who are in the same and under certain criteria comparable conditions. The principle of equality allows and even requires different treatment of persons who are in different circumstances, as well as in equal circumstances, if there is an objective and reasonable basis for this"[37] and in the judgement of 30 August 2000, referring to the judgement of the European Court of Human Rights: "The European Court of Human Rights considers that Article 14 of the Convention does not include the prohibition of any difference in treatment regarding the realization of the rights and freedoms recognized in the Convention. The principle of equal treatment is recognized

---

35 Judgements of the Constitutional Court of 4 February 2003 in case no. 2002-06-01, of 5 March 2002 in case no. 2001-10-01. Available: satv.tiesa.gov.lv.

36 The cases of the European Court of Human Rights: judgement of the European Court of Human Rights (Plenary) of 21 February 1975: *Golder v. United Kingdom*, application no. 4451/70; judgement of the European Court of Human Rights (Chamber) of 21 September 1990: *Fayed v. the United Kingdom*, application no. 17101/90. Available: hudoc.echr.coe.int.

37 Judgement of the Constitutional Court of 10 January 2003 in case no. 2002-17-0103. Available: satv.tiesa.gov.lv.

as violated only if there is no objective or reasonable justification and legitimate aim for determining the differences. The existence of such justification must be evaluated in relation to the objectives and consequences of the issue under consideration, which usually prevails in a democratic society."[38]

The *principle of proportionality*, which is recognized also as one of the most important principles of European Union law, is specified in the judgements of the Court of Justice of the European Union in the way that "state institutions may not impose obligations on citizens that exceed the defined limits of necessity arising from the public interest in order to achieve the goal" and if "the duties imposed are clearly disproportionate to the objective to be achieved, the remedy will be annulled".[39]

The development of the substantive scope of the principle of proportionality has to be particularly emphasized, because as a result of the development of the legal arrangement of Democratic States based on the Rule of Law, it has become applicable in the private law field before being solely a general principle of law applicable in the public law. Thus, the judgement of the Supreme Court Senate states: "The contractual penalty has the function of punishment as well as compensatory function. In cases where it can be concluded from the circumstances of the case that the contractual penalty, in terms of its amount, compared to the possible damages caused by the violation, performs primarily a punitive function, its application shall be evaluated according to the general principles of the application of legal remedies of a punitive nature, including the *principles of proportionality* and *justice of the penalty* [author's emphasis]. The general principles of law are generally accepted guidelines arising from

38 Judgement of the Constitutional Court of 30 August 2000 in case no. 2000-03-01. Available: satv.tiesa.gov.lv; The cases of the European Court of Human Rights: judgement of the European Court of Human Rights (Plenary) of 23 July 1968: *Belgian Linguistic case*, application nos. 1474/62; 1677/62; 1691/62; 1769/63; 1994/63; 2126/64; judgement of the European Court of Human Rights (Chamber) of 18 July 1994: *Karlheinz Schmidt v. Germany*, application no. 13580/88. Available: hudoc.echr.coe.int.

39 The cases of the European Court of Justice: judgement of the European Court of Justice of 17 December 1970: C-11/70 *Internationale Handelsgesellschaft mbH v. Einfuhr– und Vorratsstelle fur Getreide und Futtermittel*; judgement of the European Court of Justice of 24 October 1973: 5/73 *Balkan-Import-Export GmbH v. Hauptzollamt Berlin Packhof*. Available: curia.europa.eu. On the principle of proportionality in European Union law, see also: Kent P. *Law of the European Union*. 2nd ed. London: Pitman Publishing, 1995, pp. 30–41.

> the principle of the Rule of Law, the main rules on which the relevant legal arrangement or field of law is based. General principles of law are the unwritten primary law of the European Union. Due to the absence of a direct regulation of the law, the issue of the proportionality and justice of the contractual penalty has to be decided at the discretion of the court in accordance with the sense of justice and general principles of law specified in Article 5 of the Civil Procedure Law."[40]

> The *principle of legality* is concretized in the judgement of the Constitutional Court of 1 October 1999: "The fact that the decision of the [parliament] gives a task to the [government] does not contradict Article 1 of the Constitution, insofar as the mutual control and balance of power and the moderation of power, as well as other principles of a Rule of Law governed state are preserved.
> One of such principles, the principle of legality, states that the law and justice are binding on every state authority, including the legislator itself. The persons into whose hands legislative power has been transferred, after they have gathered in a certain order and created the laws, themselves are subject to the operation of these laws.
> In a democratic republic, the parliament must follow the constitution and other laws, including those passed by the parliament itself.
> Thus, the [parliament] has the right to give binding tasks to the [government], but they must not contradict the law."[41]

The concretization of general principles of law in the legal arrangement of Latvia has been carried out not only by the Constitutional Court or the Supreme Court Senate, but also at the lower levels of the courts of general jurisdiction.

> Thus, for example, the court of Riga city Vidzeme district, referring to Article 1 of the Constitution, which states that Latvia is an independent Democratic Republic, in the reasoning of its judgement of 27 December 2001, simultaneously recognized that "from it follows that in Latvia the *general principles of law* are observed and respected, including the *principle of proportionality* [author's emphasis]. When issuing an administrative act, a state official must observe the principle of proportionality. This means that the possible gains must be proportionate to the possible

40 Augstākās tiesas Senāta 2008. gada 14. maija spriedums lietā nr. SKC-212. Pieejams: at.gov.lv.

41 Judgement of the Constitutional Court of 1 October 1999.

losses that may occur to the rights, freedoms, and interests of individuals when an administrative act is issued. The means chosen must be appropriate and applied in the right place and cannot be more restrictive than necessary to achieve the legitimate aim."[42]

In this case, the official of the State Revenue Service imposed a fine on the representative of the state joint-stock company "Latvijas Nafta", without ascertaining whether the representative was also the liable person in the case, and confiscated almost 100,000 liters of diesel fuel, justifying this action only by the fact that the diesel fuel was stored in a place the address of which was not mentioned in the licenses of the company. The Court concluded that the adopted administrative act on the punishment of the representative of the state joint-stock company violated the principle of the procedural rights of the individual – the personality, degree of guilt, property status, mitigating and aggravating circumstances of the violator were not taken into account.

Furthermore, within the framework of this case, analysing another decision in a similar case, the Court also found a violation of the principle of equality: "According to Section 240 of the Code of Administrative Offenses of Latvia, administrative offense cases must be considered in accordance with the principle that all persons are *equal before the law* [author's emphasis] and institution, which examines the case. It follows that any difference established in the administrative act must be objectively justified. […] The complainant's objection that the State Revenue Service does not observe the principle of equality when applying an administrative penalty is well-founded, because […] although the State Revenue Service officials found the same violation in both cases – storage of fuel products at an address not specified in the license, but in the second case – also the sale of fuel products in the place unspecified in the license, which is recognized as a more serious violation, and as that was also admitted by the defendant's representative at the court session, a more harsh penalty is applied in the first case. At the court hearing, no evidence or explanations were obtained that this difference, applying opposite penalties for the same violation (imposing the maximum penalty in the first case, and exempting from administrative responsibility due to the minor nature of the violation in the second case), is objectively justified."[43]

42 Rīgas pilsētas Vidzemes priekšpilsētas tiesas 2001. gada 27. decembra spriedums lietā nr. C30-3554/5 2001. g. Nav publicēts.

43 Ibid.

> The *principle of proportionality* also manifested itself in the judgement of the Riga city Northern district court on 7 December 1999 in a case in which the decision of the Registry Department of Riga city Northern district was challenged. The Registry refused to issue a birth certificate to a child whose parents had given him the names Ferdinand Christopher Martin and whose surname after the father's surname of German nationality is Mentzen, changing the names and discarding the third name in accordance with then valid normative legal acts. In the reasoning of the judgement, the court referred to the European Convention for the Protection of Human Rights and Fundamental Freedoms and the case law of the European Court of Human Rights, concluding that "the right to privacy of person guaranteed in the Article 96 of the Constitution, as well as Article 8 of the European Convention for the Protection of Human Rights and Fundamental Freedoms [...] can be limited only if it is necessary in a democratic society [...], that is, if the granting of certain rights to a person could harm public interests", but "necessity in a democratic society" has to be understood as proportionality between what the state gains and what the individual loses". Thus, "refusing to register a child with the names 'Ferdinand Christopher Martin' and the surname 'Mentzen' the *principle of proportionality* [author's emphasis] between the state's benefit and the individual's loss is not respected", because "the fact that the child is given three names without Latvianizing them, and a surname identical to that of his father cannot in any way harm the public interest. On the other hand, refusing to register a child with three names chosen by his parents and Latvianizing the names and surname may harm the interests of the child, as doubts may arise about his kinship with the father, whose surname would be then significantly different from the child's surname."[44]

However, the concretization of general principles of law in the courts of Latvia has not always been successful. One of the main shortcomings in concretization is insufficient arguments provided by a court; that is, a court has referred to the application of general principles of law in an abstract way but has not specified them in relation to certain factual circumstances.

> Thus, for example, when checking compliance with the principle of proportionality, the court's justification for not taking this principle into

44 Rīgas pilsētas Ziemeļu rajona tiesas 1999. gada 7. decembra spriedums lietā nr. 2-3353/9 1999. g. Nav publicēts.

account in the case was based only on the statement "other means could have been used" not identifying at least one other means detected by the court.[45]

Similarly, insufficient concretization was allowed in the judgement of the Riga city Northern district court on 21 May 2003,[46] in which the Court, overruling the decision of the Riga City Council on the demolition of an arbitrary construction object in Riga, referred to the principle of proportionality and the principle of equality.[47] The Court, weighing the interests of the society and the individual within the scope of the principle of proportionality, recognized the economic aspect as the most important, and the only benefit of the society by demolishing the object of arbitrary construction, according to the court, was an attempt to preemptively convince the society not to carry out arbitrary construction. On the other hand, the Court had used the principle of equality to justify the overruling of the decision, because in none of the cases of arbitrary construction discovered in Riga in 2002, a decision had been made to demolish the object of arbitrary construction. Consequently, the complainant was put in a discriminatory position. Thus, the Court did not take into account the fact that the principle of equality does not create the right to equal treatment if the comparable situation is illegal. If one has obtained an illegal benefit, then the other cannot, based on principle of equality, consider that he also has the right to obtain such an illegal benefit. The system of laws is aimed at limiting illegal situations, not expanding them,[48] and the court has not only the right, but also the obligation to cast aside incorrect previous case law.

Identification of general principles of law is an important task of the legal doctrine; it is the task of legal scholars. By applying logical procedures, which are subject to various restrictions set by experience, methods and assessment of the public needs, the scholars indicate those basic concepts or general principles of law, which provide an opportunity for a judge to overcome the problem caused by the gaps in the law and pass a harmonized and rational judgement.[49]

45 Skujeniece V. *Latvijas tiesu spriedumu kvalitātes problēmas*. Rīga: Providus, 2003, 50. lpp.
46 Rīgas pilsētas Ziemeļu rajona tiesas 2003. gada 21. maija spriedums lietā nr. C-322182-02, C-397-03/3. Nav publicēts.
47 On the analysis of this case in detail see Čepāne I., Meiere S. 2003.
48 Cf.: Levits E. Par tiesiskās vienlīdzības principu. 2003.
49 See more Cueto-Rua J.C. 1981, p. 122.

For example, the doctrinally concretized *principle of good faith* means that "everyone should exercise their subjective rights and fulfil their subjective duties, respecting the legitimate interests of other persons".[50]

The *principle of legal security* guarantees a predictable environment and states that people should be able to plan their lives safely, being aware of the legal consequences of their actions.[51] The doctrinally concretized content of the *principle of legal certainty* which alongside with the principle of protection of legitimate expectations[52] are derived from the general principle of law of legal security means that "an individual should have the opportunity to learn the content of the applicable legal norms so that he/she can plan his/her actions accordingly".[53] In the concretization of the principle of protection of legitimate expectations, the following theses can be found in the legal doctrine: "[A] fundamental prerequisite for the protection of legitimate expectations is the Rule of Law. [...] Administrative decisions favourable to [a person] cannot be revoked if the beneficiary has relied on the permanence of the administrative act and his/her reliance is worthy of protection, balancing the public interest of the revocation. [...] For example, the legitimate expectations of the beneficiary are not protected if he/she has obtained the administrative act by fraudulent deception, threats, or bribery. [...] The legal content of the protection of legitimate expectations also is not fulfilled in cases where the beneficiary has obtained an administrative act by providing information that was incorrect or incomplete in essential aspects. [...] Finally, the legal content of protection of legitimate expectations is not fulfilled when the beneficiary knew about the illegality of the administrative act or did not know it due to gross negligence."[54] Referring to the law of Germany, the Netherlands and the European Union, the doctrine states that "the principle of protection of legitimate expectations is

50 See Balodis K. 2002, 280. lpp.; Brox H. *Allgemeiner Teil des BGB*. 25. Aufl. Köln, Berlin, Bonn, München: Carl Heymanns Verlag, 2001, Rn. 640; Hartkamp A., Hesselink M., Hondius E., Joustra C., du Perron E. (Eds.) *Towards a European Civil Code*. 2nd ed. Nijmegen: Ars Aequi Libri; The Hague, London, Boston: Kluwer Law International, 1998, p. 288.

51 Turk A. *Judicial Review in EU Law*. Cheltenham: Edward Elgar Publishing Ltd., 2009.

52 Rezevska D. 2011.

53 Tridimas T. *The General Principles of EC Law*. Oxford: Oxford University Press, 2000, p. 163.

54 See Briede J. Par labvēlīga un prettiesiska akta atcelšanu. *Likums un Tiesības*, 2002, 4. sēj., nr. 5 (33), 153. lpp.; Cf. arī: Peine F.J. *Allgemeines Verwaltungsrecht. Schwerpunkte.* Heidelberg: Müller C.F. Verlag, 1998, S. 204-206.

> considered an expression of subjective rights arising from the principle of legal security".[55]

As was already mentioned above, the main methodological guideline that the applier of legal norms should keep in mind when determining the content or concretizing a general principle of law is that those principles have to be oriented to a reasonable and just solution – the one which corresponds to the Basic Norm, and that in the determination of the content of the relevant principle the method of comparison and typification ("belonging to the same type") is used. The case to be solved is compared with other similar cases, which have already been solved in the case law based on certain principles. Each new case, new event, contains different factual circumstances that have occurred at different stages of the development of the legal arrangement in different legal, social, economic, ethical, etc. situations. Each such new case reveals a new nuance of the content in the concretization of the general principle of law, which, until this new and specific case, had not yet been grasped or realized by those applying the legal norms, although at the unwritten level of the legal norm it was already an element of the content of the general principle of law.

> Thus, for example, two cases examined consecutively by the Court, which contained similar factual compositions, very clearly show how a general principle of law is filled with ever new, developed content. In the first case, the protection of legitimate expectations was referred to by a pensioner who had applied to the institution with a request to stop the payment of a pension so that he could later receive a pension again, based on the promise of an employee of the institution that this is possible according to the existing legal framework. However, it turned out that the written legal norm that granted the pensioner such a subjective right had lost its validity a few days before the institution's employee made the promise, which now turned out to be illegal. Without delving into the further nuances of the case, which was legally qualified as a hard case, and the Court turned to the Constitutional Court during its review, it must be concluded that in this case the Court recognized a person's right to protection of legitimate expectations.[56]

55 Onževs M. Nodokļu regulējuma grozījumu spēks laikā: Satversmes tiesas prakse. *Jurista Vārds*, 2011, nr. 17.

56 Administratīvās apgabaltiesas 2004. gada 14. decembra spriedums lietā nr. AA21-04/2. Nav publicēts.

On the other hand, in the second case, where the institution again made an illegal promise, in the opinion of the Court the person did not have the right to the protection of legitimate expectations. It was determined by new factual circumstances, which were different from the factual circumstances of the first case and, therefore, demanded from the Court a new element of concretization in the content of the principle of protection of legitimate expectations. In this case, the person was the authorized person of the voters' union, who submitted the list of candidates for deputies to the Election Commission. Since the document was found to be incomplete, the chairman of the Election Commission verbally offered the representative to submit the corrected document containing the list of candidates the next day, even though the normative legal acts clearly and unequivocally set the date on which the deadline for submitting the candidate lists expires, and it was the day when the inaccuracies in the document were found.

Therefore, the Court, concretizing the content of the principle of protection of legitimate expectations, concluded that legal expectations cannot be protected if the promise given by the institution is *clearly* illegal and the person could easily realize it – an illegal promise can enjoy legal protection only if the normative regulation was unclear, one that requires special legal expertise to interpret. Besides, unlike the first case where the person was a pensioner, in this case the person was a potential election candidate who had to be familiar with the law governing elections. Consequently, the Court established a new factual circumstance, namely, the *person knew or should have known* that the institution's promise was illegal, which was the reason why legitimate expectations could not be created.[57]

1.2 *Solving of Mutual Collisions*

Collisions or competitions between legal norms may be solved in two ways:

1) by reinterpreting these norms and trying to harmonize them, or
2) by setting an order of priority for the colliding norms.[58]

The order of priority may be established on the basis of:

1) legal force, according to the hierarchical relation;

---

57 Administratīvās apgabaltiesas 2005. gada 29. aprīļa spriedums lietā nr.: AA1124-05/1. Nav publicēts. Later, the legislator approved this legal norm found by the courts and reflected in the case law, making it positive in paragraph 5 of the second part of Section 86 of the Administrative Procedure Law.

58 See Iļjanova D. 2000.

2) connection of speciality, according to the number of characteristic features of the legal content;
3) temporal applicability, according to the time of origin of the relevant legal norms.

Therefore, in order to determine in what way to solve the collision between the colliding principles of law, the mechanism of their functional effect should be analysed, respectively, it has to be determined whether the mutual hierarchy of the principles exists – that is, whether general principles of law have different legal force, or if the principles may be distinguished based on the number of characteristic features of their legal content, or time of their origin.

The Western legal system provides for several approaches in respect of the issue of mutual hierarchy of general principles of law. Firstly, two different opinions can be found, namely, that general principles of law differ by the aspect of legal force; and secondly, that all general principles of law are similar as of the aspect of legal force. Further, there are several opinions in respect of the criterion, which determines that general principles of law have a different legal force. The most widespread is the opinion that the legal force of general principles of law can be various and depends on the legal force of that normative legal act, in which a principle is positivised or from which it is discovered.[59]

> Thus, for example, the Constitutional Court of Belgium in the case of harmonizing the pension system, in which the legal norm had an eight-year retroactive effect, but only in relation to one category of pensioners (those who retired after 31 December 1993), writes in the argumentation of the judgement: "The principle of the prohibition of retroactive force is not a constitutional principle in itself. It is revealed from legislative acts, mainly from Section 2 of the Civil Code, and has the character of a general principle of law. [...] The constitutional principle of equality and non-discrimination means that no category of population can be discriminated against by applying the retroactive force of the norm; the principle of legal security is also important here. The guarantee of equal treatment gives these latter principles, when combined with the principles of equality and non-discrimination, constitutional status."[60]

However, this opinion hardly stands criticisms, and, looking at the above-mentioned argumentation, it has to be concluded that it looks more like a legal

59 For example, see Levits E. 2000, 262.–270. lpp.
60 Venice Commission. *Bulletin on Constitutional Case Law*. BEL-1997-1-002.

fiction, in order not to depart from the legal positivism doctrine, but to justify, in the Court's opinion, the necessary constitutional status of the principle of inadmissibility of retroactive effect in this case. As stated in Chapter 2, all of the general principles of law are deemed to be those principles that are derived from the Basic Norm, functioning in a Democratic, Rule of Law governed State, and the generally binding character of these principles comes not from the written legal norms, but from the sovereign, whose act of will formulated the Basic Norm. Hence, the opinion that the legal force of a general principle of law depends on the normative legal act in which it is positivised or from where it is discovered, could be called the positivist approach for the determination of the hierarchy of general principles of law.

The second approach that supports the statement that general principles of law have different legal force is based on the opinion that some of the principles have a higher, exclusive legal force than others. Namely, as all general principles of law are based on justice, it would always prevail over other principles of law. However, this opinion also can be criticized and as exemplified below, there are cases when justice has to retreat in the face of, for example, proportionality.

The author supports the opinion that there are no *a priori* existing hierarchical relations between general principles of law based on the factor of legal force. Namely, the functional difference between general principles of law and the written legal norms lies in the fact that the principles have the "dimension of weight".[61]

In addition, a collision of principles differs from a collision of written legal norms as the content-conflicting principles are valid at the same time, despite the collision, and must be taken into account at the same time of consideration; their validity is a prerequisite for collision. On the other hand, not all mutually contradictory written legal norms can be valid at the same time, that is to be true, for example, when legal norms of higher and lower legal force collide. Principles having a "dimension of weight" means that if a collision occurs among the principles, one has to determine which principle has a bigger "weight" in the relevant situation,[62] taking into consideration specific

61 Cf.: Peczenik A. 1989, pp. 418–425; Alexy R. 1986, S. 77 ff; Sieckamnn von J.R. 1994; Iljanova D. 2000, 251. lpp.

62 MacCormik N. *Legal Reasoning and Legal Theory*. Oxford, Oxford University Press, 1995, p. 155. It is necessary to distinguish the hierarchical relations of principles, which would be based on the criterion of legal force, from the relations of priority, which are clarified in each specific case, by ascertaining the "weight" of the principles. Therefore, the term "hierarchy" should not be used when talking about the mutual priority of the principles to be evaluated and established for a given case. For example, see Levits E. 2003, 200. lpp.

social, economic, political, and other circumstances in the relevant country at the specific moment in time. This "weighing and balancing" of the principles is a complicated, time-consuming intellectual process that the judge must carry out based on his/her experience, intuition, and knowledge.

Solving the collision of principles by the *method of weighing and balancing*, the *best possible compromise* is obtained. In order to perform the best possible weighing of the principles, one should consider as many relevant arguments for and against the conclusion in the respective issue as possible, and the relative weight of these arguments should be determined. Respectively, objectively the best evaluation is the evaluation where the applier of legal norms has taken into consideration all relevant arguments in respect of the decision as well as all relevant counterarguments, i.e., those arguments, which support the opposite conclusion in the relevant issue.[63]

Similarly, it is impossible to establish the order of priority for general principles of law based on the connection of speciality or temporal applicability because it is not possible to determine which of the general principles of law in respect of their contents is "more general", namely, contains less characteristic features of the legal content than any other "special or less general" principle.[64] It is impossible for the reason that considering their contents all general principles of law are just or are the principles of "right law",[65] as they are derived from the ideas of the Rule of Law governed State and justice, and they are all equally general in terms of the certainty of the legal content of a legal norm. It is also impossible to set an order of priority for general principles of law taking into consideration their time of origin due to the simple reason that all general principles of law of the relevant legal arrangement become valid simultaneously – they become valid, generally binding legal norms in the relevant country at the moment of origin of the legal arrangement.[66] Therefore, a collision between general principles of law can be solved not by setting an order of priority, but by harmonizing them.

As already mentioned above, the process of the application of a general principle of law will always be accompanied by another principle, because principles, unlike written legal norms, have a "dimension of weight". The collision of principles involves a number of complex problems.

63 Peczenik A. Legal Rules and Moral Principles. *Rechtstheorie*, 1991, no. 11, pp. 152–153.

64 On the understanding of the connection of speciality and the problems of contrasting of more general and less general legal norms see Buls M. 2003.

65 See Larenz K. 1979, S. 43–44.

66 See similarly Kalniņš E. 2000, 216. lpp.

The complete logical incompatibility of written legal norms can be analysed analytically and *in abstracto*, without the need to take into account the differences of a specific case, when one norm prohibits exactly the same thing that the other allows or commands. On the other hand, the collision of principles occurs only in specific cases.[67] This means that the collision of principles can be resolved only based on the materials of a specific case – on the specific social, economic, political, etc. situation at the specific moment in time when the collision of principles is resolved, weighing and evaluating the importance or, on the contrary, the insignificance of the colliding principles.

Thus, following one principle rarely completely excludes the possibility of following another principle as well. Therefore, we have to talk about the so-called weighing and comparison, or evaluation: increasing adherence to one principle leads to decreasing adherence to some other principle. Suppose one principle requires justice and the other requires economic efficiency or proportionality. In some cases, increased justice leads to decreased efficiency and *vice versa*.

> For example, on 11 March 1998, the Constitutional Court issued a judgement in case no. 04-05(97)[68] regarding the compliance of the so-called normative legal acts – "explanation" and "joint explanation" of the Ministry of Finance and Ministry of Economy regarding the re-evaluation of fixed assets in the accounting of privatized companies with the legal norms of higher legal force. In this case the collision of several general principles of law was directly encountered, therefore it was necessary to evaluate how these principles should be applied in the specific case:
>
> "When deciding the question of the time from which the contested legal acts could lose their force, the Constitutional Court evaluated in connection such principles of law as the principle of justice, the principle of legality, the principle of separation of power and the principle of trust in law. When comparing the *importance of these principles of law in this case* [author's emphasis], such elements of the principle – trust in law, as: the effect of the retroactive force of the judgement on public and private interests, are of essential importance; the long-term nature of the legal relationship that arose on the basis of the joint explanation; possible changes in the legal status of those privatization subjects who relied on the legality of the joint explanation [...] and explanation, and others."

---

67 Peczenik A. 1989, pp. 418–425; Iļjanova D. 2000, 251. lpp.

68 Judgement of the Constitutional Court of 11 March 1998.

> In this decision, solving the collision between the principle of justice and the principle of trust in law the considerations of economic efficiency prevailed over those of justice, and as a result, the state treasury and thus taxpayers lost several millions, but the Constitutional Court, weighing the importance of the principles, concluded that the economic and social situation of the time did not allow for another solution. If justice were to prevail, the employees of many privatized companies would lose their jobs, many privatized companies would go bankrupt, and this could have unpredictable consequences for the country's economic system. On the other hand, after ten years, if examining the same case and reassessing the importance of the colliding principles, it is possible that the decision would be completely opposite, because the economic situation would have stabilized, the unemployment benefit would be such as being able to compensate the real life expenses, etc., respectively, the social and economic conditions would have changed, and then, considering the colliding principles, the scales would by great chance tip in favour of justice.

Weighing and balancing, or re-evaluation, is not only a method of resolving a collision of principles, but it should also be used in cases of incompatibility of written legal norms as the first collision norm stipulates that any collision of legal norms should be in the first place prevented by re-interpreting (and thus harmonizing) these norms and only if it is not possible – determining the order of priority between them.

In case of collision of written legal norms, when one of the conflicting norms is followed, very often the other norm is not followed. In terms of principles, as was shown above, such a case could rather be an exception. In some situations, increased freedom leads to decreased equality and *vice versa*, but a decision should not be made without fully considering both: the right to freedom and the right to equality of the people involved.

However, in some cases one of the colliding principles must be completely excluded in the sense that, taking into account all the circumstances of the case, it cannot affect the decision.

> Thus, for example, the principle of *pacta sunt servanda*, positivised in Sections 1587 and 1588 of the Civil Law, providing that "[a] contract legally entered into shall impose on a contracting party a duty to perform that which was promised, and neither the exceptional difficulty of the transaction, nor difficulties in performance arising later, shall give the right to one party to withdraw from the contract, even if the other party is

compensated for losses. [...] One party may not withdraw from a contract without the consent of the other party, even if the latter fails to perform it and due to the failure to perform it",

can be excluded if the case is related to an unreasonable contract that does not have to be fulfilled at all: "Unilateral withdrawal from a contract shall be permitted only when it is based on the nature of the contract, or when the law provides for it in certain circumstances, or when such right was expressly contracted for" (Section 1589 of the Civil Law).

Or another example: the Court of Riga city Zemgale district, while examining the application of a state gymnasium for postponing the execution of the court judgement, found that two principles of law had collided, namely, the principle that the contract and the judgement must be fulfilled – *pacta sunt servanda*, and the principle of protection of the best interests of a child. The gymnasium asked the Court to postpone the obligation imposed on it by the judgement to fulfil the contract concluded with company "A" for providing food services, arguing that at the given time it is the middle of a school year, and another company provides food for the students. If the contract with the company that provides school food services were terminated in the middle of a school year, students would not be provided with these services for an indefinite period of time. Although company "A" promised to install the necessary equipment for the providing of food services within one month, the Court decided that, "evaluating the case materials in its entirety [...], the postponement of the execution of the court judgement is justified [...], [because] state gymnasium for the school year of 2000/2001 had already before the court judgement concluded a contract for the provision of food services with another company, and the compulsory enforcement of the court judgement is related to the suspension of food services at the school for at least one month; the court finds it possible to postpone the enforcement of the judgement, *because otherwise the interests of the children would not be respected, which are valued higher than the interests of company ["A"] to immediately resume the execution of the interrupted contract* [author's emphasis]".[69] However, if such a question were to be examined, for example, during the school's summer holidays, based on the specific moment

69 Rīgas pilsētas Zemgales priekšpilsētas tiesas 2001. gada 2. aprīļa lēmums lietā nr. 2-420/2000. Nav publicēts.

in time and circumstances, the principle of protection of the best interests of a child would not even be able to affect the decision.

1.3 *Evaluative Subsumption*

In its true meaning the subsumption of the factual composition to the legal content of a legal norm is possible only in the case where characteristics (elements) or features of the legal content are sufficiently determined and may be defined. But undefined or open-ended legal concepts, which have to be filled with certain content, including also general principles of law, have no such closed definitions, although they are analysed in the legal science, applied in judicial practice etc. Subordination of a life situation to such concepts is not subsumption but "evaluative subordination" or "evaluative subsumption". Instead of the conclusion that the life situation "presents" features of the legal content we have the conclusion that the life situation is similar to another life situation that has already been settled.[70]

Thus, the "evaluative subsumption" is needed in the so-called hard cases, where the simple or regular subsumption is not sufficient. In these cases, one faces a moral dilemma and that is why it is impossible to pass a decision only on the grounds of the written legal norm and description of facts. In order to understand the concept "hard cases" it is easier to find out what is meant by the opposite – easy or routine cases.

Easy cases may be characterized by several features, for example, they are adjudicated quite "mechanically",[71] where "mechanically" shall not be understood in the literal meaning. Application of legal norms as an intellectual and individual activity of each judge cannot be expressed by a precise and universal formula for all cases. Mechanical adjudication of easy cases can be seen in the procedure of decision-making and creation of arguments for supporting these decisions. The case to be adjudicated is unambiguous: the written legal norm (the basis of the legal syllogism or Major Premise) after application of the interpretation method is clear, and it is legitimate or constitutional; the established facts do not cast doubt; and there is only one possible solution to the case, which also provides a just (in accordance with the principle of a Democratic State governed by the Rule of Law) answer to the case and it is

---

70 See Larenz K., Canaris C.W. 1995, S. 95; Kalniņš E. Tiesību normu piemērošanas loģiskā shēma. 2000, 152. lpp.

71 Aarnio A. 1986, p. 1; Lyons D. Justification and judicial responsibility. *Legal Reasoning*, 1992, Vol. I, p. 147; Gaidele I. Tiesas nolēmumu argumentācijas problēmas. *Likums un Tiesības*, 2003, 5. sēj., nr. 8 (48), nr. 9 (49).

determined by that written legal norm.[72] Any doubts and uncertainties on the applicable written legal norm, its content, purposes, and cases of application are prevented by the legal method: interpretation, collision norms etc., so the judge does not need to choose from different competing possible solutions of the case with the help of additional considerations. Secondly, easy cases are supported only with legal arguments, i.e., arguments arising from sources of law. The empirical basis here serves only to prove the legal contents of the argument. In addition, the outcome of easy cases is very predictable, and these cases make up the majority of all cases adjudicated in the courts of general jurisdiction or administrative courts.[73]

> So, for example, Peczenik gives the example of the evaluative subsumption which manifested itself in the following hard case adjudicated by the judiciary of Sweden: [74] the facts of the case were such that person K., threatening the bank cashier with a gun, obtained a certain amount of money. It later turned out that he had a toy gun in his hands. Although the Criminal Code of Sweden stipulated that the threat must be real in the case of robbery, the Swedish Supreme Court ruled that such actions do not qualify as theft, but as robbery. This decision was based on the following subsumption:
> Major Premise – if someone steals using violence or real threats, then [he/she] should be punished for robbery.
> Minor Premise – person K. obtained money by threatening the victim, who (incorrectly) interpreted it as a real threat.
> Conclusion – person K. should be punished for robbery.
> This conclusion does not follow from premises 1 and 2, so for the conclusion to be logically correct, one more premise must be added:
>
> Major Premise – if someone steals using violence or real threats, then [he/she] should be punished for robbery.
> Minor Premise – person K. obtained money by threatening the victim, who (incorrectly) interpreted it as a real threat.
> The Third Premise – threats that the victim interpreted as real should be treated the same as threats that are actually real.
> Conclusion – person K. should be punished for robbery.

---

72 Klami H.T. General norms and legal reasoning. Legal, social and teleological norms as explanations of legal decision meaning. *Legal Reasoning*, 1992, Vol. 11, p. 170.

73 Aarnio A. 1986, p. 1.

74 See Peczenik A. 1989, pp. 19–20.

The Third Premise is a legal norm that was *found* by the court itself in the form of an unwritten legal norm in the system of laws. Here of course the question of the legitimacy of such a "found legal norm" arises or more precisely, the legitimacy of the courts, which are not directly legitimized by the sovereign, actions itself. The answer follows directly from the theory of the general principles of law and their direct connection with the Basic Norm which in turn is the act of the will of the sovereign. Namely, legal methods are general principles of law, and they or rather the application of them legitimize the actions of a court; evaluative subsumption where the court finds the legal norm can happen only on the basis of a written legal norm as the Major Premise of the syllogism. Thus, there has to be a written legal norm adopted by a democratically directly legitimized legislator and this written legal norm has to be modified because the legislator did not manage to write it down properly – in compliance with the general principles of law and the Basic Norm, and that is why now it is the courts' turn to correct the situation[75] *using legal methods*[76] authorized to them by the sovereign on the basis of another general principle of law derived from the Basic Norm: the principle of separation of power. Further, according to the principle of separation of power, the court always has to give a justification for such a norm – the Third Premise – as it has to prove to the sovereign that such a legal norm, as derived from the Basic Norm of a Democratic State based on the Rule of Law, in reality already existed and was valid in the system of laws.

> In the above example, the Third Premise is based on the following value judgements, which are given to the sovereign proving that the found legal norm already existed in the system of laws as valid unwritten legal norm: the existing threat was "no better" than a real threat, because the victim perceived it as a real threat; expected consequences: a lighter sentence will increase the number of such crimes; it will also lead victims to believe that the weapons they are being threatened with are game weapons, which in turn will lead to situations when victims would ignore the threats and thus put their lives at risk; another value judgement: such a risk is unacceptable.[77]

75 That follows from the general principle of prohibition of legal obstruction. See also in Chapter 2.2.4.

76 Of course, it is needless to add that legal methods should be applied in a correct manner and only then they legitimize the actions of a court.

77 Peczenik A. 1989, p. 20.

> In this particular case, the court derived the Third Premise from the general principles of law of justice, equal treatment, and right to life actually evading the principle of prohibition of analogy in public law to the detriment of the defendant.[78]

Therefore, the process of application of general principles of law will always be in the form of evaluative subsumption, with the court finding the Third Premise, which is the concretization of the general principle of law in relation to the specific factual circumstances. The Third Premise of a legal syllogism is called both a value judgement and an axiological premise,[79] thus indicating the evaluative nature of the process of its finding and formulation.

On the other hand, if there is no written legal norm which regulates a similar actual situation, there is nothing to put in the legal syllogism in the place of the Major Premise, then it means that the rare situation of a "gap of law" exists (and not the gap of the law). This means that there is a lack of an entire legal institute, a set of the written legal norms regulating a specific legal issue, and in this case according to the principle of separation of power, legislators' action is needed as courts do not have such authorisation from the sovereign and by the Basic Norm, and according to the natural law doctrine to create new legal institutes or new legal rights. While within legal positivism if the case cannot be resolved by the written legal norm, which is adopted by any state institution in advance, the judge has a "discretion" to decide the case either way in reality legislating new legal rights and applying them retrospectively to the case at hand,[80] and that is completely opposite to what contemporary legal theory pertaining to Democratic States based on the Rule of Law stands for, according to the doctrine and legal understanding of natural law.[81]

---

78 The principle of prohibition of analogy in public law, worsening the condition of the subject, has developed in the continental European legal system compared to the understanding of the Soviet legal system. This development is based on the principle of justice and the principle of "equality before the law" derived from it. In other words, substantially similar human actions should be regulated and treated similarly, that is, ethical evaluations and essentially similar results created by persons' actions are considered (See Peczenik A. 1989, p. 400; Iļjanova D. 2002, 104.–106. lpp.; Slaņķe G. Tiesību tālākveidošana krimināltiesībās. *Jurista Vārds*, 2012, nr. 37.).

79 Wroblewski J. *The Judicial Application of Law.* Bankowski Z., MacCormick N. (Eds.) Dordrecht, Boston, London: Kluwer Academic Publishers, 1992, p. 210; Peczenik A. 1989, p. 20.

80 Dworkin R. 1977, 1978, p. 81.

81 On filling the gaps of the law applying the legal method of further development of law see Chapter 4.2.3.

The most recent example of this type of gap – gap of law – which is to be considered as rare gap presented itself in the judgement of 21 January 2021[82] in the case of Supreme Court Senate on the registration of the relationship between same-sex couple, where the Court states:

"[17] [I]t can be concluded that the first sentence of Article 110 of the Constitution, in connection with the principle of human dignity, establishes a legal obligation for the state to ensure the possibility for families of same-sex couples to legally strengthen their family relationships and be recognized by the state. The legislator has not fulfilled this obligation, because neither the Civil Status Act Registration Law nor any other law provides for the recognition and registration of such family relationships. Nor can it be established that any significant public interests would justify non-fulfilment of this obligation, that is, no legally justified reason for non-fulfilment of this obligation can be established.

[...] [21] [...] However, as follows from the decisions of the panels of the Constitutional Court of 7 July 2021 and 8 October 2021, the legislator can decide from a legal policy point of view whether to regulate the legal recognition of the family relations of a same-sex couple as the registration of a civil status act in the Civil Status Act Registration Act or in some other law determining some other mechanism. Therefore, the court cannot to impose an obligation on [...] the registry office to register the applicants' family relationships as a civil status act.

[...] [23] [...] Until the legislator has created the appropriate legal framework, such a judgement, which has established that the relationships of certain persons are recognized as family relationships within the meaning of Article 110 of the Constitution, will also replace the registration of these relationships implemented by the state. Therefore, it can be used in other situations when it is necessary to justify that these persons are guaranteed some rights intended for families."

Namely, the court stated that *the gap of the law* could be detected in this case, and it is regarding the legal recognition of the family relationship between same-sex couple, but regarding in what way this legal recognition will be regulated *the gap of law* exists and thus it falls under the discretion of the legislator.[83]

---

82 Augstākās tiesas Senāta 2021. gada 21. janvāra spriedums lietā nr. SKA-[B1]/2021. Pieejams: at.gov.lv.

83 On the issue of the legal recognition of the family relationship of same-sex couples see also: judgements of the Constitutional Court of 12 November 2020 and of 8 April 2021 in case no. 2020-34-03. Available: satv.tiesa.gov.lv. Judgements of the European Court of

As is mentioned above, the Court has a duty before the sovereign always to substantiate the derivation or discovery of such a norm, providing a *coherent chain of value judgements*, as without them the argumentation of the decision will be unintelligible and obscure to the public.[84] It lacks legitimacy, as the sovereign is not able to follow the legal thinking process, which led the Court to the given result showing the legal methods applied. The absence of such value judgements in the case of evaluative subsumption would allow the Court decision to be recognized as illegal due to its insufficient reasoning and thus inconsistent with the principle of necessity for justification and prohibition of arbitrariness. Thus, when a decision is based on the general principle of law, it must be comprehensively and widely justified, showing all the value judgements that lie at the basis for the finding and formulating of the Third Premise. When giving the coherent chain of value judgements, the Court has to answer the questions of what would happen or what general principles of law would be violated if the Court would not have found such an unwritten legal norm in the system of laws.

> An example of how a Court should apply a general principle of law in the form of evaluative subsumption, providing a long and coherent chain of value judgements, is, for example, the judgement of the Supreme Court Senate of 14 January 2008[85] in the case regarding the refusal of the registry office to make changes in the birth register of a person due to gender change. In this case, a person asked the state to make corrections to her birth record by recording her gender following gender reassignment surgeries that the person had been unable to complete due to objective circumstances beyond her control. The Court was faced with the lack of written regulation and, referring to the principle of prohibition of legal obstruction, applied the principles of justice, equality, protection of legitimate expectations, and right to private life in resolving the case.

Human Rights reflecting the level of the European consensus on this issue: judgement of the European Court of Human Rights (Grand Chamber) of 17 January 2023: *Fedotova and Others v. Russia*; judgement of the European Court of Human Rights (Section) of 21 July 2015: *Oliari and Others v. Italy*, applications nos. 18766/11 and 36030/11; judgement of the European Court of Human Rights (Grand Chamber) of 7 November 2013: *Vallianatos and Others v. Greece*, applications nos. 29381/09 and 32684/09; judgement of the European Court of Human Rights (Section) of 22 November 2010: *Schalk and Kopf v. Austria*, application no. 30141/04. Available: hudoc.echr.coe.int.

84 On the importance of general principles of law in the reasoning of the decision, see more detailed Chapter 4.2.4.

85 Augstākās tiesas Senāta 2008. gada 14. janvāra spriedums lietā SKA-5/2008. Pieejams: tiesas.lv.

The Court concluded that "in general, the general principle in European countries is the legal recognition of gender change, if it has occurred. From the [written] legal norms of Latvia, it can be concluded that the country allows the possibility of both changing the gender and supplementing the entry in the birth register accordingly. On the other hand, there is a lack of [written] legal norms[86] that would determine the criteria to be followed in order to establish whether gender change in the sense of the law has taken place. The state should determine in a person-friendly way as much as possible if and when there is an objective basis for supplementing birth register entries. In addition, in the course of the administrative procedure, in the course of clarifying the circumstances and making a decision on supplementing the birth register, the *prohibition of legal obstruction* must be observed, that is, the institution and the court must not refuse to decide on the issue arguing that the issue is not regulated by the law or other external normative act. *Since there is currently no more specific legal regulation, the institution and the court must fill the concept of "gender change" with content*, respecting human rights norms as much as possible [author's inserts and emphasis]."

The scheme of evaluative subsumption in this case looks like this:
Major Premise: If a person (F1)[87] has undergone all gender reassignment surgeries (F2), then has the right to correct their gender record.
Minor Premise: A person (F1) has undergone gender reassignment surgery, but has not completed it due to objective, impartial circumstances(F3), the changes are irreversible (F4), the person looks and identifies himself/herself psychologically and socially according to the new gender (F5).
The Third Premise: If a person (F1) has undergone all gender reassignment surgeries (F2) or has undergone gender reassignment surgery and has not completed it due to objective, impartial circumstances (F3), and the changes are irreversible(F4), and he/she looks and identifies himself/herself psychologically and socially according to the new gender (F5), then [the person] has the right to amend the birth record.
\+ Right to private life
The principle of equality

86 Here the Court obviously thinks that there is a lack of *written* legal norms. Thus, the Court concludes that there is an open gap in the law, which can be eliminated through further development of the law, applying the method of analogy.

87 Where "F" is a feature of legal or factual content, composition.

The principle of justice
The principle of protection of legitimate expectations

Conclusion of the Syllogism: A person has the right to an amendment regarding the change of gender in the birth register.

Value judgements:

1 Medical progress, especially gender reassignment surgery, today makes it possible to perform body corrections, matching physical and psychological gender and thus giving a person gender identity, which is a defining characteristic of personality. Such changes should be reflected accordingly in the data on the person's civil status – otherwise, transsexual persons would be subject to discrimination and significant invasions of private life, arising from the discrepancy between the position in society assumed by the person after the operations and the legal status.

2 Gender includes not only the biological features characterizing women and men, which are basically determined by the differences in the genitals, but also psychological features (how a person identifies himself/herself) and social features, which are a set of specific characteristics formed under the influence of culture, which determine the social behaviour of women and men.

3 When determining the gender of a transsexual person, relying solely on the statement of a doctor or a medical institution about a gender change is insufficient and inadequate, since a wider set of factors must be evaluated in determining the gender change.

4 Actual changing of biological features of gender requires multiple and serious medical manipulations and causes significant physical changes, including irreversible ones. Therefore, a person's choice to change gender cannot be considered a frivolous or arbitrary choice. The difficulty or impossibility of performing the operations necessary for a complete gender change in a short period of time cannot limit a person's right to belong to the social group to which he/she feels he/she belongs, if the person performs voluntary and, moreover, irreversible actions to achieve this goal.

5 The State is obliged to recognize a person's gender change in order to prevent situations where a person has a difference between his/her actual gender (including its perception in society) and legal status. The State must fulfil this obligation, regardless of whether the regulatory framework provides or does not provide for the criteria by which gender change can be determined and the procedure by which it is determined. If the relevant issue is

not regulated in detail in the country, the institution and the court must fill the concept of "gender change" with content, respecting human rights norms as much as possible.

2 The Impact of General Principles of Law on the Application of Written Legal Norms

2.1 *Collisions and Validity*

When it is possible to solve the case based on any written legal norm, general principles of law are also highly significant in this process; they regulate and accompany the entire process of the application of legal norms. The main issue discussed in this chapter is how the functional effect of the general principles of law finds expression in the application of a written legal norm, taking into account that they determine the contents of written legal norms and act as the criteria of their legitimacy.[88]

Speaking about the functional effect of general principles of law the issue of their legal force and place in respect of the normative legal acts should not be forgotten. It is also important to note the emergence of collisions between general principles of law and written legal norms, and the problem of solving such collisions.

The problem of hierarchy of independent sources of law in general is discussed in Chapter 2.1., where it is concluded that general principles of law in the legal arrangement of Latvia (and thus in the legal arrangement of any Democratic State based on the Rule of Law) have supra-positive force in the hierarchy of independent sources of law or they are above the normative legal acts.

The judgement of the Supreme Court Senate of 12 January 2005[89] is an example of the confirmation of the supra-positive force of general principles of law. The Court concludes:

"Having familiarized with the case materials and checked the legality of the judgement with regard to the arguments relating to the cassation complaint, which are determined in the first part of Section 473 of the Civil Procedure Law, which regulates the limits of examination of the case in the court of cassation instance, the Senate recognizes that

---

88 Compare with conclusions of Chapter 2 and Chapter 3.

89 Augstākās tiesas Senāta 2005. gada 12. janvāra spriedums lietā nr. SKC-22. Nav publicēts.

the court's judgement has to be annulled, because, *in adjudicating the dispute, the principle of justice was ignored* [author's emphasis].

[…] The Senate believes that the mentioned aspects cannot serve as an obstacle to the settlement of the dispute, based on the general principle of justice established in Section 1 of the Civil Law, which, first of all, presumes the prevention of infringement of personal rights and legal interests, which are related to the specific nature of the dispute (basically, the collision between the property rights and obligation rights regulation), relegating legal nuances behind for achieving this purpose."

Likewise, the Administrative District Court, in the judgement of 2 November 2004, in the case regarding the maternity allowance of an official of the specialized civil service, a police officer, which was determined by the written legal norm to be several times smaller compared to the amount of the maternity benefit set for general civil service officials, the collision between the general principle of law and the written legal norm is resolved in a way, that the general principles of law – the principle of justice and equality – prevail over the written legal norm adopted by the legislator: "The court considers that, in accordance with the stated objective of the law, when deciding to grant some benefit to state civil service officials, the state should, in accordance with the principle of legal equality, observe *equal treatment in relation to all civil servants under the same conditions* [author's emphasis]. Different treatment is necessary when civil servants are in different circumstances."[90]

Moreover, in the judgement of 8 March 2007,[91] the Supreme Court Senate determined: "The state of Latvia is obliged to ensure a fair balance between the individual's right to family life and the interests of society in the field of immigration control. The legislator is not always able to achieve such a balance when adopting legal norms, therefore the obligation to observe the balance also rests with the law applier, who evaluates each case individually. Therefore, when issuing *any type* of administrative act, *including a mandatory* administrative act, the institution must assess whether it does not *disproportionately restrict a person's fundamental rights* [author's emphasis]." Therefore, when applying even an imperative

90 Administratīvās rajona tiesas 2004. gada 2. novembra spriedumā lietā nr. A42140204. Nav publicēts.

91 Augstākās tiesas Senāta 2007. gada 8. marta spriedums.

written legal norm of public law, the applier of legal norms should check its compliance with general principles of law.

General principles of law in the hierarchy of legal norms have supra-positive force, constitutional force; that is, they are on the same level as the material Constitution in terms of legal force. Of course, the legal thought in the legal arrangements of Democratic States based on the Rule of Law has undergone development in the course of time.

This thesis is most clearly demonstrated by the practice of France.[92] Until the adoption of the Constitution of 1958, it was considered that general principles of law were at the level of the laws in the hierarchy of legal norms. They were mandatory for the administration as an unwritten law. The legislature could revoke a general principle of law just as it could amend or repeal a previously enacted law. However, this was not particularly presumed. The Council of State had such a positive attitude towards certain general principles of law that, in order to preserve them, it refused to consider the laws, the meaning and force of which did not cause any doubts, as being in contradiction with general principles of law.[93]

In France, it is widely believed that general principles of law are not directly based on the provisions of the Preamble of the Constitution or the Universal Declaration of Human Rights. The Council of State considers the Preamble and the Declaration only as an accession to the general principles of law and not as their source. The Council of State refers to sources that are more extensive (for example, the laws) or more uncertain (for example, the traditions of the Republic). With the entry into force of the Constitution of 1958, a new problem arose for the Council of State. If general principles of law are nothing but a synthesis of legislative acts and their legal force is equal to the force of the law, it becomes obvious that these general principles of law are not mandatory for the administration in those areas that are removed from the competence of the legislature and in which the administration can act independently of the law. Such a position would seriously weaken the role of judicial control over "autonomous regulations", as they can only be controlled in terms of their competence and form, but the content of these regulations can be controlled by an administrative court only in case of violation of the Preamble of the Constitution or the acts which it refers to. However, some general principles of law are not directly established in the Preamble or in the acts referred to in it. Thus, the Council of State can provide much stricter judicial control of

92 Cf.: Iljanova D. 1997; Iljanova D. 1999, 105.–106. lpp.

93 Cf. Vedel G. *Droit Administratif*. Paris: PUF, 1968; *The French Legal System. An Introduction*. London: Fourmat Publishing, 1992.

"autonomous regulations" if it recognizes that general principles of law have a higher force than the laws or the constitutional legal force. In that case, the administration is subject to general principles of law even in those matters that are not regulated by the law. This is precisely the approach chosen by the Council of State in determining the legal force of general principles of law in the legal arrangement of France. It remains only to find out how the overriding force of general principles of law can be theoretically justified. It is undeniable that some part of them is formulated in the Preamble of the Constitution, or at least in the legal acts to which the Preamble refers. The conclusion about the supremacy of other general principles of law is based on the existence of constitutional custom, which is formulated by issuing relevant legislative acts based on the legislator's belief that the constitutional principles impose an obligation to make such decisions.[94] Such an analysis is clearly recognized by French legal doctrine.

In this study it is maintained that general principles of law do not only have a constitutional rank, but that in the legal arrangement of a Democratic State based on the Rule of Law they are to be recognized as supra-positive prescriptions.[95] This means that all written legal norms as the ones created by a legislator have to be subject to a test of general principles of law. Theoretically, it is quite possible that a parliament includes in the formal Constitution such written legal norms that do not comply with general principles of law derived from the Basic Norm, a Democratic State based on the Rule of Law. In this case there should be a mechanism for declaring such norms as null and void.[96]

The author of this study supports the thesis that in all situations where the collision between general principles of law and written legal norms has arisen general principles of law shall prevail over the conflicting written legal norms because general principles of law are derived from the basis of the entire legal arrangement: the Basic Norm. They reflect the spirit of this arrangement and define its content. It is the legislator's task to find the objective norms that exist in the relevant legal arrangement and regulate actual cases taking place in this arrangement. If any separate written legal norm is in contradiction with these principles due to the legislator's failure, then it is obvious that it is in conflict with the entire legal arrangement; this written legal norm then goes beyond the relevant legal arrangement and in this case it has to be declared

---

94 Cf.: Iļjanova D. 1999.

95 Cf. also Jelāgins J. 1999, 80. lpp., 154. vēre; Ziemele I. Starptautisko tiesību vieta un nacionālo tiesību attiecības. *Juristu Žurnāls*, nr. 5/ *Cilvēktiesību Žurnāls*, nr. 6, 67. lpp.

96 Similar opinion see Rodiņa A. *Konstitucionālās sūdzības teorija un prakse Latvijā.* Rīga: Latvijas Vēstnesis, 2009, 126.–137. lpp.

null and void. Declaration of such a written legal norm as null and void is the task of constitutional courts (constitutional review institution), respectively, the constitutional court has to evaluate not only the compliance of written legal norms with the Constitution, but also the compliance of written legal norms included in the Constitution with general principles of law.

2.2 *Interpretation*

In the discussion of the axiology of general principles of law in Chapter 3 it is stated that interpretation of all written legal norms – both substantiation of the necessity for interpretation and the application of interpretation methods or criteria – is based on and determined by general principles of law. Even if a legislator would not include the possibility or necessity of interpretation and interpretation methods and criteria in the texts of normative legal acts, none of the written legal norms could be applied without interpretation on the basis of these unwritten legal norms – principles of interpretation.

In any case when any or several general principles of law are applicable in respect of the subject regulated by any definite written legal norm, the norm shall be interpreted in a way most corresponding to this principle or principles.[97]

The task of interpretation of written legal norms is shared by the court practice (case law) and legal doctrine in that the court practice faces the interpretation problem discovering the specific life situation, indicating to the possible solutions of this problem, which are always examined from the aspect of the legal doctrine. Although a judge is encouraged by a certain life situation to interpret one or another written legal norm, he or she at all times should do the interpretation in such a way that it can be applied not only in the adjudication of this specific case, but also to similar cases. If any written legal norm is interpreted differently in respect of similar cases, it also comes into conflict with the principle of justice and legal security.

Certainly, the Court is not bound by the previous, generally accepted interpretation of written legal norms. The Court can deviate, and it even has an obligation to deviate from the previous interpretation if it has established grounds for a new interpretation. On the other hand, according to the principle of legal security, such cases should be relatively rare. Continuity of judicial practice or judicature upholding trust in the adjudication of cases based on the

---

97 Cf.: MacCormick N., Summers R. (Eds.) *Interpreting statutes. A comparative study.* Aldershot: Dartmouth Publishing Company Limited, 1981, p. 514; Gaidele I. Nolēmumu argumentācija: teorija un prakse. *Likums un Tiesības*, 2002, 4. sēj., nr. 8 (36), nr. 10 (38), 247. lpp.

fact that all disputes will be resolved according to the principles that have been applied up to now, is a value in itself. On the other hand, the interpreter must not ignore a principal change in the orientation of common values, especially if this change is reflected in the new laws.[98]

The functionality of general principles of law is expressed in the application of any of the sub-methods of interpretation – literal, historical, systemic, or teleological – regulating the way of the application of a specific interpretation sub-method (for example, that the literal interpretation consists of four elements: logical, lexical, syntactical, and stylistic) or which tool should be used in interpreting the text of a written legal norm (for example, that the interpretation tools used within the historical interpretation sub-method, among others, are *travaux préparatoires* of the legislations process and the records of all of the committees of legislature involved in the preparation of the text of the written legal norm, as well as transcripts of the plenary sessions of the parliament). In the systemic and teleological interpretation sub-methods, the role of general principles of law is also part of the content of what these interpretation sub-methods are looking for in the text of a written legal norm.

The purpose of the systemic method or criterion of interpretation is to determine which of the several variants of multiple meanings of individual words or sentences of the written legal norm, which result from the use of language and have been clarified as a result of the application of the literal interpretation method, should be taken into account in the specific case. Usually, it can be determined according to the context in which the specific word is used or in which the specific sentence is understood. The mentioned connections determine the understanding of both individual words and sentences, taking into account their location in the system of laws.[99]

Thus, the systemic interpretation means:

1) the use of a legal norm for the purpose of interpreting another written legal norm;
2) interpretation that is related or depends on the systemic structure of the normative legal act. When interpreting a written legal norm, the following must be taken into account: a) title of the section, b) location of the written legal norm to be interpreted in a certain part of the system of laws, in a certain normative legal act and in a certain part of this normative legal act;

98 See Larenz K., Canaris C.W. 1995, S. 135–136.
99 Cf.: Ibid., S. 145.

3) interpretation, which is related to all other types of sources of law existing in the relevant legal arrangement, including general principles of law.[100]

As a result of the application of this interpretation sub-method the true content and sense of the thought expressed in the written legal norm is determined in interrelation with general principles of law of the legal arrangement.[101] This is determined by both the first and the third understanding aspect of the systemic interpretation method mentioned above.

The teleological method or criterion of interpretation of the written legal norms looks at the goals. Each legal framework is aimed at achieving a specific goal. These goals may be directly expressed in the written legal norm or may be derived indirectly from the content of the legal framework. Regardless of the specific goal of the legal framework, in each individual case it is necessary to take into account the common goals of the entire legal arrangement. In this regard, it is usually the question of utility, proportionality, and justice as the ultimate ideal.[102] Here, the central place is for the idea of justice, where one of the principles is the principle of equal treatment, which requires similar treatment for similar contents in accordance with the general evaluations of the legal arrangement. Different evaluation of similar legal contents leads to the fact that contradictions appear in the evaluations, but this is not compatible with the idea of justice. Mitigating or preventing such contradictions is not only the task of a legislator, but also of the applier of legal norms – to interpret the written legal norm in such a way as to mitigate as much as possible or prevent contradictions in evaluations altogether, applying general principles of law (for example, the principle of protection of legitimate expectations, principle of legal security, *bona fide* principle, etc.).[103]

2.3 *Further Development of Law*

A precondition for the further development of law is the existence of such a gap or loophole in the law (in the broader sense, normative legal act), which has to be eliminated, because in such cases the court (judge) cannot refuse to adjudicate the case alleging that the law lacks a written norm that would be

100 See similarly Larenz K., Canaris C.W. 1995, S. 146 ff.

101 MacCormick N., Summers R. (Eds.) 1981, pp. 513–514; Zippelius R. *Juristische Methodenlehre*. 7. Aufl. München: C.H. Beck, 1999, S. 57–59; Meļķisis E. Tiesību normu iztulkošana. 2000, 281. lpp.; Meļķisis E. 2003, 118. lpp.

102 See Wank R. 1997, S. 79–80.

103 See Larenz K., Canaris C.W. 1995, S. 155.

directly related to the case of adjudication.[104] A gap in the law is only such a gap, which is opposite to the original plan of the legislator or teleology of the law itself.

Further development of law is closely related to the controversy between the concepts "the law" (normative legal acts) and "law", which are not identical.[105] On the one hand, a normative legal act is always the same as the positive law; however, law is not limited to the concept of the normative legal act[106] (moreover, equalization of the "normative legal act" and "law" does not agree with the idea of a Democratic State based on the Rule of Law[107]) respectively, a normative legal act does not cover all law (any normative legal act is objectively incomplete), and next to the normative legal act *inter alia* as a generally binding source of law there are also general principles of law.[108] Although it is impossible to avoid gaps in the normative legal acts, the system of laws in itself has to be considered as a system without gaps,[109] as the concept of the so-called gaps in the system of laws is not compatible with the perception of an "open ended" system of laws.[110] In a system of laws, which objectively consists of both written and unwritten legal norms, there exists the totality of all those regulations, which are necessary for solving actual cases. However, the legislator will never be able to positivise all these instructions – find, identify, and include in the normative legal acts. With the help of the further development of law, the applier of legal norms fills the gaps and corrects the errors of the legislator by discovering and deriving valid legal norms existing within the system of laws in the form of general principles of law.

Analogy is allowed both in private and public law, and the possibility of applying the analogy in the legal arrangement of Latvia is also determined in the respective normative legal acts.

> For example, Section 4 of the Civil Law states: "The provisions of this Law shall be interpreted firstly in accordance with their direct meaning; where

---

104 See Palandt. *Bürgerliches Gesetzbuch* (*Beck'sche Kurz-Kommentare*). 56. Aufl. München, 1997, S. 7; Kalniņš E. Tiesību tālākveidošana. *Likums un Tiesības*, 2001, 3. sēj., nr. 9 (25), 278. lpp.

105 See Chapter 2.2.4.

106 Cf.: Kalniņš E. 2001, 115. lpp.

107 See Jelāgins J. 1999, 61. lpp.; Larenz K., Canaris C.W. 1995, S. 189–190.

108 On the role of judges in the further development of law in connection with general principles of law, see also Picker E. Richterrecht oder Rechtsdogmatik – Alternativen der Rechtsgewinnung? *Juristen Zeitung*, 1998, no. 1.

109 Kramer E.A. *Juristische Methodenlehre*. Bern: Stampfli Verlag AG, 1998, S. 137.

110 Larenz K., Canaris C.W. 1995, S. 198.

> necessary, they may also be interpreted in accordance with the structure, basis and purposes of this Law; and, finally, they may also be interpreted through *analogy*"; in the fifth part of Section 5 of the Civil Procedure Law it is determined: "If there is no law governing the contested relation, a court shall apply *a law governing similar legal relations*, but if no such law exists, a court shall act according to general principles of law and meaning of law"; in the second part of Section 17 of the Administrative Procedure Law it is stated: "If an institution or a court finds a gap in the legal system, it may rectify such gap by also using the *method of analogy*, that is, by a systematic analysis of the legal regulation of similar cases and by applying the principles of law determined as a result of this analysis to the particular case. Such administrative act as infringes human rights of an addressee may not be based on analogy [author's emphasis]."

Analogy in the legal sense is "transferring" of legal consequences set forth in normative legal acts for one or several legal contents to similar factual content or factual composition not regulated in the normative legal acts. Such transferring is based on the fact that due to the essential similarity of these contents they should be evaluated and treated similarly, based on the principle of justice. The essential similarity can be detected by assessing the interests protected by the law and the interests involved in the unregulated factual composition. So, analogy is a method of prevention of imperfections or deficiencies in the normative legal acts, as a result of which, to the factual contents not regulated in the normative legal acts are applied either: 1) legal consequences of the written legal norm regulating similar factual compositions, or 2) a common principle discovered from several written legal norms regulating similar factual compositions, which on the basis of justice and equality, covers both directly regulated in the normative legal acts as well as unregulated factual compositions.[111]

In the case of analogy, it is not about the conclusion from the particular to the particular (from the individual to individual), but about the conclusion from the particular (individual) to the general – a direct conclusion is made not from the individual to the individual, but by finding the common, joint aspects between the legal content provided for in the written legal norm and the factual composition of the life event to be decided.[112]

---

111 See Larenz K., Canaris C.W. 1995, S. 204; Kalniņš E. Tiesību tālākveidošana. 2003, 150.–153. lpp.

112 Kalniņš E. 2001, 139.–142. lpp.

Discovery of a common principle in the event of analogy in case of similar written legal contents is based on the fact that *ratio legis* of all summarized separate norms comprises not only the cases regulated by a normative legal act, but also applies to all those life situations presenting the required general preconditions. However, it is always necessary to carefully check the extent to which such a goal of the law is generalizable and whether the peculiarities of certain groups of cases do not require a different assessment.[113]

Since the establishing of essential similarity between legal and factual contents or discovery of these common aspects or principles in cases of similar written legal contents have to comply with and in fact are reflections of the general principles of law, and as already stated above, is far from easy, but is a complex and demanding process, there are possible cases when the applier of legal norms makes a mistake while doing it.

> Thus, for example, when considering a case regarding the separation of real estate for capital shares, the Court after five years of litigation ruled that as a result of the refusal to separate the property, an illegal act was committed against the plaintiff and at that time possession in bad faith had already been established over the subject of the dispute. The Court also recognized the plaintiff's property rights to these real estates, but the judgement did not specify the moment when the property rights are recognized. On the other hand, in the trial for the recovery of the unobtained fruits from the possessor in bad faith, the court recognized that the plaintiff acquired the property right not from the moment when the rights were violated, and also not from the moment when the plaintiff turned to the Court for the protection of the violated rights, but only from the moment when the court judgement came into force, recognizing the plaintiff's property rights.[114] However, no normative legal act contains a norm that would determine such a regulation. So, the Supreme Court Senate had based the judgement on some principle, which could be conditionally called the principle of minimum rights protection,[115] which contradicts both the positivised norms of private law, Articles 92 and 105 of the Constitution, as well as general principles of law.[116] How

113 See Larenz K., Canaris C.W. 1995, S. 205.

114 Škutāns D. Vai Latvijā pastāv minimālās tiesību aizsardzības princips? *Likums un Tiesības*, 2003, 5. sēj., nr. 1(41), 2.–9. lpp.

115 Augstākās tiesas Senāta 2002. gada 11. septembra spriedums lietā nr. SKC-451. Nav publicēts.

116 See analyses in detail Škutāns D. 2003, 2.–9. lpp.

should a person act in such a case, when his/her rights have been violated because the Court has applied an incorrectly discovered principle? In a Democratic State based on the Rule of Law there should be a mechanism to check the legitimacy of such discovered principles as this is a part necessary for recognition of the legitimacy of the Court's actions. In this case, all the courts of the judicial system up to the cassation instance, when checking the legitimacy of this principle, did not conclude that it was wrongly discovered. The next step in the protection of individual rights is the Constitutional Court, and it was also used in this case. The competence of the Constitutional Court is determined in Section 16 of the Constitutional Court Law: "The Constitutional Court shall examine cases regarding:

1) conformity of [the] laws with the Constitution;
2) conformity of international agreements signed or entered into by Latvia (also until the confirmation of the relevant agreements in the [parliament]) with the Constitution;
3) conformity of other laws and regulations or parts thereof with the norms (acts) of a higher legal force;
4) conformity of other acts of the [parliament], the Cabinet, the President, the Speaker of the [parliament] and the Prime Minster with [the] law, except for administrative acts;
5) conformity with [the] law of such an order by which a Minister authorized by the Cabinet has suspended a decision taken by a local government council;
6) conformity of Latvian national legal norms with those international agreements entered into by Latvia that are not in conflict with the Constitution."

In this enumeration, the legislator did not directly include the examination of the legality and legitimacy of the legal norms found by a judge as a result of the process of further development of law, because the basic task of a constitutional court is first of all to control the activity of a legislator in the adoption of written legal norms. The legal norms found as a result of the further development of law are real legal norms with all their inherent characteristics (including the generally binding force), which the legislator was not able to formulate in a normative legal act.[117] Therefore, the opinion expressed in the argumentation of the decision of

117 On the generally binding force of judge made law, as a result of the application of further development of law, see comprehensively: Sniedzīte G. 2013.

the Constitutional Court on the refusal to initiate a case stating that: "The competence of the Constitutional Court includes only the evaluation of generally binding legal norms. It follows from the application and the materials attached to it that the applicant disputes the legal norm established by the Supreme Court Senate. The Supreme Court Senate derived this legal norm by interpreting the content of other legal norms. The (derivative) legal norms established by the court *are not generally binding* [author's emphasis], therefore their evaluation is not within the competence of the Constitutional Court" is to be criticized.[118]

The unwritten form of general principle of law, as already analysed above, does not deprive it of its generally binding character – all subsequent similar cases are adjudicated on its basis: it is generally binding, applies to an indefinite group of persons (including persons involved in similar cases), and its application is ensured by the state (court) with the help of coercive mechanism.

What is the just solution in this case? In the specific case, the principle revealed by the judges is not legitimate, even though it has created legal consequences for an individual. The consequences of such an illegitimate prescription must be eliminated in a Democratic State based on the Rule of Law. If the competence of the Constitutional Court includes the evaluation of generally binding legal norms, then obviously this competence also has to be extended in relation to the legal norms found in the process of application of the legal method of the further development of law, thus expanding the competence of the Constitutional Court with the right to control the coherence of the entire system of laws. In addition, it must not be allowed that normative regulations exist in the legal arrangement of a Democratic State based on the Rule of Law, the constitutionality of which cannot be challenged, verified, and in case of non-compliance with legal norms of higher legal force, these regulations must be recognized as null and void.[119]

Argumentum a fortiori or argument "even more" – the general principle of law – a legal method, which is closely connected with the analogy as its

118 Satversmes tiesas 4. kolēģijas 2002. gada 13. novembra lēmums par atteikšanos ierosināt lietu. Nav publicēts.

119 On the necessity of expanding the competence of the Constitutional Court in cases of unconstitutional silence of the law see Feldhūne G. "Likumu klusēšana" un Satversmes tiesas kompetence. *Likums un Tiesības,* 2002, 4. sēj., nr. 3 (31), 83.–86. lpp. Other view on parliamentary control of judge made law see Sniedzīte G. 2013, 254.–257. lpp.

strengthening argument, has been applied to find a just and reasonable solution in the following case.[120]

> The applicant submitted an application to the Court claiming for the reimbursement for the serious (grave) moral damages, after she was confined into the mental hospital against her own will when she came to the municipal police office to submit an application, and to impose an obligation on the municipal police to apologize to her in writing. The law states that if the court in assessing the circumstances of a particular case establishes, that the infringement of the rights or interests protected by the law is not serious (grave), then the amount of the compensation for moral damage shall be up to 3000 EUR or independent or additional compensation for the moral damage in a form of written or public apology can be imposed to the institution. If serious (grave) moral damage has done, the amount of the compensation can be set at up to 5000 EUR. The court of the first instance satisfied the application partially by requiring the municipal police to pay to the applicant the reimbursement for moral damage in amount of 5000 EUR, while refusing to grant to the applicant of the additional compensation – a written apology by the municipal police. The Court reasoned that, in accordance with the provisions of the law the written apology as an additional compensation can be imposed only in cases where the infringement of the rights or interests protected by the law is not serious (grave).
> The scheme of the legal syllogism would be as follows:
> Determining the structure of the written legal norm – finding legal content and legal consequences
> *Major Premise*: If the court (F1) in assessing the circumstances of a particular case (F2) establishes, that the infringement of the rights or interests protected by the law is not serious (grave) (F3), then additional compensation for the moral damage in a form of written or public apology can be imposed to the institution.
> *Minor Premise*: The court (F1) in assessing the circumstances of a particular case (F2) establishes, that the infringement of the rights or interests protected by the law is serious (grave) (F4).
> Assessing the interests protected by the law (1) and interests infringed by the given factual composition (2):

120 Augstākās tiesas Senāta 2010. gada 16. februāra spriedums lietā nr. SKA-104/2010. Pieejams: at.gov.lv.

1) to provide the protection to the persons' right to dignity and honour – to receive as an additional compensation apology of the institution even in cases when the infringement has not been severe (grave);
2) persons rights have been infringed in a severe (grave) way and she wants along with the compensation in money also to receive additionally the compensation in a form of written apology in order to restore the infringed right to dignity and honour.

The essential similarity can be detected – the written legal norm and the factual composition is connected with the protection of the right to dignity and honour.

To transfer the consequences of the written legal norm to the non-regulated factual composition:

..., then additional compensation for the moral damage in a form of written or public apology can be imposed on the institution.

The Third Premise: If in cases when the Court (F1) in assessing the circumstances of a particular case (F2) establishes, that the infringement of the rights or interests protected by the law is not serious (grave) (F3), the additional compensation for the moral damage in a form of written or public apology can be imposed to the institution, then *even more* in cases when the infringement of the rights or interests protected by the law is serious (grave) (F4), the additional compensation for the moral damage in a form of written or public apology can be imposed on the institution.

\+ Right to dignity and honour
The principle of equality
The principle of justice

Conclusion of the Syllogism: The applicant has the right to an additional compensation in a form of written apology.

Value judgements:

1. If in case of not grave infringement of right to dignity and honour the institution has the duty as an additional punishment to issue an apology to the applicant, then even more that is the case when the infringement has been grave.
2. The principle of equality would be violated if person suffering from great infringement of the basic right would not be able to ask for the apology while a person who suffered not serious infringement of the basic right would be able to ask for the apology.
3. That would contradict the principle of justice – "there would be 1) no harmony and balance, 2) equal treatment of persons in

> similar circumstances and 3) the benefits would not be distributed on the basis of merits."[121]

Analogy to the detriment of the defendant is excluded according to the general principle of law *nulla poena sine lege*. However, as already mentioned above,[122] in public law, the principle of prohibition of analogy in the Western legal system has developed in a way, and the practice of applying legal norms indicates that, based on the principles of justice and equality, which determine that essentially similar human activities should be regulated and treated in a similar way, ethical evaluations and essentially similar results created by the actions of individuals are taken into account.

The legal practice of developed Democratic countries shows that evaluative subsumption is used in so-called hard cases. The cases are dealt with in a similar way when the result of the actions of persons are essentially similar to the results provided by the legal norms as those for which responsibility arises, despite the fact that the possibilities of interpretation have been exhausted with the broadest possible meaning of the words used in the written legal norm.

> Thus, for example, in Sweden the written legal norm determines that criminal liability arises for the illegal spending of money left in one's possession. A person, while checking the status of his account, has discovered that money has been transferred to it that does not belong to him, and realizing this, he spends this money anyway. Of course, in such a case, we cannot talk about possession in its usual legal sense, however, the Swedish court makes a judgement by analogy, applying to the person the legal consequences, which were provided in the Criminal Law norm for illegal spending of money given into someone's possession. Or another example: two persons left a radioactive substance unattended at the workplace. These persons were sentenced according to the norm of the Criminal Law, which provided the responsibility for creating a general threat associated with the spreading of poison or similar substances, respectively, leaving substances unattended was recognized as analogous to their spreading.[123]

---

121 On the scope of principle of justice see: Satversmes tiesas tiesneses Daigas Rezevskas atsevišķās domas lietā nr. 2016-14-01 "Par Solidaritātes nodokļa likuma 3., 5., 6., 7. un 9. panta atbilstību Latvijas Republikas Satversmes 91. panta pirmajam teikumam un 109. pantam". Pieejams: satv.tiesa.gov.lv.

122 See Chapter 4.1.3.

123 Peczenik A. 1989, p. 400.

> In this regard, the position of the legislator in Latvia on the issue of illegal cutting of trees seems interesting. Section 161 of the Criminal Code of Latvia provided for liability for illegal cutting of trees. Here, even without further determination of the plan and teleology of the law, it was obvious that the legislature intended to punish anyone who destroys a tree without a permit, not thinking that cutting is the only type of tree destruction that should be punished. Already in 1997, the decision of the Supreme Court's Plenary Session On the Application of the Laws in Criminal Cases Regarding Illegal Cutting of Trees, Destruction or Damage of the Forest continued to further develop what was established by the legislator, stipulating that "illegal (arbitrary) cutting of trees in the sense of Section 161 of the Criminal Code should be understood as the separation of wild or dead trees from the soil by any means (by sawing, felling, breaking, uprooting, etc.) without the relevant permission". Apparently, the Supreme Court's Plenary Session has been engaged in summarizing the further development of law done by the courts (this time in a positive sense), because the goal of the illegal action is the same: no matter how the tree is destroyed, it ends its existence. It is also clear that even if the tree were to be poisoned, which in any case is not cutting even in the broadest sense of the word, and as a result would be destroyed, taking into account the principles of justice and equality, as well as moral evaluations, the responsibility should be the same.
>
> However, the first part of Section 109 of the Criminal Law, adopted in 1998, once again determines responsibility only for cutting down trees, while the second part of this Section determines responsibility for "arbitrary cutting down, destruction or damage of trees [...] in specially protected areas of the state", which, applying interpretation methods, clearly indicates that with the first part, the legislator wanted to limit liability, providing it only for a specific type of tree destruction – cutting. Should this be considered as an indication of the unwillingness or inability of the legislator to take into account the results of the case law and the further development of law?

While analogy and *argumentum a fortiori* as legal methods of further development of law are applicable to fill open gaps in the law, where there is a lack of positive regulation, and on the basis of a requirement to treat similar contents similarly, there also exists the method of further development of law: teleological reduction, which in turn is applicable to fill the hidden gaps, where the positive regulation is enacted but is contrary to the general principles of law and the Basic Norm because of being too wide: regulating the factual compositions which the written legal norm should not provide specific legal consequences for; so exemption on the too broad text of the written legal norm has to be imposed by treating different contents differently.[124]

2.4 *Elaboration of Decision*

As mentioned above, general principles of law belong to that group of independent sources of law that may serve as the ground for a judgement – the basis for the operational (holding) part of a decision. However, this does not mean that generally binding sources of law may not be used in the argumentation of a judgement. On the contrary, written legal norms, generally binding interpretations of the authorised courts as well as general principles of law are an integral part of the argumentation in appropriately drafted acts of the application of legal norms.

> Since its first judgements, the Constitutional Court has used both general principles of law and written legal norms in the reasoning of its judgements.[125] Thus, for example, in its first judgement issued on 7 May 1997, the Court wrote: "According to the *general principles of law* [author's emphasis], a normative legal act loses its force in the following cases: 1) if a deadline or condition has reached, limiting the force of the normative legal act in time, 2) if the normative legal act is abolished or 3) if another normative legal act with the same or higher legal force, which regulates the same issues, enters into force."[126]

Over time, general principles of law have become an integral part of the work of the Constitutional Court. Currently, it is difficult to imagine a judgement of the Constitutional Court in which general principles of law are not mentioned (in the facts) or applied (in the motives, argumentation or holding part). Other

124 As an example of the necessity to apply a teleological reduction in the case where the written legal norm is formulated too wide (a hidden gap of the law exists) Article 58 of the Constitution can be mentioned. It states that the administrative institutions of the State shall be subordinated to the Cabinet of Ministers; no exceptions are provided in the written text of the norm. While in a Democratic State governed by the Rule of Law several functionally independent administrative institutions should exist that are not subordinated to the Cabinet of Ministers in performing their duties, for example, the Central Bank or Public Utilities Regulator. Thus, in applying Article 58 of the Constitution an exemption should be imposed on the too wide formulated text of the written legal norm.

125 Nikuļceva I. Satversmes tiesas pieci gadi: ieskats tiesas jurisprudencē. *Likums un Tiesības,* 2001, 3. sēj., nr. 12 (28), 364.–365. lpp.

126 Judgement of the Constitutional Court of 7 May 1997.

courts of Latvia, and especially the administrative courts, have also shown a significant development applying general principles of law in the reasoning of judgements.

> The Supreme Court Senate wrote in the argumentation of the judgement of 8 January 2003: "The Senate believes that the judgement cannot be recognized as legal also because the court, when deciding the case, did not analyse the conformity of the contested decision of the [agency] with the *principles of protection of legitimate expectations and proportionality recognized in the continental European legal system* [author's emphasis]."[127]
>
> The Court of Riga city Zemgale district wrote in the argumentation of the judgement of 14 September 2001: "Consequently, the action of the State Revenue Service, when adopting the contested decision, *was not proportionate* to the circumstances [author's emphasis]. [...] [The company] *in good faith* [author's emphasis] relied on the correctness of the specified information, as normative legal acts do not provide the recipient of the goods with an obligation to verify the correctness of the specified information."[128]
>
> In the reasoning of the judgement of the Supreme Court Senate adopted on 22 March 2010, one can read: "In accordance with the fourth part of Section 349 of the Administrative Procedure Law, the Senate joins the motivation contained in the judgement of the regional court, recognizing the decision of the council of the foundation as illegal, as it violates the principle of the prohibition of arbitrariness. The *principle of prohibition of arbitrariness* requires that there is a reasonable justification for the state's action and that everyone can be convinced of the existence of this justification. Since the justification of the state's action is reflected in the argumentation, the principle of prohibition of arbitrariness is closely related to the *principle of necessity to provide the justification*. [...] The court, when reviewing the institution's decision, must assess whether the institution has evaluated all the facts relevant to adopt the decision on the issue and whether the grounds for the institution's decision are

127 Augstākās tiesas Senāta 2003. gada 8. janvāra spriedums lietā nr. SKC-27 2003. g. Nav publicēts.

128 Rīgas pilsētas Zemgales priekšpilsētas 2001. gada 26. septembra spriedums lietā nr. C 31345300 1045/1. Nav publicēts.

based on such facts and objective and rational legal considerations arising from them."[129]

Doctrinal studies are of great practical importance for the possibility to refer to general principles of law in court judgements because general principles of law are filtered and systematized based on normative legal acts, cases, historical and social facts in there.

The practice of the Senate of Latvia in time before the occupation regarding the application of the general principles of law is noteworthy and instructive. In the reasoning of its judgements, there were references not only to legal doctrine[130] (therefore indirectly also to general principles of law), but also directly to general principles of law.[131]

Thus, for example, in the judgement of the Civil Cassation Department of the Senate of 8 December 1921, can be read: "Latvia, as a country based on the Rule of Law, can only recognize as legal and binding orders of a foreign country that correspond to *the general principles of the legal arrangement* [author's emphasis], with which the liquidation of all insurance companies in principle is incompatible", or

in the judgement of the Civil Cassation Department of the Senate of 23 January 1939, regarding the application of the Law on the Entry into Force of the Civil Law and the Transitional Provisions, the court referred to the general principle of intertemporal applicability of legal norms in private law: "In the Paragraph 3 of the Transitional Provisions it is provided that the legal relationship, which started on the basis of the law before the entry into force of the Civil Law, is regulated according to the previous laws. From this *general principle* [author's emphasis] in Paragraph 15 of the same regulations an exception is provided, which stipulates the legal relations of guardianship cases, even though they have arisen on the basis of the previous laws, are regulated in the future according to the provisions of the new Civil Law. [...] Therefore, those legal relations in guardianship cases that have arisen during the effect of the old Civil Law of 1864 and were not realized until the entry into force of the new Civil

129 Augstākās tiesas Senāta 2010. gada 22. marta spriedums lietā nr. SKA-58/2010. Pieejams: at.gov.lv.

130 See *Ieskats Latvijas Senāta spriedumos un senatora Augusta Lēbera rakstos (1920–1938)*. Rīga: Latvijas Enciklopēdija, 1992, 23. lpp.

131 Cf.: Lēbers D.A. Latvijas Senāts viņdienās un mūsdienās. *Latvijas Vēstnesis*, 1998, nr. 387.

Law are also regulated according to the norms of the new Civil Law. (cf. Sen. judgement 38/550)",[132]

but in the judgement of 24 May 1939 in the case regarding the application of the Law on Cooperative Societies and Their Unions the Senate referred to the general principle of law of intertemporal applicability of legal norms in public law: "Section 139 of the Law on Cooperative Societies and Their Unions contains a procedural norm, [...] [that] the material rights of the member, including his right to demand the protection of material rights through court, have not been affected [by this Law], but, as already pointed out, [it] only sets the procedure and deadline for filing complaints. Therefore, this Section, as a new procedural law, is applicable after its entry into force also to cases such as the one in question [...]. Such an opinion is consistent with the *general principle* [author's emphasis] that each newly adopted procedural law is applicable to all procedural actions that the court has to perform in a case after the entering into force of the new procedural law, and that the court cannot apply to the substantive legal relations that arose during the existence of a previous procedural law the old procedural norms (cf. Sen. judgement 29/455, see also Prof. Bukovsky's civil procedure study book para. 22, 1)."[133]

Likewise, in the judgement of 28 April 1939 the Senate argues: "*Constant case law* has recognized [author's emphasis] that according to commercial law the buyer, by the way, has the right to demand from the seller, in case of delay, the execution of the contract; it is a *general principle* [author's emphasis], which applies not only to the term purchase, as the defendant thinks (judgements No. 430, No. 1462, etc.)", or

in the judgement of 26 April 1939: "The *general principle* [author's emphasis] expressed in Section 6 of the Civil Procedure Law, according to which the judicial authorities can decide cases only after hearing the explanations of the opposing party or after the expiration of the time set for submitting explanations, also applies to the magistrates' courts."[134]

132 Izvilkumi no Latvijas Senāta Civilā kasācijas departamenta spriedumiem. Konradi F., Valters A. (Sast.) XV. sēj. *Tieslietu ministrijas Vēstneša pielikums*, 1939, nr. 1, 245. lpp.

133 Ibid., 400.–401. lpp.

134 Ibid., 308. lpp.

> Also, the Senate already in the judgement of 23 January 1939 in the case of the complaint about the decision of the Minister of the People's Welfare emphasizes the inevitable necessity of the reasoning of the decision: "Until special procedural rules have yet been issued on the deciding of requests and complaints, in the meantime the *general principle that every official and state institution must justify their decisions as from the point of view of usefulness, as well as from the point of view of legality* [author's emphasis], because otherwise it is not possible for the relevant minister to check and monitor whether the institutions and officials under his authority have acted correctly",[135] or
>
> in the judgement of 16 May 1938 in the case of complaint regarding the decision of the Ministry of People's Welfare, concretizing the *principle of equality*: "It is unimaginable that one state institution, on the same issue under the same circumstances, comes to a completely opposite conclusion than another",[136] or
>
> in the judgement of 13 June 1938 in the case of complaint regarding the decision of the Council of Customs Affairs, confirming the doctrinally concretized general principle of law – legal method of interpretation that "Section 836 of the Import Customs Tariff, as a *norm of exception, cannot be broadly interpreted according to the general principle*."[137]

This practice of the Senate really shows that the concept of general principles of law has not been unknown to the legal arrangement of Latvia and that the courts have referred to general principles of law in their decisions and judgements (even to those principles of law that are not defined in normative legal acts).

The Greek philosopher Aristotle, as one of the first to search for the legitimacy and conditions of true argumentation, pointed out that only such arguments can be used in argumentation that participants of the dialogue and others will accept. They are phrases that "either to everyone, or to the majority, or to the wise seem to be true".[138] Argumentation is additionally stabilized by the procedural law. In any case, a fair process requires that each party of the

---

135 Senāta Administratīvā Departamenta spriedumu izvilkumi. Kalacs J., Ripke A. (Sast.) *Tieslietu ministrijas Vēstneša pielikums*, 1939, 292. lpp.

136 Ibid., 398. lpp.

137 Ibid., 402. lpp.

138 Cueto-Rua J.C. 1981.

process be heard, that the right to representation is ensured, that the time limits are set, and that reasons are presented. The role of the general principles of law is especially significant in supporting the contents of the judgement[139] and when the process of application of legal norms is discussed in its dynamics and considering its creative aspect, exactly general principles of law have the decisive meaning in the argumentation of judgements.[140] The outcome is appropriately and sufficiently justified, when:

1) such reasons are expressed clearly, from which
2) may be directly concluded which principles are taken as the basis, and
3) when the train of thought resulting from these principles and leading to the objective is clearly expressed. If the enlisted reasons lead any reasonably thinking person to the same result, the judgement is justified appropriately.[141]

According to the argumentation theory, all arguments used in judgements can be divided into two basic types: legal arguments and non-legal arguments. Legal arguments are those that legally justify the judge's decision and give legal meaning to the reasoning. On the other hand, arguments not related to jurisprudence, that is, those based on experience or practical considerations, are called non-legal or general arguments. General principles of law together with written legal norms, case law, other sources of law belong to the group of legal arguments – they are only the arguments characteristic of legal science, which must be included in every reasoning of the decision.[142]

Legal reasoning should show the general principles of law:

1) from which the results are derived;
2) according to which the relevant truthfulness of the circumstances of the case are evaluated;
3) according to which the most important thought processes leading to the result are shown. The decision should present the most important arguments that highlight the necessary evaluations.

For example, in the argumentation part of the judgement of the Supreme Court Senate of 12 September 2006, it is written: "According to the case law of the Department of Administrative Affairs, which was formed,

139 Sauer W. *Juristische Elementarlehre.* Basel: Verlag für Recht und Gesellschaft, 1944.

140 MacCormick N. 1974, p. 222.

141 Cf.: Horns N. Ievads tiesību zinātnē un tiesību filozofijā. *Likums un Tiesības*, 2000, 2. sēj., nr. 9 (13), 260. lpp.

142 Cf.: Gaidele I. 2002, 244.–245. lpp.; Peczenik A. 1989, p. 156.

> also observing the practice of the European Court of Human Rights, the court is obliged to justify the judgements, but this is not understood as a requirement to answer in detail to any argument. Judges must hear the arguments, but they are not obliged to argue in detail any submission or clearly respond to any explanation. The court is allowed to evaluate the arguments that it considers to be relevant from a legal point of view. Only if the court has not analysed any significant or decisive argument, a violation can be found. How much the judgement should be argued depends on the circumstances of the case."[143]

These requirements apply both to judgements and other decisions of legal practice (such as administrative acts) as well as to the works of legal science.[144] Legal reasoning must formally show the train of thought.[145] Moreover, no logical contradiction should arise, as this would not comply with the principle of prohibition of arbitrariness and, therefore, with the principle of equality before the law.[146]

However, the formal logical precision of the judgement's reasoning is not sufficient for a complete justification of the ruling. In particular, the evaluations underlying the decision should be emphasized, and they should be in accordance with the applicable legal norms.[147] Judgements are evaluations,[148] which must be in accordance with general principles of law. The written legal norms are not an end in themselves in the realization of power but are only means to implement the general public good and justice. Thus, judgement is always related to general principles of law. Evaluations according to general principles of law is the last and also the highest goal of a legal decision, which gives it an internal justification, a deeper, greater meaning, an ethical undertone.[149]

143 Augstākās tiesas Senāta 2006. gada 12. septembra spriedums lietā nr. SKA-280/2006. Nav publicēts.

144 On styles of judgement and legal opinion see Horns N. 2000, 261. lpp.

145 Hartmane L. Juridiskā argumentācija tiesu nolēmumos. *Likums un Tiesības,* 2001, 3. sēj., nr. 11 (27), 344.–349. lpp.

146 See *Principles of Administrative Law Concerning the Relations Between Administrative Authorities and Private Persons.* Directorate of Legal Affairs, Strasbourg, 1996; Sauer W. 1944.

147 Sauer W. 1944.

148 Cueto-Rua J.C. 1981.

149 Cf.: Ibid.; Sauer W. 1944.

3 Conclusions

Regarding the functional meaning or mechanism of functional effect in the legal arrangement, general principles of law differ from written legal norms, as they have a "dimension of weight".

The content of general principles of law is determined by the concretization method, unlike written legal norms, the content and true meaning of which are determined by the method of interpretation.

There is no hierarchical relationship between general principles of law in terms of legal force. It is also impossible to establish the order of priority for the general principles of law based on the connection of speciality or temporal applicability because, first, all general principles of law are equally general in terms of the certainty of the legal content of the legal norm, and, secondly, all general principles of law of the relevant legal arrangement become valid simultaneously – they become generally binding in the relevant country with the moment of origin of the legal arrangement. The conflict between the principles is resolved by the method of weighing and balancing, determining which of them has more "weight" in the given situation, taking into account the specific social, economic, political and other conditions of the relevant country at a certain point in time, with the aim of achieving the best possible compromise.

The actions of the courts are legitimized by the use of legal methods, which are general principles of law themselves. A written legal norm adopted by the democratically directly legitimized legislator is always a Major Premise in a syllogism. In a case of evaluative subsumption this written legal norm has to be modified because the legislator did not manage to write it down properly – in compliance with general principles of law and the Basic Norm – and that is why now it is the courts' turn to correct the situation, according to the general principle of law, the principle of prohibition of legal obstruction, using legal methods authorized to them by the sovereign on the basis of another general principle of law derived from the Basic Norm, the principle of separation of power.

When providing the Third Premise in an evaluative subsumption scheme, the Court has a duty before the sovereign always to substantiate the discovery of such a norm with a coherent chain of value judgements. When giving the coherent chain of value judgements, the Court has to answer the questions of what would happen or what general principles of law would be violated if the court would not have found such an unwritten legal norm in the system of laws.

In all cases where there has been a conflict between the general principles of law and written legal norms, general principles of law have priority over the written legal norm, which is in conflict with them, because general principles of law are derived from the act of the sovereign's will – the Basic Norm of a Democratic State based on the Rule of Law – they reflect the spirit of the legal arrangement and determine its content.

If any individual written legal norm contradicts general principles of law due to the failure of the legislator, then it also contradicts the entire legal arrangement. This norm falls outside the scope of the specific legal arrangement, and in that case the norm has to be recognized as null and void. Recognizing these written legal norms as null and void is the task of the constitutional review institutions, for example, Constitutional Courts. Thus, the Constitutional Court should assess not only the compliance of the written legal norms with the formal Constitution but also the compliance of the written legal norms contained in the Constitution with the general principles of law.

Bibliography

Legal Literature

Aarnio A. *The Rational as Reasonable.* Dordrecht, Boston, Lancaster, Tokyo: D. Reidel Publishing Company, 1987.

Alchourron C.E., Bulygin E. The Expressive Conception of Norms. In: Stanley L. Paulson (Ed.) *Normativity and Norms. Critical Perspectives on Kelsenian Themes.* Oxford: Clarendon Press, 1999.

Alexy R. Zum Begriff des Rechtsprinzips. *Rechtstheorie,* Beiheft 1, 1979.

Alexy R. *Theorie der Grundrechte.* Aufl. 1. Frankfurt am Main: Suhrkamp, 1986.

Atienza M., Manero J.R. *A Theory of Legal Sentences.* Dordrecht, Boston, London: Kluwer Academic Publishers, 1996.

Balodis K. Labas ticības principa loma mūsdienu Latvijas civiltiesībās. *Likums un Tiesības,* 2002, 4. sēj., nr. 9 (37).

Banneberga Br. Pierādījumu nastas pārnešana? Mantas konfiskācija korupcijas gadījumos. *Likums un Tiesības,* 2001, 3. sēj., nr. 12 (28).

Bērziņš M. Objektīvās izmeklēšanas princips *Administratīvā procesa likumā. Likums un Tiesības,* 2003, 5. sēj., nr. 6 (46).

Bīriņu domnīca – jau desmito gadu pēc kārtas. *Jurista Vārds,* 2013, nr. 32.

Boulanger J. *Principes généraux du droit et droit positif, Le droit prive français au milieu du 20e siècle.* Vol. I, 1950.

Briede J. Tiesiskās paļāvības aizsardzība – viens no administratīvā procesa principiem. *Cilvēktiesību Žurnāls,* 1997, nr. 5.

Briede J. Par samērīgumu administratīvajā procesā. *Latvijas Vēstnesis,* 2000, nr. 16.

Briede J. Par tiesisko paļāvību administratīvajā procesā. *Latvijas Vēstnesis,* 2000, nr. 19.

Briede J. Par vienlīdzību administratīvajā procesā. *Latvijas Vēstnesis,* 2000, nr. 25.

Briede J. Par labvēlīga un prettiesiska akta atcelšanu. *Likums un Tiesības,* 2002, 4. sēj., nr. 5 (33).

Briede J. 10. pants. Tiesiskās paļāvības princips. Grām.: *Administratīvā procesa komentāri.* Briede J. (Zin. red.) Rīga: Tiesu namu aģentūra, 2013.

Brox H. *Allgemeiner Teil des BGB.* 25. Aufl. Köln, Berlin, Bonn, München: Carl Heymanns Verlag, 2001.

Buchwald D. The Rule of Law: A Complete and Consistent Set of (Legal) Norms? *Rechtstheorie,* Beiheft 17, 1997.

Buls M. Vispārīgās un speciālās tiesību normas. *Likums un Tiesības,* 2003, 5. sēj., nr. 6 (46), nr. 7 (47).

Butāns M. Valsts atbildības izpratne (*Satversmes* 92. pants). *Likums un Tiesības,* 2000, 2. sēj., nr. 1 (5).

Bydlinsky F. *Juristische Methodenlehre und Rechtsbegriff.* 2. Aufl. Wien, New York: Springer Verlag, 1991.

Cipeliuss R. *Vispārējā mācība par valsti.* Rīga: AGB, 1998.

Cipeliuss R. Par tiesisko apsvērumu racionālu strukturēšanu. *Likums un Tiesības,* 2000, 2. sēj., nr. 4 (8).

Cueto-Rua J.C. *Judicial Methods of Interpretation of the Law.* Louisiana: The Publications Institute Paul M.Hebert Law Center, 1981.

Čepāne I., Meiere S. Patvaļīgā būvniecība, Satversme un vispārīgie tiesību principi. *Latvijas Vēstneša* pielikums *Jurista Vārds,* 2003, nr. 36 (294).

D'Aspremont J. *International Law as a Belief System* (Cambridge Studies in International and Comparative Law) Cambridge: Cambridge University Press, 2017.

David R. Sources of Law. In: *International Encyclopedia of Comparative Law.* Vol. II, Tübingen: J.C.B. Mohr, 1971.

David R. *Major Legal Systems in the World Today.* London: Steven&Sons, 1985.

Dišlers K. *Tautu pašnoteikšanās principa tiesiskais saturs.* Rīga: Latvijas Universitāte, 1932.

Dreier R. *Recht – Moral – Ideologie.* Frankfurt am Main: Suhrkamp Verlag, 1981.

Dworkin R. *Taking Rights Seriously.* Cambridge, Massachusetts: Harvard University Press, 1977, 1978.

Dworkin R. *A Matter of Principle.* Cambridge: Harvard University Press, 1985.

Eiropas Cilvēktiesību tiesa. Spriedumu izlase I. Mits M. (Red.) Rīga: Latvijas Vēstnesis, 2003.

Eiropas Savienības tiesību īstenošana Latvijā. Alehno I. (Red.) Rīga: Latvijas Vēstnesis, 2003.

Esser J. *Grundsatz und Norm in der richterlichen Fortbildung des Privatrechts.* 4. Aufl. Tübingen: J.C.B. Mohr (Paul Siebeck), 1990.

European Committee on Legal Co-operation, Project Group on Administrative Law. A Handbook: Principles of Administrative Law Concerning the Relations Between Administrative Authorities and Private Persons. Strasbourg: Directorate of Legal Affairs, 1996.

Fabian O.R. *General Principles of Law in the Decisions of International Criminal Courts and Tribunals.* Leiden: Martinus Nijhoff Publishers, 2008.

Feldhūne G. "Likumu klusēšana" un Satversmes tiesas kompetence. *Likums un Tiesības,* 2002, 4. sēj., nr. 3 (31).

Ferrari Fr. General Principles and International Uniform Commercial Law Conventions: A Study of the 1980 Vienna Sales Convention and the 1988 Unidroit Conventions. *RDU,* 1997, no. 3.

Fogels A. Eiropas Savienība starptautisko un Eiropas Savienības tiesību skatījumā. *Likums un Tiesības,* 2003, 5. sēj., nr. 7 (47).

Foster N.G. *German Law and Legal System.* Cardiff: Blackstone Press Ltd., 1993.

Freeman M.D.A. *Lloyd's Introduction to Jurisprudence.* London: Sweet & Maxwell ltd., 1994.

Gaidele I. Nolēmumu argumentācija: teorija un prakse. *Likums un Tiesības,* 2002, 4. sēj., nr. 8 (36), nr. 10 (38).

Gaidele I. Tiesas nolēmumu argumentācijas problēmas. *Likums un Tiesības,* 2003, 5. sēj., nr. 8 (48), nr. 9 (49).

Gardner J. *Law as a Leap of Faith*. Oxford: Oxford University Press, 2012.

Gatawis S., Broks. E., Bule Z. *Eiropas tiesības.* Rīga: Eirofakultāte, 2002.

Glendon M.A., Gordon M.W., Osakwe Chr. *Comparative Legal Traditions.* St.Paul.: West Publishing co., 1985.

Grigore-Bāra E., Kovaļevska A., Liepa L., Levits E., Mits M., Rezevska D., Rozenvalds J., Sniedzīte G. 1. Latvija ir neatkarīga demokrātiska republika. Grām.: *Latvijas Republikas Satversmes komentāri.* Balodis R. (Zin. vad.) Rīga: Latvijas Vēstnesis, 2014.

Harbo T-I. The Function of the Proportionality Principle in EU Law. *European Law Journal,* 2010, Vol.16, no. 2.

Hart H.L.A. *The Concept of Law.* Oxford: Clarendon Press, 1993.

Hartkamp A., Hesselink M., Hondius E., Joustra C., du Perron E. (Eds.) *Towards a European Civil Code.* 2nd ed. Nijmegen: Ars Aequi Libri; The Hague, London, Boston: Kluwer Law International, 1998.

Hartmane L. Juridiskā argumentācija tiesu nolēmumos. *Likums un Tiesības,* 2001, 3. sēj., nr. 11 (27).

Horns N. Ievads tiesību zinātnē un tiesību filozofijā. *Likums un Tiesības,* 2000, 2. sēj., nr. 9 (13).

Hübner U., Constantinesco V. *Einführung in das französische Recht.* München: Verlag Beck C.H., 1994.

Ieskats Latvijas Senāta spriedumos un senatora Augusta Lēbera rakstos (1920–1938). Rīga: Latvijas Enciklopēdija, 1992.

Iļjanova D. Vispārīgie tiesību principi kā tiesību avots. *Latvijas Vēstnesis,* 1997, nr. 277/278.

Iļjanova D. Vispārīgie tiesību principi un to funkcionālā nozīme. Grām.: *Mūsdienu tiesību teorijas atziņas.* Rīga: Tiesu namu aģentūra, 1999.

Iļjanova D. Tiesību normu un principu kolīzija. *Likums un Tiesības,* 2000, 2. sēj., nr. 8 (12).

Iļjanova D. Vispārējo tiesību principu aksioloģiskie un funkcionālie aspekti Latvijas tiesību sistēmas pārejas periodā. Grām.: *Tiesību transformācijas problēmas sakarā ar integrāciju Eiropas Savienībā.* Starptautiskās konferences materiāli. Rīga: LU, 2002.

Iļjanova D. Vispārējo tiesību principu izpratnes izcelšanās vēsturiskā perspektīva. *Latvijas Vēsture. Jaunie un Jaunākie Laiki,* 2003, nr. 3 (51).

Iļjanova D. Labas pārvaldības princips kā vispārējais tiesību princips: konkretizācija un piemērošana. Grām: Zin. red. Ozoliņa Ž., Reinholde I. *Laba pārvaldība.* Rīga: Zinātne, 2009.

Jelāgins J. Tiesību pamatavoti. Grām.: *Mūsdienu tiesību teorijas atziņas.* Rīga: Tiesu namu aģentūra, 1999.

Kalniņš E. Publiskas ticamības princips tiesu praksē. *Likums un Tiesības*, 1999, 1. sēj., nr. 2.

Kalniņš E. Tiesību normu piemērošanas loģiskā shēma. *Likums un Tiesības*, 2000, 2. sēj., nr. 5 (9).

Kalniņš E. Tiesību normas spēkā esamība un intertemporālā piemērojamība. *Likums un Tiesības*, 2000, 2. sēj., nr. 7 (11).

Kalniņš E. Tiesību tālākveidošana. *Likums un Tiesības*, 2001, 3. sēj., nr. 9 (25).

Kalniņš E. Tiesību normu piemērošanas loģiskā shēma. Grām.: *Juridiskās metodes pamati. 11 soļi tiesību normu piemērošanā*. Meļķisis E. (Red.) Rīga: Ratio iuris, 2003.

Kalniņš E. Tiesību tālākveidošana. Grām.: *Juridiskās metodes pamati. 11 soļi tiesību normu piemērošanā*. Meļķisis E. (Red.) Rīga: Ratio iuris, 2003.

Kaufmann A. *Rechtsphilosophie*. München: C.H.Beck'sche Verlagsbuchhandlung, 1997.

Kelsen H. *Pure Theory of Law*. Translation from the Second (Revised and Enlarged) German Edition by Max Knight. Berkeley and Los Angeles: University of California Press, 1967.

Kennedy D. A Transnational Genealogy of Proportionality in Private Law. In: *The Foundations of European Private Law*. Brownsword R., Micklitz H.W., Niglia L., Weatherill S. (Eds.) Oxford: Hart Publishing Ltd., 2011.

Kent P. *Law of the European Union*. 2nd ed. London: Pitman Publishing, 1995.

Klami H.T. General norms and legal reasoning. Legal, social and teleological norms as explanations of legal decision meaning. *Legal Reasoning*, 1992, Vol. II.

Kramer E.A. *Juristische Methodenlehre*. Bern: Stampfli Verlag AG, 1998.

Krastiņš I. *Valsts un tiesību teorija*. Rīga: Zvaigzne, 1985.

Krons M. Intertemporālo tiesību mācība un Civillikuma trešais pants. *Tieslietu Ministrijas Vēstnesis*, 1938, nr. 1.

Krūmiņa V., Skujiņa V. *Normatīvo aktu izstrādes rokasgrāmata*. Rīga: Valsts kanceleja, 2002.

Kusiņš G., Levits E., Liepa L., Mits M., Rezevska D., Ziemele I. *Par Latvijas valsts konstitucionālajiem pamatiem un neaizskaramo Satversmes kodolu. Konstitucionālo tiesību komisijas viedoklis un materiāli*. Rīga: Latvijas Vēstnesis, 2012.

Larenz K. *Methodenlehre der Rechtswissenschaft*. Berlin, Heidelberg, New York: Springer Verlag, 1969.

Larenz K. *Richtiges Recht*. München: C.H. Beck, 1979.

Larenz K., Canaris C.W. *Methodenlehre der Rechtswissenschaft*. 3. Aufl. Berlin, Heidelberg: Springer-Verlag, 1995.

Latviešu valodas vārdnīca. Rīga: Avots, 1987.

Latviešu valodas vārdnīca. 2. izd. Rīga: Avots, 1998.

Legrand P. European Legal Systems Are Not Converging. *The International and Comparative Law Quarterly*, 1996, Vol. 45, no. 1.

Levits E. Starp tiesību normu un tiesisko realitāti. Intervija. *Diena*, 1996. 10. oktobris.

Levits E. Tiesību normu interpretācija un Satversmes 1. panta *demokrātijas* jēdziens. *Cilvēktiesību Žurnāls*, 1997, nr. 4.

Levits E. Cilvēktiesības Eiropas Savienības tiesību sistēmā. *Likums un Tiesības*, 2000, 2. sēj., nr. 11 (15).

Levits E. Samērīguma princips publiskajās tiesībās – *jus commune europaeum* un *Satversmē* ietvertais konstitucionāla ranga princips. *Likums un Tiesības*, 2000, 2. sēj., nr. 9 (13).

Levits E. Normatīvo tiesību aktu demokrātiskā leģitimācija un deleģētā likumdošana: teorētiskie pamati. *Likums un Tiesības*, 2002, 4. sēj., nr. 9 (37).

Levits E. Pārveidojot PSRS tiesiskās sistēmas mantojumu. *Likums un Tiesības*, 2002, 4. sēj., nr. 6 (34).

Levits E. Ģenerālklauzulas un iestādes (tiesas) rīcības brīvība. Funkcijas likumā, piemērošana konkrētā gadījumā, kontrole augstākā iestādē un tiesā. *Likums un Tiesības*, 2003, 5. sēj., nr. 6 (46), nr, 7 (47).

Levits E. Par tiesiskās vienlīdzības principu. *Latvijas Vēstnesis*, 2003, nr. 68.

Lēbers D.A. Latvijas Senāts viņdienās un mūsdienās. *Latvijas Vēstnesis*, 1998, nr. 387.

Liepa L. Pozitīvās tiesības. Grām.: *Mūsdienu tiesību teorijas atziņas*. Rīga: Latvijas Universitāte, 1997.

Līcis A. Vai tiesām jāievēro patiesības princips civillietās? *Likums un Tiesības*, 2000, 2. sēj., nr. 3.

Līcis A. Taisnīguma princips civilprocesā. *Likums un Tiesības*, 2001, 3. sēj., nr. 10 (26).

Lorenz W. General Principles of Law: Their Elaboration in the Court of Justice of the European Communities. *The American Journal of Comparative Law*, 1964, Vol. 13.

Lyons D. Justification and judicial responsibility. *Legal Reasoning*, 1992, Vol. I.

MacCormick N. "Principles" of Law. *Juridical Review*, 1974, Vol. 19.

MacCormick N., Summers R. (Eds.) *Interpreting statutes. A comparative study*. Aldershot: Dartmouth Publishing Company Limited, 1981.

MacCormik N. *Legal Reasoning and Legal Theory*. Oxford: Oxford University Press, 1995.

Maurer H. *Staatsrecht I. Grundlagen, Verfassungsorgane, Staatsfunktionen*. 6. Aufl. München: C.H. Beck, 2010.

McCreary J.M. Retroactivity of Laws: An Illustration of Intertemporal Conflicts Law Issues Through the Revised Civil Code Articles on Disinherison. *Louisiana Law Review*, 2002, Vol. 62, no. 4. Available: digitalcommons.law.lsu.edu/lalrev/vol62/iss4/16.

Meļķisis E. Likuma burts, likuma gars, Satversmes tiesa. *Latvijas Vēstnesis*, 1997, nr. 125.

Meļķisis E. *Attīstības tendences dažos tiesību teorijas un prakses jautājumos*. Rīga: Latvijas Universitāte, 2000.

Meļķisis E. Kontinentālās Eiropas tiesību loks Rietumu tiesībzinātnieku skatījumā. *Juristu Žurnāls*, nr. 6.

Meļķisis E. Tiesību normu abstraktums un tā sekas. *Juristu Žurnāls*, nr. 8.

Meļķisis E. Tiesību normu iztulkošana. *Likums un Tiesības,* 2. sēj., 2000, nr. 9 (13).

Morton P. *An Institutional Theory of Law. Keeping Law in its Place.* Oxford: Clarendon Press, 1998.

Nedjati Z.M., Trice J.E., Dashwood A.A. *English and Continental Systems of Administrative Law.* Amsterdam, New York, Oxford: North Holland Publishing Company, 1978.

Neimanis J. *Ievads tiesībās.* Rīga: zv. adv. J.Neimanis, 2004.

Neimanis J. *Tiesību tālākveidošana.* Rīga: Latvijas Vēstnesis, 2006.

Nikuļceva I. Satversmes tiesas pieci gadi: ieskats tiesas jurisprudencē. *Likums un Tiesības,* 2001, 3. sēj., nr. 12 (28).

Onževs M. Nodokļu regulējuma grozījumu spēks laikā: Satversmes tiesas prakse. *Jurista Vārds,* 2011, nr. 17.

Onževs M. *Tiesību normu laika aspekti tiesiskā un demokrātiskā valstī.* Rīga: Latvijas Vēstnesis, 2016.

Onževs M. Atpakaļejoša un tūlītēja spēka noškiršana praksē. *Jurista Vārds,* 2021, nr. 30.

Osipova S. Nacionālo tiesību nenacionālie avoti. *Jurista Vārds,* 2011, nr. 51.

Osipova S. Latvijas tautas tiesiskā apziņa un Latvijas valsts. *Jurista Vārds,* 2012, nr. 52.

Paine F.J. *Vācijas vispārīgas administratīvas tiesības. Vācijas Administratīvā procesa likums.* Rīga: Tiesu namu aģentūra, 2002.

Palandt. *Bürgerliches Gesetzbuch (Beck'sche Kurz-Kommentare).* 56. Aufl. München, 1997.

Peine F.J. *Allgemeines Verwaltungsrecht. Schwerpunkte.* Heidelberg: Müller C.F. Verlag, 1998.

Penski U. Rechtsgrundsatze und Rechtsregeln. *Juristen Zeitung,* 1989, no. 3.

Peczenik A. Principles of Law. The Search for Legal Theory. *Rechtstheorie,* 1971, no. 2.

Peczenik A. *On Law and Reason.* Dordrecht, Boston, London: Kluwer Academic Publishers, 1989.

Peczenik A. Legal Rules and Moral Principles. *Rechtstheorie,* 1991, no. 11.

Picker E. Richterrecht oder Rechtsdogmatik – Alternativen der Rechtsgewinnung? *Juristen Zeitung,* 1998, no. 1.

Pleps J. Normatīvo tiesību aktu hierarhija: profesors *Hanss Kelzens* un mūsdienas (I). *Likums un Tiesības,* 2007, 9. sēj., nr. 2 (90).

Pleps J. *Satversmes iztulkošana.* Rīga: Latvijas Vēstnesis, 2012.

Pleps J. The Principle of Good Legislation. In: *The Quality of Legal Acts and its Importance in Contemporary Legal Space.* Materials of the International Scientific Conference. Riga: University of Latvia Press, 2012.

Pleps J. Autoritāras valsts izpratne un pamatprincipi: Kārļa Ulmaņa režīms. Grām.: *Tiesību efektīvas piemērošanas problemātika.* Latvijas Universitātes 72. zinātniskās konferences rakstu krājums. Rīga: LU Akadēmiskais apgāds, 2014.

Pleps J., Pastars E., Plakane I. *Konstitucionālās tiesības.* Rīga: Latvijas Vēstnesis, 2014.

Plotnieks A. *Padomju sociālistiskās tiesības.* Rīga: Zvaigzne, 1975.

Radbruch G. Five Minutes of Legal Philosophy (1945). *Oxford Journal of Legal Studies*, 2006, Vol. 26, no. 1; Available: https://idv.sinica.edu.tw/philaw/Jurisprudence_Reading/Five%20Minutes%20of%20Legal%20 Philosophy%20 (1945).pdf.

Rechtsworterbuch. München: C.H.Beck, 1994.

Redgwell C. General Principles of International Law. In: Vogenauer S., Weatherill S. Eds. *General Principles of Law. European and Comparative Perspectives*. Oxford and Portland: Hart Publishing, 2017.

Reich N. *General Principles of EU Law*. Cambridge: Intersentia Publishing Ltd., 2014.

Rezevska D. Judikatūra kā tiesību avots: izpratne un pielietošana. *Latvijas Republikas Augstākās Tiesas Biļetens*, 2010, nr. 1.

Rezevska D. Legal Methods in Latvia's Legal Arrangement and European Integration. In: *European Integration and Baltic Sea Region: Diversity and Perspectives*. Collection of Papers of International Conference held by the University of Latvia. Riga: The University of Latvia Press, 2011.

Rezevska D. Tiesiskās paļāvības principa satura konkretizācija un attīstība judikatūrā. Grām.: *Apvienotā pasaules latviešu zinātnieku III kongresa un Letonikas IV kongresa rakstu krājums*. Rīga, 2011.

Rezevska D. The Content of the General Principles of Law and Normative Legal Acts. In: *The Quality of Legal Acts and its Importance in Contemporary Legal Space*. International Scientific Conference, 4–5 October, 2012. Riga: University of Latvia Press, 2012.

Rezevska D. 17. pants. Tiesību normu interpretācija un analoģija. Grām. : *Administratīvā procesa likuma komentāri*. Briede J. (Zin. Red.) Rīga : Tiesu namu aģentūra, 2013.

Rezevska D. *Vispārējo tiesību principu nozīme un piemērošana*. Rīga: D.Rezevskas izd., 2015.

Rezevska D. Legislation in Latvia. Chapter 17. In: Karpen U., Xanthaki H. Eds. *Legislation in Europe: A Country by Country Guide*. Oxford: Hart Publishing, 2021.

Rezevska D. Nacionālās tiesību avotu doktrīnas attīstība gadsimta laikā. Grām.: *Tiesības un tiesiskā vide mainīgos apstākļos*. Latvijas Universitātes 79. starptautiskās zinātniskās konferences rakstu krājums. Rīga: LU Akadēmiskais apgāds, 2021.

Rezevska D. The Temporal Effect of Legal Norms and Case Law of the Constitutional Court of the Republic of Latvia. In: *The Materials of the 8th International Scientific Conference of the Faculty of Law of the University of Latvia, 21–22 October 2021*. Rīga: LU Akadēmiskais apgāds, 2021.

Rodiņa A. *Konstitucionālās sūdzības teorija un prakse Latvijā*. Rīga: Latvijas Vēstnesis, 2009.

Satversmes 1. panta komentārs. Grām.: Balodis R. (Zin.red.) *Latvijas Republikas Satversmes komentāri. I nodaļa. Vispārējie noteikumi*. Rīga: Tiesu namu aģentūra, 2014.

Sauer W. *Juristische Elementarlehre*. Basel: Verlag für Recht und Gesellschaft, 1944.

Scandinavian Studies in Law. Stockholm: Almqvist & Wiksell International, 1991.

Schmalz D. *Methodenlehre für das juristische Studium.* 3. Aufl. Baden-Baden: Nomos-Verlagsgesellschaft, 1992.

Sieckamnn von J.R. Logische eigenschaften von principien. *Rechtstheorie*, 1994, Band 25, Heft 2.

Sinaiskis V. Taisnības princips Latvijas civiltiesībās. *Jurists*, 1937, nr. 7/8.

Sinaiskis V. Civillikuma principi un ģimenes tiesības. *Tieslietu Ministrijas Vēstnesis*, 1938, nr. 1.

Skujeniece V. *Latvijas tiesu spriedumu kvalitātes problēmas.* Rīga: Providus, 2003.

Slaņķe G. Tiesību tālākveidošana krimināltiesībās. *Jurista Vārds*, 2012, nr. 37.

Sniedzīte G. Tiesību palīgavoti, piemērojot tiesību normas. *Jurista Vārds*, 2005, nr. 39.

Sniedzīte G. *Tiesnešu tiesības. Jēdziens un nozīme Latvijas tiesību avotu doktrīnā.* Rīga: Latvijas Vēstnesis, 2013.

Sonenscher M. (Ed.) *Sieyès: Political Writings: Including the Debate Between Sieyes and Tom Paine in 1791.* Indianapolis, Cambridge: Hackett Publishing Company, Inc., 2003.

Stromberg T. *Inledning till den allmanna rattslaran.* Lund, 1970.

Szladits Ch., Germain C.M. *Guide to Foreign Legal Materials: French.* New York: Oceana Publications Inc., 1985.

Škutāns D. Vai Latvijā pastāv minimālās tiesību aizsardzības princips? *Likums un Tiesības*, 2003, 5. sēj., nr. 1(41).

Šulcs L. *Tiesības kā ētikas minimums.* Rīga: [B.i.], 1936.

Šulcs L. Dabisko tiesību jēdziens. *Jurists*, 1937, nr. ½.

The French Legal System. An Introduction. London: Fourmat Publishing, 1992.

Tridimas T. *The General Principles of EC Law.* Oxford: Oxford University Press, 2000.

Turk A. *Judicial Review in EU Law.* Cheltenham: Edward Elgar Publishing Ltd., 2009.

Unger R.M. *Law in Modern Society.* New York: The Free Press, 1977.

Vainovskis M. Nodokļu krimināllietu aktuālā problemātika un atšķirības tiesu praksē. *Likums un Tiesības*, 4. sēj., nr. 2 (30).

Vedel G. *Droit Administratif.* Paris: PUF, 1968.

Vildbergs H.J., Feldhūne G. *Atsauces Satversmei: mācību līdzeklis.* Rīga: Latvijas Universitāte, 2003.

Višķere I. 5. pants. Privātpersonas tiesību ievērošanas princips. Grām.: *Administratīvā procesa likuma komentāri.* Briede J. (Zin. red.) Rīga: Tiesu namu aģentūra, 2013.

Vīnzarājs N. Jēdzienu jurisprudence. *Tieslietu Ministrijas Vēstnesis*, 1937, nr. 1.

Wank R. *Die Auslegung von Gesetzen.* München: Carl Heymanns Verlag KG, 1997.

Weinberger O. The Expressive Conception of Norms: An Impasse for the Logic of Norms. In: *Normativity and Norms. Critical Perspectives on Kelsenian Themes.* Oxford: Clarendon Press, 1999.

West A., Desdevises Y., Fenet A., Gaurier D., Heussaff M.C. *The French Legal System. An Introduction.* London: Fourmat Publishing, 1992.

Wheatley S. Revisiting the Doctrine of Intertemporal Law. *Oxford Journal of Legal Studies*, 2021, Vol. 41, no. 2.

Wroblewski J. *The Judicial Application of Law*. Bankowski Z., MacCormick N. (Eds.) Dodrecht, Boston, London: Kluwer Academic Publishers, 1992.

Ziemele I. Mazākumgrupu tiesiskās aizsardzības nodrošināšana Latvijā: dažas mācību stundas Eiropai. *Likums un Tiesības*, 2001, 3. sēj., nr. 10 (26).

Ziemele I. Starptautisko tiesību vieta un nacionālo tiesību attiecības. *Juristu Žurnāls*, nr. 5/ *Cilvēktiesību Žurnāls*, nr. 6.

Zippelius R. *Juristische Methodenlehre*. 7. Aufl. München: C.H. Beck, 1999.

Case Law

Administratīvās apgabaltiesas 2004. gada 14. decembra spriedums lietā nr. AA21-04/2. Nav publicēts.

Administratīvās apgabaltiesas 2005. gada 29. aprīļa spriedums lietā nr.: AA1124-05/1. Nav publicēts.

Administratīvās rajona tiesas 2004. gada 2. novembra spriedumā lietā nr. A42140204. Nav publicēts.

Augstākās tiesas Senāta 2002. gada 11. septembra spriedums lietā nr. SKC-451. Nav publicēts.

Augstākās tiesas Senāta 2003. gada 8. janvāra spriedums lietā nr. SKC-27 2003. g. Nav publicēts.

Augstākās tiesas Senāta 2005. gada 12. janvāra spriedums lietā nr. SKC-22. Nav publicēts.

Augstākās tiesas Senāta 2006. gada 12. septembra spriedums lietā nr. SKA-280/2006. Nav publicēts.

Augstākās tiesas Senāta 2007. gada 8. marta spriedums lietā nr. SKA-89/2007. Pieejams: tiesas.lv.

Augstākās tiesas Senāta 2008. gada 14. janvāra spriedums lietā SKA-5/2008. Pieejams: tiesas.lv.

Augstākās tiesas Senāta 2008. gada 14. maija spriedums lietā nr. SKC-212. Pieejams: *at.gov.lv*.

Augstākās tiesas Senāta 2010. gada 16. februāra spriedums lietā nr. SKA-104/2010. Pieejams: at.gov.lv.

Augstākās tiesas Senāta 2010. gada 22. marta spriedums lietā nr. SKA-58/2010. Pieejams: at.gov.lv.

Augstākās tiesas Senāta 2021. gada 21. janvāra spriedums lietā nr. SKA-[B1]/2021. Pieejams: at.gov.lv.

Decision of the Constitutional Court of 21 October 2016 on termination of proceedings in case no. 2016-03-01. Available: satv.tiesa.gov.lv.

Decision of the Constitutional Court of 27 May 2022 on termination of proceedings in case no. 2021-34-01. Available: satv.tiesa.gov.lv.

Decision of the Constitutional Court of 28 February 2007 on termination of proceedings in case no. 2006-41-01. Available: satv.tiesa.gov.lv.

Izvilkumi no Latvijas Senāta Civilā kasācijas departamenta spriedumiem. Konradi F., Valters A. (Sast.) xv. sēj. *Tieslietu ministrijas Vēstneša pielikums*, 1939, nr. 1.

Judgement of the Constitutional Court of 7 May 1997 in case no. 04-01(97). Available: satv.tiesa.gov.lv.

Judgement of the Constitutional Court of 20 April 1999 in case no. 04-01(99). Available: satv.tiesa.gov.lv.

Judgement of the Constitutional Court of 24 March 2000 in case no. 04-07(99). Available: satv.tiesa.gov.lv.

Judgement of the Constitutional Court of 15 March 2010 in case no. 2009-44-01. Available: satv.tiesa.gov.lv.

Judgement of the Constitutional Court of 12 April 2018 in case no. 2017-17-01. Available: satv.tiesa.gov.lv.

Judgement of the Constitutional Court of 5 March 2021 in the case no. 2020-30-01. Available: satv.tiesa.gov.lv.

Judgement of the Constitutional Court of 8 April 2021 in the case no. 2020-34-03. Available: satv.tiesa.gov.lv.

Judgement of the Constitutional Court of 11 March 1998 in case no. 04-05(97). Available: satv.tiesa.gov.lv.

Judgement of the Constitutional Court of 10 June 1998 in the case no. 04-03(98). Available: satv.tiesa.gov.lv.

Judgement of the Constitutional Court of 9 July 1999 in case no. 04-03(99). Available: satv.tiesa.gov.lv.

Judgement of the Constitutional Court of 1 October 1999 in case no. 03-05(99). Available: satv.tiesa.gov.lv.

Judgement of the Constitutional Court of 30 August 2000 in case no. 2000-03-01. Available: satv.tiesa.gov.lv.

Judgement of the Constitutional Court of 5 March 2002 in case no. 2001-10-01. Available: satv.tiesa.gov.lv.

Judgement of the Constitutional Court of 10 January 2003 in case no. 2002-17-0103. Available: satv.tiesa.gov.lv.

Judgement of the Constitutional Court of 4 February 2003 in the case no. 2002-06-01. Available: satv.tiesa.gov.lv.

Judgement of the Constitutional Court of 25 March 2003 in case no. 2002-12-01. Available: satv.tiesa.gov.lv.

Judgement of the Constitutional Court of 4 January 2005 in case no. 2004-16-01. Available: satv.tiesa.gov.lv.

Judgement of the Constitutional Court of 21 November 2005 in case no. 2005-03-0306. Available: satv.tiesa.gov.lv.

Judgement of the Constitutional Court of 16 December 2005 in case no. 2005-12-0103. Available: satv.tiesa.gov.lv.

Judgement of the Constitutional Court of 20 April 2012 in case no. 2011-16-01. Available: satv.tiesa.gov.lv.

Judgement of the Constitutional Court of 26 October 2017 in case no. 2016-31-01. Available: satv.tiesa.gov.lv.

Judgement of the Constitutional Court of 29 June 2018 in case no. 2017-25-01. Available: satv.tiesa.gov.lv.

Judgement of the Constitutional Court of 6 March 2019 in case no. 2018-11-01. Available: satv.tiesa.gov.lv.

Judgement of the Constitutional Court of 23 April 2019 in case no. 2018-12-01. Available: satv.tiesa.gov.lv.

Judgement of the Constitutional Court of 13 November 2019 in case no. 2018-22-01. Available: satv.tiesa.gov.lv.

Judgement of the Constitutional Court of 12 March 2020 in case no. 2019-11-01. Available: satv.tiesa.gov.lv.

Judgement of the Constitutional Court of 25 June 2020 in case no. 2019-24-03. Available: satv.tiesa.gov.lv.

Judgement of the Constitutional Court of 16 July 2020 in case no. 2019-25-03. Available: satv.tiesa.gov.lv.

Judgement of the Constitutional Court of 28 September 2020 in case no. 2019-37-0103. Available: satv.tiesa.gov.lv.

Judgement of the Constitutional Court of 12 November 2020 in case no. 2019-33-01. Available: satv.tiesa.gov.lv.

Judgement of the Constitutional Court of 19 February 2021 in case no. 2020-23-01. Available: satv.tiesa.gov.lv.

Judgement of the Constitutional Court of 23 February 2022 in case no. 2021-22-01. Available: satv.tiesa.gov.lv.

Judgement of the Constitutional Court of 25 March 2022 in case no. 2021-25-03. Available: satv.tiesa.gov.lv.

Decision of the Constitutional Court of 27 May 2022 on termination of proceedings in case no. 2021-34-01. Available: satv.tiesa.gov.lv.

Judgement of the Constitutional Court of 8 June 2022 in case no. 2021-40-0103. Available: satv.tiesa.gov.lv.

Judgement of the Constitutional Court of 15 December 2022 in case no. 2021-36-01. Available: satv.tiesa.gov.lv.

Judgement of the European Court of Human Rights (Chamber) of 18 July 1994: *Karlheinz Schmidt v. Germany*, application no. 13580/88. Available: hudoc.echr.coe.int.

Judgement of the European Court of Human Rights (Chamber) of 21 September 1990: *Fayed v. the United Kingdom*, application no. 17101/90. Available: hudoc.echr.coe.int.

Judgement of the European Court of Human Rights (Grand Chamber) of 17 January 2023: *Fedotova and Others v. Russia*, applications nos. 40792/10, 30538/14 and 43439/14: Available: hudoc.echr.coe.int.

Judgement of the European Court of Human Rights (Grand Chamber) of 7 November 2013: *Vallianatos and Others v. Greece*, applications nos. 29381/09 and 32684/09. Available: hudoc.echr.coe.int.

Judgement of the European Court of Human Rights (Grand Chamber) of 16 March 2006: *Ždanoka v. Latvia*, application no. 58278/00. Available: hudoc.echr.coe.int.

Judgement of the European Court of Human Rights (Plenary) of 21 February 1975: *Golder v. United Kingdom*, application no. 4451/70. Available: hudoc.echr.coe.int.

Judgement of the European Court of Human Rights (Plenary) of 23 July 1968: *Belgian Linguistic case*, application no. 1474/62; 1677/62; 1691/62; 1769/63; 1994/63; 2126/64. Available: hudoc.echr.coe.int.

Judgement of the European Court of Human Rights (Section) of 21 July 2015: *Oliari and Others v. Italy*, applications nos. 18766/11 and 36030/11. Available: hudoc.echr.coe.int.

Judgement of the European Court of Human Rights (Section) of 22 November 2010: *Schalk and Kopf v. Austria*, application no. 30141/04. Available: hudoc.echr.coe.int.

Judgement of the European Court of Justice of 12 July 1957: C-7/56 *Algera and Others v. Joint Assembly*. Available: curia.europa.eu.

Judgement of the European Court of Justice of 17 December 1970: C-11/70 *Internationale Handelsgesellschaft mbH v. Einfuhr- und Vorratsstelle fur Getreide und Futtermittel*. Available: curia.europa.eu.

Judgement of the European Court of Justice of 24 October 1973: 5/73 *Balkan-Import-Export GmbH v. Hauptzollamt Berlin Packhof*. Available: curia.europa.eu.

Latvijas Republikas Augstākās tiesas Senāta spriedumi un lēmumi 1996. Rīga: Latvijas Tiesnešu mācību centrs, 1997.

Rīgas apgabaltiesas 2002. gada 13. maija lēmums lietā nr. CA-2736/02, C-31 184994. Nav publicēts.

Rīgas pilsētas Vidzemes priekšpilsētas tiesas 2001. gada 27. decembra spriedums lietā nr. C30-3554/5 2001. g. Nav publicēts.

Rīgas pilsētas Zemgales priekšpilsētas 2001. gada 26. septembra spriedums lietā nr. C 31345300 1045/1. Nav publicēts.

Rīgas pilsētas Zemgales priekšpilsētas tiesas 2001. gada 2. aprīļa lēmums lietā nr. 2-420/2000. Nav publicēts.

Rīgas pilsētas Zemgales priekšpilsētas tiesas 2002. gada 6. februāra lēmums lietā nr. 2-00987/98. Nav publicēts.

Rīgas pilsētas Ziemeļu rajona tiesas 1999. gada 7. decembra spriedums lietā nr. 2-3353/9 1999. g. Nav publicēts.

Rīgas pilsētas Ziemeļu rajona tiesas 2003. gada 21. maija spriedums lietā nr. C-322182-02, C-397-03/3. Nav publicēts.

Satversmes tiesas 4. kolēģijas 2002. gada 13. novembra lēmums par atteikšanos ierosināt lietu. Nav publicēts.

Senāta Administratīvā Departamenta spriedumu izvilkumi. Kalacs J., Ripke A. (Sast.) *Tieslietu ministrijas Vēstneša pielikums*, 1939.

Legal Acts

Administrative Procedure Law: the Law of the Republic of Latvia. Adopted on 25.10.2001. Available: likumi.lv/ta/en/en/id/55567-administrative-procedure-law.

Citizenship Law: the Law of the Republic of Latvia. Adopted on 22.07.1994. Available: likumi.lv/ta/en/en/id/57512-citizenship-law.

Civil Law: the Law of the Republic of Latvia. Adopted on 28.01.1937. Available: likumi.lv/ta/en/en/id/225418-civil-law.

Civil Procedure Law: the Law of the Republic of Latvia. Adopted on 14.10.1998. Available: likumi.lv/ta/en/en/id/50500-civil-procedure-law.

Constitutional Court Law: the Law of the Republic of Latvia. Adopted on 05.06.1996. Available: likumi.lv/ta/en/en/id/63354-constitutional-court-law.

Convention for the Protection of Human Rights and Fundamental Freedoms: International Convention. Available: echr.coe.int/documents/convention_eng.pdf.

Deklarācija par Latvijas valsti: Latvijas Satversmes sapulces deklarācija. *Likumu un Valdības Rīkojumu Krājums*, 1920, nr. 4.

Environmental Protection Law: the Law of the Republic of Latvia. Adopted on 02.11.2006. Available: likumi.lv/ta/en/en/id/147917-environmental-protection-law.

International Covenant on Civil and Political Rights: International Convention. Available: likumi.lv/ta/en/starptautiskie-ligumi/id/705-international-covenant-on-civil-and-political-rights.

International Covenant on Economic, Social, and Cultural Rights: International Convention. Available: treaties.un.org/Pages/ViewDetails.aspx?src=TREATY&mtdsg_no=IV-3&chapter=4&clang=_en.

Latvijas pilsoņiem!: Latvijas Tautas padomes Latvijas Republikas proklamēšanas akts. *Pagaidu Valdības Vēstnesis*, 1918, nr. 1.

Law on Official Publications and Legal Information: the Law of the Republic of Latvia. Adopted on 31.05.2012. Available: likumi.lv/ta/en/en/id/249322-law-on-official-publications-and-legal-information.

On Judicial Power: the Law of the Republic of Latvia. Adopted on 15.12.1992. Available: likumi.lv/ta/en/en/id/62847-on-judicial-power.

Par likumu un citu Saeimas, Valsts prezidenta un Ministru kabineta pieņemto aktu izsludināšanas, publicēšanas, spēkā stāšanās kārtību un spēkā esamību: LR likums. Nav spēkā. Pieejams: likumi.lv.

State Administration Structure Law: the Law of the Republic of Latvia. Adopted on 06.06.2002. Available: likumi.lv/ta/en/en/id/63545-state-administration-structure-law.

The Charter of Fundamental Rights of the European Union. Available: eur-lex.europa.eu/legal-content/EN/TXT/?uri=CELEX:12012P/TXT.

The Constitution of the Republic of Latvia: the Constitutional Law of the Republic of Latvia. Adopted on 15.02.1922. Available: likumi.lv/ta/en/en/id/57980-the-constitution-of-the-republic-of-latvia.

The Treaty on the Functioning of the European Union: European Union Treaty. Available: eur-lex.europa.eu/LexUriServ/LexUriServ.do?uri=CELEX:12012E/TXT:en:PDF.

Universal Declaration of Human Rights. Available: un.org/en/udhrbook/pdf/udhr_booklet_en_web.pdf.

Other

Interinstitutional Agreement between the European Parliament, the Council of the European Union and the European Commission on Better Law-Making of 13 April 2016. Available: eur-lex.europa.eu.

OECD Guiding Principles for Regulatory Quality and Performance of 2005. Available: oecd.org/fr/reformereg/34976533.pdf.

OECD Recommendation of the Council on Regulatory Policy and Governance of 22 March 2012. Available: oecd.org/gov/regulatory-policy/49990817.pdf.

Principles of Administrative Law Concerning the Relations Between Administrative Authorities and Private Persons. Directorate of Legal Affairs, Strasbourg, 1996.

Rule of law checklist of European Commission for Democracy through Law (Venice Commission) of 11–12 March 2016. Available: venice.coe.int.

Satversmes tiesas tiesneses Daigas Rezevskas atsevišķās domas lietā nr. 2016-14-01"Par Solidaritātes nodokļa likuma 3., 5., 6., 7. un 9. panta atbilstību Latvijas Republikas Satversmes 91. panta pirmajam teikumam un 109. pantam". Pieejams: satv.tiesa.gov.lv.

Valsts Prezidenta Egila Levita uzruna konstitucionālo tiesību ekspertu domnīcā Satversmes tiesā. 13.12.2019. Pieejams: president.lv/lv/jaunums/valsts-prezidenta-egila-levita-uzruna-konstitucionalo-tiesibu-ekspertu-domnica-satversmes-tiesa.

Venice Commission. *Bulletin on Constitutional Case Law.* BEL-1997-1-002.

Index of Names and Subjects

Alexy, Robert 13
Aristotle 18, 143
Atienza, Manuel 13

Balodis, Kaspars 12
Basic Norm VII–VIII, 2–4, 11–12, 14, 16–17, 29–32, 40, 52–53, 62, 66, 68, 70, 82–85, 88–94, 97–99, 107, 110, 117–118, 126, 138, 146–147
Boulanger, Jean 13, 41
Briede, Jautrīte 12

Case Law 26*n*42, 39
Coercive Measures (Mechanism) 23, 25–26, 37, 134
Collisions 110, 112–113, 123–124, 126, 146–147
- Connection of speciality 17, 109, 111, 111*n*64, 146
- Priority Order 108, 110*n*62, 111, 113, 146
- Temporal Applicability 109, 111, 146

Contemporary Legal Theory Pertaining to Democratic States Based on the Rule of Law 1, 3, 14, 24, 26, 31, 37, 118
Constitutional Review (Control) 70, 83, 126–127, 133–134, 147
Core of Constitution 18*n*16
Cueto-Rua, Julio C. 89

Decision (judgement) 64–65, 81, 139–140, 143–145, 145*n*144
- Just and Reasonable 63, 82–83, 85, 87, 89, 98, 107, 115, 135

Deduction 90–91, 96
Democratic State based on the Rule of Law VII, 1–2, 7, 55, 58, 66, 66*n*26, 68, 70, 73, 77, 88, 94, 102, 111, 115, 130, 133–134, 139*n*124, 141
- Duties (Obligations) 71–72
- *See also* general principles of law; legal arrangement; system of laws

Dišlers, Kārlis 6
Dworkin, Ronald VII, 1, 13, 35–36, 80–81

European Union VII, 10, 67
- Member State 46

Esser, Joseph 13

General Clause 19, 69, 69*n*38, 84, 97*n*22
General Principles of Law
- Adversarial Proceedings 17
- Axiology 11, 40, 53–54, 54*n*1, 80, 87, 89, 127
- Bona Fide 94, 129
- Concept 15–16
- Content Guideline 42–44, 47, 53, 69, 69*n*36, 83, 88
- Core 91–92, 94, 97, 97*n*22, 98
- Democracy 17
- Derived 3, 8, 17, 21, 47, 47*n*112, 52, 60, 66, 68, 71, 88–91, 91*n*9, 92, 94, 98, 100, 110, 117, 120, 126, 130, 134, 146
- Dimension of Weight 11, 110–111, 146
- Discovered 47, 48*n*112, 48, 60, 88–91, 91*n*9, 94, 98, 109–110, 120, 131
- Equality 33*n*68, 44–47, 50–51, 70–72, 96, 97*n*22, 100, 103, 105, 109, 113, 118, 118*n*78, 120–121, 124, 129, 131, 136–138, 143, 145
- Functional Effect 11, 41–42, 88–89, 109, 123, 128, 146
- General Acceptance 99
- Good Faith 58, 106, 140
- Good Governance 40*n*89, 59
- Good Legislation 67*n*30, 68, 74–75, 87, 92–94
- Hierarchy 17, 109–110, 146
- Impartial Investigation 17, 47
- Impartiality of Judge 51
- Independence
  - of Judge 80*n*68, 100
- In Dubio Pro Reo 48, 48*n*113
- Inter-Institutional Loyalty 94
- Justice VIII, 1–2, 6, 14, 21, 22, 29, 33*n*68, 35, 45–46, 48–49, 58–59, 62, 69–72, 77, 80*n*68, 82–83, 90, 92, 100–102, 110–113, 118, 118*n*78, 120, 122, 124, 127, 129, 131, 136, 137, 137*n*121, 138, 145
- Necessity to Justify a Decision 6, 49, 85, 89, 120, 140
- Legal Certainty 96, 106
- Legality 8, 102, 112
- Legal Security 39, 75, 106–107, 109, 127, 129
- Militant Democracy 30, 30*n*62

General Principles of Law (*cont.*)
Mutual Collision 82*n*75, 88, 108–110, 110*n*62, 111–113
National State 17
Nemo Auditor 57
No-Retroactive Force of the Law 51, 74–75, 109–110
Origin 22, 27
Pacta Sunt Servanda 113–114
Positivisation 42, 45
Presumption of Innocence 46
Private autonomy 6
Procedural Rights 103
Prohibition of Analogy (Nulla Poena Sine Lege) 118, 118*n*78, 137
Prohibition of Arbitrariness 6, 47, 85, 89, 120, 140, 145
Prohibition of Legal Obstruction 31–32, 52, 117*n*75, 120–121, 146
Proportionality 6, 8, 17, 47, 75, 82, 96, 100–101, 101*n*39, 102, 104–105, 110, 112, 140
Protection of Legitimate Expectations 6, 8, 39–40, 40*n*89, 47, 74–76, 106–108, 120, 122, 129, 140
Rational Legislature 73, 93
Reasonable Application of Legal Norms (Interpretation) 21*n*27, 47, 83–84
Retroactive Effect of the Rule which is Favourable to a Person in Public Law 76–77
Right to Court Protection 31–32
Right to Defence 50
Right to Fair Trial 70–71, 83, 99–100
Right to Family Life 4*n*9, 10, 119, 124
Right to Freedom 21, 113
Right to Freedom of Conscience 51
Right to Freedom of Expression, Prohibition of Censorship 21*n*27, 67*n*28
Right to Health 32*n*68
Right to Human Dignity VII, VIII, 1–4, 14, 21*n*27, 70, 81, 119, 136
Right to Life 21, 32*n*68, 118
Right to Private Life (Privacy) 104, 120–122
Right to Property 21, 70, 96, 132
Right to Protection of Personal Data 67*n*28
Right to Protection of the Best Interests of a Child 33*n*68, 114–115
Right to Recognition as a Person Before the Law 33*n*68
Right to Social Security 70–71
Rule of Law 18, 47, 77, 93, 100, 102, 106
Scope (Content) 39, 92–93, 96–99, 101, 106–108, 111, 137*n*121, 146
Separation of Power 6, 8, 20, 21*n*27, 31–33, 51–53, 70, 73, 77–79, 80*n*68, 80, 85, 89, 100, 112, 117–118, 146
Socially Responsible State 3, 17–18
Subsidiarity 59
Sustainable Development 94
System 11, 21–22, 70, 77, 85
Trust in Law and State 68, 92, 112–113
Types 15, 41–42
See also Democratic State based on the Rule of Law; human rights; natural rights; unwritten legal norms

Hart, Herbert L.A. VII, 1–2, 12, 28–29
Human (Fundamental) Rights 4, 11, 20–21, 25, 45, 51, 67, 67*n*28, 70–71, 81–82, 85, 94, 99, 122, 123–124, 131, 135–136
See also general principles of law; natural rights; unwritten legal norms

Judiciary 32–33, 49, 54, 78, 99, 116

Kelzen, Hans VII, 1–2, 13, 27–29

Law 1*n*2, 15, 24–25, 130
Gap 118–119
Meaning 22, 60, 63
Legal Arrangement 16, 61, 63, 98, 107, 146–147
Democratic State based on the Rule of Law VII, 1–2, 8–9, 12, 21, 21*n*27, 24–27, 29–31, 40–41, 52–53, 54*n*2, 60, 62, 65, 71–72, 82–83, 85, 101, 110, 123–124, 126, 134
Latvia's 5–7, 10, 29, 55, 58, 60, 62, 64*n*22, 64, 78, 91, 102, 123, 130, 143
Ratio Iuris 84
Transitional (Transformation) VII, 55–56, 56*n*7, 62
Legal Culture 6–8
Western 46

Legal Force 17, 17*n*14, 18, 43, 66, 78, 93, 108–110, 110*n*62, 112, 123, 125–126, 133–134, 146
Legal Methods 1, 11, 21–22, 32, 43, 70, 73, 82–85, 87, 117, 117*n*76, 120, 146
  Analogy 32, 38, 53, 73*n*51, 84–85, 121*n*86, 130–132, 134, 137–138
  Argumentation (Legal Reasoning) 44, 80, 84–85, 87, 89, 120*n*84, 139–140, 143–145
  Argumentum a Fortiori 85, 134, 138
  Argumentum e Contrario 84
  Collision Norms 44, 85, 87, 89, 113, 116
  Comparative Law 97–98
  Comparison and Typification 98, 107
  Concretization 9, 39, 73, 83–84, 88–89, 91, 93, 96–97, 97*n*22, 98–100, 104–108, 118, 146
  Construction of Factual Content 84
  Diversity of Sources of Law 62, 84
  Further Development of Law 84–85, 87, 118*n*80, 121*n*86, 129–130, 130*n*108, 133, 133*n*117, 134, 138
  Higher Critique 39, 82, 84
  Interpretation 33, 39, 44, 73, 75, 79–80*n*68, 80, 82–84, 87, 89, 96, 115–116, 127–131, 134, 137–139, 143, 146
  Intertemporality Principles 73, 73*n*54, 74, 74*n*55, 77, 84, 141–142
  Lower Critique 39, 84
  Subsumption 85
  Teleological Reduction 32, 38, 53, 84–85, 138, 139*n*124
  Transitional Provisions 75, 84
  Weighing and Balancing 85, 88, 111, 113, 146
  See also general principles of law
Legal Norm
  Application Process 5–6, 12, 18, 22, 42, 62, 67, 69, 73, 78, 80–85, 115–116, 123, 144
  Complete 36, 38
  Expressive Understanding 26
  Generally Binding 8–11, 15, 22–23, 24, 26, 33, 37, 40, 43, 53, 63–64, 68, 79, 79*n*68, 80, 82, 87, 92, 99, 110–111, 130, 133, 133*n*117, 134, 146
  See also general principles of law
  Hierarchy 43, 66*n*26, 78, 84–85, 125
  Hyletic Understanding 26
  Imperative attributive nature 34, 40, 83
  Ratio Legis 32, 38, 52, 132
  Real (Valid for Direct Application) 8–9, 11, 21, 21*n*27, 24, 33, 35, 39–40, 53, 82, 85, 87, 89
  See also general principles of law
  Structure 11, 25, 33–34, 37–40, 52–53, 82–83, 96
  Substantial Criteria 37
  Temporal Effect 74–77
  Unwritten 3, 24–25, 29, 32*n*68, 33*n*68, 36, 38, 40–41, 41*n*90, 42–43, 49, 53, 67*n*26, 69*n*36, 74*n*55, 80, 83, 89, 91*n*9, 94, 96, 98, 102, 107, 117, 120, 125, 127, 130, 134
  See also general principles of law
  Validity VII, 28–29, 110–111, 117, 146
  Written 11–12, 14, 20, 23–24, 26*n*42, 27, 32, 36–44, 49, 51, 53, 58, 62, 65–66, 68–70, 72–74, 82–85, 87–90, 92, 95–96, 110, 113, 115–118, 120–121, 121*n*86, 123–131, 133, 136–138, 139*n*124, 144–147
Legal Order 28–29
Legal Positivism VII, 1, 5, 7, 18, 22–25, 29, 88, 91, 110, 118
Legal Reason VII, 2, 14, 29, 98
Legal Sylogism 12, 88–89, 115–118, 135–136, 146
  Evaluative Subsumption 85, 88, 115–118, 120–121, 137, 146
  Hard Case 107, 115–116, 137
  Subsumption (Regular) 115
  The Third Premise (Judge Made Law) 89, 117–118, 120–121, 133*n*117, 134*n*119, 136, 146
  Value Judgements 117–118, 120, 122, 136, 146
Legal System 61, 63, 97
  Anglo-American 16, 54–55, 55*n*6
  Concept 16
  Continental European 6, 10–11, 57, 60, 62, 77, 80, 118*n*78, 140
  Islamic 54–55
  Romano-Germanic 10, 16, 42, 44, 47, 54–55, 55*n*6, 56, 58, 62–64, 67, 81–82
  Soviet 5, 5*n*12, 6, 10–11, 24, 62, 77–78, 118*n*78
  Western VII, 6, 9–11, 16–17, 22, 54, 54*n*1, 63, 65, 67–68, 88, 99, 99*n*33, 109, 137
Legislative Process (Legislation) VIII, 28, 73, 78, 87, 92, 92*n*11
  Delegated 73, 78–79
  Justification 75–77

Legislature (Legislator) 7, 9–10, 12, 24, 26, 26*n*42, 27, 31–32, 32*n*68, 38, 40, 42–45, 52–54, 57–58, 60–61, 63, 65–66, 68–69, 69*n*37, 71–78, 81–83, 87, 90, 91*n*9, 93–94, 99, 102, 108*n*57, 117, 119, 124–127, 129–130, 133, 138, 146–147
Legitimacy (Lawfulness) 5, 56, 66–67, 70, 75, 79, 82–83, 87, 115–117, 117*n*76, 120, 123, 133–134, 143, 146
Levits, Egils 5, 10–12, 67
Līcis, Aivars 12
Lorca-Navarrete 66*n*26

Manero, Ruiz 13
Meļķisis, Edgars 12–13
Moral Norms (Morality) 25, 42

Natural Law 23–26, 29*n*59
  Doctrine VII, 1, 14, 22–25, 29, 31, 37, 42, 66, 81, 118
Natural Rights 21–22, 24, 26, 26*n*42, 69
  See also general principles of law; human rights
Normative Legal Act 5, 5*n*12, 11–12, 18, 24–26, 26*n*42, 27, 32*n*68, 40, 42, 44, 52–53, 55, 57, 59–62, 64–67, 93, 98–99, 108–110, 112, 121, 123, 127–133, 139–141
  Drafting 67, 69–70, 72–73
  Hierarchy 11, 20–21, 48, 70
  Null and Void 67, 70, 83, 85, 126, 134, 147
  Validity 67, 123, 139
  See also the law; written legal norms

Peczenik, Aleksander 13, 18, 65, 72, 116
Penski, Ulrich 13
Plato 18
Principles of Law 21, 40

Radbruch 49

Sinaiskis, Vasilijs 6
Sources of Law 1, 6–7, 24–25, 45–46, 48, 55, 57, 89, 116, 129, 144
  Basic 65
  Case Law (Judicature) 60, 64, 64*n*22, 80, 85, 98–99, 105, 107, 108*n*57, 127, 138, 142, 144
  Customary Law 41*n*90, 58, 61*n*18, 64–65, 65*n*23, 66, 98
  Constitutional Court Judgement 59
  Dissenting or Concurring Opinions of Judges 64, 98
  Diversity (Variety) 5, 54, 62–63, 73, 89
  Doctrine 9, 56, 60, 60*n*17, 62
  European Union Law 59, 68, 93, 101–102, 106
  Generally Binding Interpretations of Legal Norms by Authorized Courts 64, 64*n*22, 65, 93, 98–99, 139
  Hierarchy 11, 65–67, 70, 87, 123
  Independent 8–9, 63–64, 64*n*22, 65, 80*n*68, 87, 93, 123, 139
  International Law 59, 66*n*26, 68, 77, 99, 133
  Legal Doctrine (Writings) 26*n*42, 39, 60, 64, 66, 93, 97–99, 99*n*33, 105–106, 126–127, 141
  Precedents 55, 66
  Subsidiary (Additional) 48, 64*n*22, 65
  Supplementary 6, 63–64, 64*n*22, 65, 80*n*68, 80, 93
  Travaux préparatoires 64, 66, 93, 98, 128
  Types 58, 60–63, 63*n*21, 65–66, 93
  See also general principles of law; normative legal act
Sovereign 1–2, 8, 25–27, 29–31, 32*n*68, 66, 110, 117–118, 120, 146–147
Soviet Occupation VII, 5–6
State Order (System) 1–3, 14, 31
  Authoritarian 30*n*63
  Totalitarian VII
System of Laws 1, 16, 26, 31–32, 46, 52, 68–69, 83, 89–90, 93, 105, 117, 120, 128, 130, 134, 146
Šulcs, Lotārs 6, 25, 34

The Law 24–25, 56, 68, 121, 124–126, 129–132, 135–136
  Gap 5, 33, 44, 48, 55, 105, 118*n*81, 119, 121*n*86, 129–131, 138, 139*n*124
  Transitional Provisions 75–76
  See also normative legal act, written legal norms

Values 11, 20, 21, 41, 52, 68, 70, 90–91, 128
Vichy 49
Vīnzarājs, Nikolajs 73*n*51

Ziemele, Ineta VIII

www.ingramcontent.com/pod-product-compliance
Lightning Source LLC
Chambersburg PA
CBHW071341230926
51846CB00002B/416
9789004690509